PS   Smith,
634   Townsend, 1938—
.S593   55894
            More plays from Off-
            Off Broadway

DATE			

MORE PLAYS FROM
OFF-OFF BROADWAY

MORE PLAYS FROM OFF-OFF BROADWAY

Edited by Michael Smith ，1938-　　　comp.

THE BOBBS-MERRILL COMPANY, INC.
Indianapolis • New York

CONTENTS

INTRODUCTION

Six years ago, introducing a first volume of Off-Off Broadway plays,* I wrote that the coffeehouses, churches, and lofts in New York City where the plays were being staged were something new—not another way into the established theater but an alternative to it. Off-Off Broadway was a declaration of freedom.

By the late nineteen-fifties Broadway was narrowing down to slick comedies, musicals, and plays imported from England. Off Broadway was going commercial, raising ticket prices and production budgets, aiming for hits. The new repertory theaters in cities across the country were stuck with respectable, quasi-educational programming as they struggled to sell subscriptions. College theaters concentrated on the literature, and as usual community theaters did revivals of standard comedies and dramas with ready-made reputations. There was no place at all to do experimental or even original work.

Then, in the early sixties, Off-Off Broadway quietly blossomed in downtown New York—an assortment of improbable spaces and a few people inspired to make fresh things happen. For many people in love with theater, this was the first active encouragement they had found. Suddenly, any place could be a theater. These were arenas of liberation; theater was whatever we wanted to make it.

The first surprise was that the magic of theater is accessible to all. This wasn't just apprenticeship, it was the real thing. Actors found themselves actually acting, not hung up taking classes, making rounds, hoping for a break. Designers took tools into their hands and found what they needed to bring their visions into the light. Directors not only directed but usually functioned as producers, too. Playwrights joined in the work of production, transforming the written words into a performance.

---

* *Eight Plays from Off-Off Broadway,* edited with Nick Orzel (New York, The Bobbs-Merrill Company, Inc.), 1966.

We had stopped waiting humbly for admission into that exclusive, narrow sub-world that was thought of as "the" theater. We had even stopped needing theaters—often we were better off without them. We could do our work wherever an audience could gather—among the tables in a crowded coffeehouse, in studios and lofts, in the choir loft or parish hall of a church, even on the set of another play in an Off-Broadway theater rented for one night. And if we were good, we could release as much pure theater power as anyone. More than most, in fact, because the audience was not held professionally at bay but included in the adventure.

Countless actors, directors, designers, and technical people were liberated from inaction. The word spread and a large number of talented, sometimes inspired playwrights appeared with scripts. Among the first were Lanford Wilson, H. M. Koutoukas, David Starkweather, Doric Wilson, Leonard Melfi, Paul Foster, Robert Heide, Sam Shepard, Soren Agenoux, Ronald Tavel, Jean-Claude van Itallie, Maria Irene Fornes, Megan Terry, Rochelle Owens, Jackie Curtis, Tom Eyen, George Dennison, Rosalyn Drexler, Ruth Krauss, Tom Sankey, Claris Nelson, Robert Patrick, Donald Kvares, William M. Hoffman.

The character of their work, as varied as their persons, was generally outside the conventional American realism. They were hip to the revolutions of technique and consciousness that vitalized other art media, while theater had bogged down in bourgeois conventions. The stages they were writing for didn't have the conventional equipment, there was no money for production, everything was do-it-yourself, and they were forced to invent a resourceful dramaturgy. Many of the plays were (and are) strikingly original, with a singularity of voice and exuberance of form that were unthinkable at the time anywhere but Off-Off Broadway.

Six years ago I named five exemplars of Off-Off Broadway: The Caffe Cino, the Judson Poets' Theater, Theatre Genesis, La Mama, and the Open Theatre. There have been and are many other places and groups. I think immediately of the American Theater for Poets, the Artists' Theater, the Hardware Poets' Playhouse, the Living Theater, the Loft Workshop, the Playwrights' Unit, the Playbox, the Extension, the Cubiculo, the Old Reliable, the Play-house of the Ridiculous, the Ridiculous Theatrical Company, WPA, the Peformance Group, the Bread and Puppet Theater; and, outside New York, the

Theater Company of Boston, the Firehouse Theater of Minneapolis (now in San Francisco), the Changing Scene in Denver, the Company Theater in Los Angeles, and the Magic Theater in Berkeley— all devoted to new work and the remaking of theater experience.

The five first named have produced a disproportionate bounty of new playwrights. The Caffe Cino was, in the first place, a coffeehouse—a narrow Greenwich Village storefront cluttered with tables and chairs, with an espresso machine on a counter at the rear. Behind the counter, making the coffee, was Joe Cino. For several years the Cino presented a new play every week, and countless people did their first creative work there. Joe turned them all on to his high personal anarchistic energy, wild and indiscriminate love of beauty, and shining faith in the honor and magic of imagination. Cino was not interested in the play and playwright so much as the whole production and all the people involved in it, and would sometimes redecorate the whole place to complement the show. Though the space was small, the scope of the work was virtually unlimited. I've never known a theater with less separation of play and audience; the actors were usually surrounded, and plays materialized in dangerous proximity to "real" life. Joe died in the spring of 1967, and the Caffe Cino closed a year later.

In the early and middle sixties Judson Memorial Church on Washington Square was a remarkable center of energy. The Judson Poets' Theater and the Judson Dance Theater had a sophisticated, loyal audience, and at the Judson Gallery artists were inventing happenings. Al Carmines, the minister and theater composer who created and runs the Judson arts program, recognized that the dancers were not just dancing but were doing astonishing theater, and that the artists were making pure theater, too. Plays, after all, drama, are only one kind of theater—and Judson's unique service was to bring poets, dancers, artists, and composers together. This produced some marvelous occasions of joy, beauty, and amazement in all forms, including plays. But as paranoia closed in later in the decade, one's own thing got obsessive and lonely even at Judson. The nucleus of dancers moved on, several of the Poets' Theater productions moved Off Broadway, Carmines increasingly reserved the space for his own work, and Judson lost its air of being the private theater of an avant-garde community.

Theatre Genesis was always a place apart, going its own way with cool Western machismo, implacable concentration, and no interest in any other theater. Ralph Cook founded Genesis and ran it until 1970. Almost all the work he directed there had a distinctive clarity and strength of style, intensely personal, often gritty. Sponsored and housed by St. Mark's Church in-the-Bouwerie, Genesis has from the start been concerned with playwrights rather than plays, and has offered them a continuing relationship with a stage and actors. Sam Shepard, Murray Mednick, Walter Hadler, and Tom Sankey are among the playwrights who have taken advantage of this offer, and Genesis has developed a community of artists who have worked together over several years. Theatre Genesis is now being run by a group of playwrights.

Ellen Stewart *is* La Mama. Inspired by Joe Cino, she started putting on plays in a tiny cellar coffeehouse in 1960, then because of municipal pressure moved into a large loft which she operated as an Experimental Theater Club. Now she owns a building with two theater spaces where she produces new plays at a phenomenal pace. In addition she sponsors La Mamas in Bogota, Amsterdam, London, Munich, Toronto, and Tokyo; a series of foreign directors have come to New York to direct plays at La Mama; and La Mama touring companies are almost constantly on the road. Ellen pours forth enthusiasm and encourages everyone to work, sustaining them with any money she can get, which is never enough. She seeks all available publicity, woos critics, and pushes toward commercial productions. The result is a unique concentration of people and energies.

The Open Theatre began as an acting workshop directed by Joseph Chaikin. The emphasis was on ensemble and on exploring and inventing techniques to go beyond individualistic psychological acting and the dead forms of the commodity theater. Collaborations with playwrights Megan Terry and Jean-Claude van Itallie were particularly fruitful, and the work has been enormously influential. Productions such as *The Serpent* and *The Mutation Show* have established the Open Theatre as one of the finest performing groups in the contemporary theater. Instead of working in commercial situations for the usual paying audiences, the Open Theatre has most often performed in prisons and at universities and has shown work-in-progress at its own rehearsal studio in New York.

Just talking about Off-Off Broadway implies that it exists, that it is something. There is no "it," only a range of possibilities, with no

fence at the horizon. It's what you make happen. These five places
are not institutions. They are five adventures in bringing theater
into the world that rely on no known structure or concept. The lesson is clear. If what you want to do is theater, go ahead, do it.

The problem this theater faces is poverty. At first, people were so
happy to be working Off-Off Broadway that they didn't expect to
be paid for what they did. They knew there was no money, and
they gave of themselves to help build situations where they could
do what they wanted to do. But no structure has developed to
support them adequately. You sell yourself or you practically starve.
Much of the work reflects the desperate circumstances in which the
artists have had to work and live if they were to work at their art
at all.

Some have moved on to other media. Some have lost their sense
of theater's creative potential. But movies and television don't com-
pete with theater; they aren't offering the same things to the artist
or the spectator. Neither can be as personal as theater, as free, as
poetic, as frank, as magical. Neither honors the spectator's actual
presence and participation. Neither can exist without big budgets
and mass audience appeal, while some of the best theater happens
in humble circumstances with only a handful of spectators. Theater
is an object lesson in freedom, creating beings and worlds fresh by
the pure power of imagination in action.

The Ford and Rockefeller foundations, the arts councils of various
states, the National Endowment for the Arts, and other sources have
given money to the new theater, but not enough. Much important
theater work will never be self-supporting, and there is an urgent
need for the development of some system of steady patronage. The
writers in this collection are not serving an apprenticeship, developing a technique, and preparing themselves for some glittering big-
time. The plays are not attempts to be popular. They are not
preliminary sketches or exercises any more than string quartets are
attempts at symphonies. Off-Off Broadway is still virtually the only
place where this work can be done; and even there the most serious
work often gets little encouragement. Good new work sometimes
does find a public and make money. But, as Chaikin has written, "It
is not possible to make discoveries under the pressure to please."

After the first exhilaration the struggle proves to be arduous and
sometimes destructive. We have had to learn about exhaustion; to
face our own failures of nerve and morale. Renewal is elusive, and

the American mood in the past few years has been bitter. In my own impatience and frustration, I personally got discouraged. I tried to give up on theater. I left the city and went to live in the country, disengaged from my brothers and sisters.

But discouragement is not honorable. I can't give up on this world, because there is no other. This is my community, and if the times seem dark, I must yet testify, with my friends, to the prevalence of light. I can't just stand back dismayed and wait for the final solution, for total revolution and/or total war. *These* are our lives; let's make them good.

This is the perpetual middle of the struggle. What is required is courage and a clear realization of theater's mission: to bring light, to liberate and quicken the human spirit. Actors are priests, they celebrate our lives, and theater's opportunity is to perform the dreams and rituals our civilization dangerously lacks. This is the challenge to its creative force—to make poets and visionaries members of the modern world, to answer the mass media with re-humanizing person-to-person messages, to embody the alternate news.

MICHAEL SMITH

MORE PLAYS FROM OFF-OFF BROADWAY

TIDY PASSIONS, or
KILL, KALEIDOSCOPE, KILL

An Epic Camp

by H. M. Koutoukas

For Tosh Carrillo and Charles Stanley

> *Tidy passions and a roundup of gall*
> *Bring myna-bird passions*
> *To the piranha ethic,*
> *Where eat-as-eat-may rules well*
> *And empty dinners*
> *Make the week go round,*
> *To where the length*
> *Of Tidy Passions abound.*

TIDY PASSIONS or KILL, KALEIDOSCOPE, KILL was performed at La Mama Experimental Theatre Club, 122 Second Avenue, New York. It was directed by the author, with music and lighting by Charles Stanley, technical coordination by Ellen Levene, and the following cast:

COBRA PRIEST	Lyn Johnson
JEAN HARLOW	Charles Stanley
NARCISSUS	Tosh Carrillo
DOVE	Mari-Claire Charba
WITCHES	Alice Turner
	Stanley Amos
	Andrew Sherwood
EROSTA	Jacque Lynn Colton

1

H. M. KOUTOUKAS was born in Athens and reared in Endicott, New York. He has had 74 plays done in New York, almost all under his own direction. *Only a Countess May Dance When She's Crazy, Pope Jean, With Creatures Make My Way, Medea, Tidy Passions, A Letter from Colette, Crumpled Christmas, The View from Sorrentino,* and *Cause Célèbre* were produced at the Caffe Cino. Among his chamber plays, created for private patrons and privately performed, are *Atlantis and More, Invocations of a Haunted Mind, The Children's Crusade, Burglars and Bunglers, Burglar on the Roof, The Methedrine Madonna,* and *The Howard Klein Trilogy;* some of these were also performed at the Elgin Theatre. A stained glass theater was built for Koutoukas by Gilly Glass, where he staged *Amphetamine Glamour. Turtles Don't Dream, or Happy Birthday, Jesus, or the Amphetamine Angel* was performed at Carnegie Hall. *Michael Touched Me* was read on WBAI. *Feathers Are for Ramming, or Tell Me Tender Tales* was performed at the Coda Gallery, and *When Clowns Play Hamlet* at La Mama. *Pomegranada,* with music by Al Carmines and choreography by Aileen Passloff, was given at the Judson Poets' Theatre. *Only a Countess May Dance When She's Crazy* and *The Last Triangle* were produced at the Actors' Playhouse under the title *Two Camps by Koutoukas. Christopher at Sheridan Squared* was presented at the Performing Garage. H. M. Koutoukas has won National Arts Club and "Obie" awards and is currently available for twenty-five dollars an hour.

(The curtains open—this camp must be performed in a theater with curtains—to reveal the innards of a huge kaleidoscope. The cast are center stage in a circle, some kneeling, some bending; in the dim opening light they resemble the passport photo of an avocado. They are circled about the COBRA PRIEST. *The setting is swirling about them, and in their archetypal poses they seem to be the only solid things.*

It is important that the setting be made of remnants of glass, cellophane, etc. It is vital that no part of the setting or costumes be bought; the designer of costumes and sets must spin them of remnants and castaway items.

The lights rise as OVERTURE *ends.*)

COBRA PRIEST

(Screams)
I have seen the best cobras of my generation
die mad—from lack of worship.

(ANCIENT TEMPLE MUSIC *up. The cast circle* COBRA PRIEST; *he joins the circle. Each of the cast members turns to audience as they circle.*)

HARLOW

Close-up—that's a technical term that
means the screen is full of you and the
whole nation goes mad!

NARCISSUS

I've fallen in love with my reflection,
on many occasions—
(Horror)
But *never, never* with *myself.*

DOVE

They've put nails on churches to
keep feathered folk off the ledges.
(Scream to count of four)

WITCHES (XEROX, CON EDISON, and IBM)
Burn us, burn us, burn us—
but don't not believe in us!

EROSTA

Perhaps if I were a nurse I could find
a life of fulfillment.

HARLOW

Who the hell is Beverly Grab?

(*All but the* COBRA PRIEST *scream and run to opposite sides of stage,
leaving him alone, center.
The* WITCHES *go downstage right and form a picture.*)

COBRA PRIEST

Bring me my viper pit——

EROSTA

Sorry, there's a fifty-cent minimum to
keep out riffraff.

COBRA PRIEST

The cobra temple is crumbling—
even the cobras have left.

DOVE

She's one of the very best-dressed——

WITCHES

Knows how to drag her furs about——

EROSTA

I hate gossip, BUT—she's in analysis,
she found out in the *Herald Tribune* that
an answering service is a defense mechanism.

DOVE

She's still the best-dressed—

WITCHES

(*To* DOVE.)
They say she often wears feathers—
dove's feathers——
(*The* DOVE *faints in horror.*)

EROSTA

He hasn't been the same since Picasso painted him!
(*The* DOVE *flutters back to consciousness.*)

1ST WITCH (XEROX)

They say, although I hate
gossip, that——

2ND WITCH (CON EDISON)

I know—I know——

3RD WITCH (IBM)

That she wears the feathers of
living birds—
(*The* DOVE *stumbles to center stage, falls into the arms of the* COBRA
PRIEST *upon hearing the words of the* 3RD WITCH.)

HARLOW

Jean loves you, America!
(*Goes to* DOVE)
Jean loves you, America!

DOVE

I'm not America—I'm
a dying dove.

HARLOW

Say what you will—everyone
has a tiny resemblance of me in
their mind.
(*Leaving center stage, sway-backed*)
Long shot! That's a technical term meaning
when the crowd sees the crowd seeing the crowd
that is seeing and adoring you!

DOVE

(*To* COBRA PRIEST)
Please help me, I'm a dying dove!

EROSTA

Die, dove, die!

COBRA PRIEST

(*Pushing* DOVE *away*)
I am of the cobra cult—
I worship only the *feathered* cobra.

DOVE

I'm a feathered friend . . .

COBRA PRIEST

The temple of the cobra cult crumbles—
without the cobra there is no incentive—
without incentive Con Edison will die—
Con Edison, don't turn off the cobra.
(*He exits*)

DOVE

I'm weak—so weak . . .

EROSTA

That's wrong—you must be strong—
strong——

DOVE

Won't someone call me an ornithologist?

HARLOW

God does not have feathered *fears*—
therefore it's all in your mind.
Don't you know about Christian Science?

EROSTA

He lacks incentive——

HARLOW

A nation is something that loves *you*
come long shot or close shot. No matter
what the shot—a nation is something
that loves *you*.

EROSTA

(*Looking at* DOVE's *feathers, plucks one*)
Perhaps I should have been a milliner.

DOVE
Saint Isabel, where are you?

1ST WITCH
(*Sadistically*)
They've put nails on the churches
to keep the birds from splattering
the saints that loved them.
(*She plucks a feather.*)

DOVE
Ahhhhhh! My pubic feather!
(1ST WITCH *rushes down to the other* WITCHES.)

1ST WITCH
Can't find a mummy's hand. Will this do?

2ND & 3RD WITCHES
Of course not—
stupid——
(1ST WITCH *goes back and stabs feather back into* DOVE.)

DOVE
Ahhhhhhhh! Oh, oh——

NARCISSUS
It's unconstitutional not being able
to love one's self. Some people—
can you imagine?—some people
have never tasted their own
come?

EROSTA
Perhaps I could have found fulfillment
in being a *snood* designer.

DOVE
(*Frightened*)
Feathered snoods?

EROSTA
Ain't you got no business sense?—
feathers just ain't stylish next year!
(DOVE *weeps, loud.*)

DOVE

Somewhere in orange—
Dark and away from pink
Feathered ecstasy waits
And birds must fly with birds
While chickens watch sad
But even they know God *has* created *meat loaf!*

EROSTA

Meat loaf—that's true fulfillment.

DOVE

(*Yearningly*)
Meat loaf . . .

WITCHES

(*All*)   Meat loaf—
(*1st*)   The goal of alchemy—
(*2nd*)   And all holy practices—
(*3rd*)   The proof of miracles and puddings!
(*All*)   Meat loaf.

NARCISSUS

There's more to magic than life——

ALL

There's meat loaf and the color orange—
And decadence convinces us that no age
Is ever really golden.
(TEMPLE MUSIC. *A single spot on* NARCISSUS. *He removes his loin-
cloth.*)

NARCISSUS

Many people have never had a spotlight
On their naked body
Tell them that there's God
In every found object
And misguided desire.
        Why love another
        When their heads are full of preconceptions?

Why give what you want
When what you want is wanting?
Only through ourselves do we know,
So why go further?
Why gild the lilies
When you can gild yourself?
And give the giving
Gave the given,
Knowing that rot is the summation
(*To* HARLOW)
Of *all* beauty.
Even marble flaws
And there is no temple for melancholia.

Fight to go into another mind—
And you'll find you've gone out of yours.
Cry only for the taste of your own tears,
Sob only for the sound of your own sobs.

You cannot vote if you can't tap dance.

Meat loaf and me,
That's quite enough
To build eternity,
Squelch sadness
As you dance——

EROSTA

(*Screams*)
You *are* the meat loaf that joined me in eternal life.

NARCISSUS

(*Shakes his head no, very slowly*)
No—my name's Narcissus.

EROSTA

(*Hostilely, with Jewish accent*)
Sounds foreign. . . .

NARCISSUS

(*Rejecting her*)
Foreign only to the touch of others
And never needing,

Save my own needs for rainy days
And when the sun is shining—
I love my reflection and
that has *little* to do with loving myself.
(DOVE *weakly goes to* NARCISSUS *and places a wreath of his own
feathers on him.*)

NARCISSUS

You are a dove and I am a man—how pretentious—
thinking that we are different.

3RD WITCH

(*Points to* DOVE)
Aren't you supposed to be dying?
(DOVE *rushes back to former position and hurriedly resumes dying.*)

NARCISSUS

There's nothing like *not* being loved
to keep one alive.

EROSTA

The unloved go on and on
Like Jews
And mousetraps,
Broken light bulbs,
Eviction notices . . .

1ST WITCH

(*Having a vision*)
It is written in the sand
On comets' tails,
Whooping-crane wings
And Government treaties with the Indians—
(*Wisely*)
We are the No-Cal generation!

EROSTA

Hang onto your meat loaf—
I've got a song——

NARCISSUS

I have a glance . . .

1ST WITCH

I have a sneer . . .

2ND WITCH

I have a leer . . .

3RD WITCH

I have a mummy's tongue . . .

DOVE

(*Proudly*)
I have my wounds . . .

EROSTA

I could have retched all night——

NARCISSUS

You saw it happen.
(*The* DOVE *puts ketchup on his wounds.*)

WITCHES

(*Beginning* WITCHES' *dance*)
We all saw it happen all of us all of us
and each saw yes we all saw it and we let
it through our eyes and into our brains
where it was squelched by *thoughts.*

EROSTA

You may be witches but you're right—
thoughts are squelching.

DOVE

There's nothing sadder than a squelched perception.

EROSTA

That's murder—when thoughts squelch perceptions.

ALL

Murder! Help, murder! Police! Police!
(*Crash of cymbals. The* COBRA PRIEST *starts crossing the stage sideways, like an Egyptian hieroglyph.*)

COBRA PRIEST

The cobra temple is crumbling——

WITCHES

Crumble, crumble, fall and tumble . . .

COBRA PRIEST

(*Reaching center stage*)
Even the cobras are leaving the temple of the
cobra cult. There's no more cobra loaf—
the cobra queen—the holy cobra cult—
bring me my viper pit!

EROSTA

Has Diane di Prima borrowed the viper pit and
forgotten to return it?

COBRA PRIEST

The cobra cult is dying! What can I become?

DOVE

(*Shyly*)
Would you like to become a . . . a . . . bird watcher?

NARCISSUS

The obscure is tumbling in around us—
We must do something or the world will wind
Its way without us.

Creatures of pretension arise?

EROSTA

Ave Maria Callas.

WITCHES

Ave Maria Callas.

DOVE

(*Sings a few notes of* "Casta Diva")

COBRA PRIEST

I shall weep by the sea for the holy cobra,
weep by the mountain for the lost cobra queen.
I shall search all the world for the cobra jewel.

NARCISSUS

And in the end you'll die—so why bother?

COBRA PRIEST

(*Leaving*)
Forgive them, cobras, they know not what they're doing!
(*Leaves*)

(*Ruth Etting's record of* "Shine On, Harvest Moon" *begins.* HARLOW
laughs as if she were alive.)

HARLOW

Glamour is *dead*—
(*Screams for count of five as she crosses center*)
Dead—dead—dead—dead—dead—dead—
(*She begins to drape herself about* NARCISSUS *like an art-nouveau
figure. Her scarf must be long enough so that when she leaves it
will still be wrapped about him.*)
Glamour is dead. Rainbows don't promise. What
the hell does a nice girl have to do to be nice?
My mistakes have been shown on screens large as
city blocks. Only creeps can give you immortality.
Blond is the color of my true sex-goddess hair.
Have you ever wondered what it's like to die?—
Can you imagine your eyes frothing and your lips
caving in? The best brains of all ages become
. . . skulls. I could teach Medea a thing or two.

The day you die, you die. The day you die, they
have you all figured out. They'll even say you
liked your own funeral.
(*Graciously*)
I gave and gave and gave and gave—they gave and
gave and gave—
(*Bitter*)
—and gave. Until it all became giving and
getting. That was all it became, it became
nothing at all else.

When I had my period, four hundred people didn't work!

The problem is glamour—no one mourned glamour—and
abstract thoughts get their revenge. Watch out—
even Electra could learn a thing or two from abstract
thoughts. Abstract thoughts do have their revenge.

I've had everything. So who needs a child? I've
even been tortured—yes, I've been tortured. I've
felt so lousy that I thought I was becoming a *Jew.*

How low can one go? You can go so low that you
never know what height is all about!
(*Music is full now.*)

Corsages worn on the breast. Red roses in long vases.
He hated me so much he sent me roses with thorns.
Chiffon gowns that teach the wind to flutter.
Long lengths of lethargy to wrap about the sad
moments when one has time to remember.

It's enough to make one weep, but tears—tears
stain the mascara, ruin the eyes. Death is
ruined eyes and that's a *post-war fact.*
(*She is still wrapping herself about* NARCISSUS.)

Glamour is dead.
(*She begins kissing all the parts of his naked body.*)

Glamour is dead. Nothing is ugly any more. There
was a time when things could be ugly, so ugly
that they were worth going after.

But now everything's the same. Split-negative-
plural-minus-negative. Formulas gave forth formulas
and glamour couldn't add or count, so it died at its
first literacy test.
(*She has kissed all of his body and now kisses his feet. Looks up
from ground. Screams. Weeps.*)

I know where I am. I damn well know where I am.
I stepped off from a pedestal to get here, so
I know where I am.
(*An amber spot comes up on her at the feet of* NARCISSUS. *She rests
her head on his thigh.*)
If we could only end with an amber spot upon us!

But no—it ends darkly as mascara from ruined
eyes—long soft chiffon—roses in white long
vases—an arched door to lean against—that's
heaven and more.

When glamour died, did it go to heaven?

I've had enough mud thrown at me to make a mummy movie.

At least Bela Lugosi was a gentleman. Why did Fatty
Arbuckle have to do that Coke endorsement!

Why is why why?

(*Stands*)
I'm a *stah* of the *cinemah*—to be seen—
to be heard. All I can say—all that I know
is that glamour's dead.

(*Starts off. Turns to audience.*)
ANYBODY WANT TO FUCK A STAR?

(*Flashbulbs. Exits.*)

DOVE
Sadness isn't even funny any more.
And cruelty just reminds us we
aren't nice. If I weren't a
feathered friend, I'd be a masochist
but that's such a cozy way out.

I thought I was going to die but I'm
just molting.

NARCISSUS
It seems as if our whole world is molting
around us. Thank God I've never put much
faith in the world.

DOVE
That's true—one never wants something
unless one *sees* it.

NARCISSUS
Desire's always outside . . .

DOVE

There's a parrot—I've missed her often—
a lady parrot that tells dirty stories.

NARCISSUS

Would that be enough?

DOVE

No, dirty stories aren't enough. In fact *all*
stories aren't enough. You have
to believe that everything ends if
you are to believe stories. Nihilism's
the cheap way out.

(*Stands*)
I may not be able to sit on churches
but I have my ideals. They can put as many
barbs on public buildings as they want to keep
me from perching—I'm an American just the same.
Negroes can go to the bathroom now
but pigeons can't nor can doves or
flamingoes—their damned statues are more
valuable to them than birds. Even the Catholic
Church's put anti-bird barbs up——

1ST WITCH

The Catholic Church is always first and
democracy is difficult.
(*Laughs*)

NARCISSUS

The trouble with democracy is that
it expects everyone to have an orgasm
at any time with anyone at all.

DOVE

Here I lie molting to death and you
discuss politics——

(*A four-second—exactly—scream is heard from offstage.*)

2ND WITCH

Did you hear that?

3RD WITCH
I guess it's time to get up.

1ST WITCH
Hully-bullie-boo-boo-boo.

DOVE
Aren't you at least going to try to buy
our souls?

3RD WITCH
(*Bored*)
We need tigers' tits—

2ND WITCH
(*Bored*)
And mummies' tongues—

1ST WITCH
(*Bored*)
Bubbling gall
by the cauldronsful.

2ND WITCH
(*Bored*)
Souls just aren't worth troubling about.
Too many are up for sale—there's no
shortage.

DOVE
Well, won't you stay and screech awhile?
You're the nearest thing we have to Muses.

NARCISSUS
Won't you stay and talk?

1ST WITCH
We didn't get to be witches by *talking*.
(WITCH MUSIC. *Softly*)
Three wicked harpies
Sitting on a fence

Counting out curses
In dollars and cents.

ALL WITCHES

Cherubs turn to gargoyles
And wine's not always safe.
We are remembrances
Who have forgotten
How to titter-tattle.

1ST WITCH

Terror's keeper,
Readers of the holy Tarot,
The Bible's even soon to fall
Into our vile keeping.

2ND WITCH

When the vogue is over we get the fashion,
When the love is over we sell the hate.

3RD WITCH

Satan is only worshiped by neurotic witches.
We worship all that's lost its time and worth,
The glamour that has decayed.

ALL WITCHES

Mix potion of dead beauties,
Combine the crumble of dead temples
With skull dust.

1ST WITCH

If it weren't for us, there'd be a fairy-dust
plague.

3RD WITCH

We're where grooviness goes when it dies—

2ND WITCH

Where swingers go when they've swung.
(WITCH MUSIC *up full.*)

ALL WITCHES

Cubicle of lost lost knowns,
Dusty bins to sort and know,
Filthy ecstasies left in trust,
Things no longer young enough to love.

Our domain the living dead,
The dream-line of dormice and lizards:
The crawly must be kept and cared for,
The old old gods need still be appeased.

The sky could fall,
The sky might fall,
And that's the only reason,
The sky could fall today!

So we brew
Forgotten tastes
With foreign objects
In jet jet dark.

More's been forgotten than
Was ever known
And we grow heavy cataloguing
All that there's no more use for.

Three wicked harpies
Sitting on a fence
Counting out curses
In dollars and cents.

(*They exit as music comes down.*)

EROSTA

Henny Penny was a prophetess
But who'd believe someone with a name like that?

DOVE

There's gossamer
And Morocco—
Little else
Except the one beautiful
Sigh, sound, or twitter each day, one thing
That makes it worth going to bed.

EROSTA

If we remembered everything
we'd be freaks—

NARCISSUS

(*Haunted*)
Yet somewhere before tomorrow
And after yesterday is . . . *now.*
Can that be enough?

DOVE

(*Passionately*)
I asked God for eternal life—
And all I got was a chocolate-chip cookie.
(*Starts walking in a circle. Smiles sadly*)
But it tasted like glamour
And smelled like fabulousness.

EROSTA

Potions are so important
And never cease to evaporate.
Can Sobo glue be the secret to eternal youth?

Vicks Vapo-Rub may be the cure to psychosis.
Why won't science give it a chance?

Little dove, you have the most peculiar walk.

DOVE

Original, isn't it?

EROSTA

Well—it is different.

NARCISSUS

No reason to lie—
He walks like a washing machine.

(DOVE *screams for the count of six, pounding his head with one hand, his breast with the other. He then faints.*)

EROSTA

(*Looking at fainted* DOVE.)
It's so seldom we have a *chance* to be alone . . .

NARCISSUS

My name is Narcissus——

EROSTA

I'm Erosta, the only whore in the history
of history who doesn't have a Golden Heart.

NARCISSUS

What do you have?

EROSTA

(*Struts*)
Bazaaz—and lotsa class . . . .

NARCISSUS

Forgive me for not having noticed—
my name's Narcissus——

EROSTA

I don't mind foreigners none—lots of 'em
make good Americans. I know some Anglicans
and Episcopalians that are real good Americans.
It's the Jews that bother me! You'd think
they'da learned that usury's a sin.

NARCISSUS

What's
in a Jew?

EROSTA

The tackiness and gauchity of all eternity
woven in a fur coat and plastic wedgie with a
rose in the heel.

NARCISSUS

Is that all you hate?

EROSTA

Fags get bothersome too—they think they're
so different—and spicks and Catholics
and eye-talians and limeys. Turks are
so ruthless and Indians are so dreary,

and now that Negroes can use public bathrooms
you notice there's a water shortage!
(*Pause*)
But let's not talk philosophy—
let's talk about *us*.

NARCISSUS

Us hasn't got a noun or verb. Perhaps
we had better discuss birth control——

EROSTA

Or fashion——

NARCISSUS

Or the market——

EROSTA

Vegetable or stock?

NARCISSUS

We could talk about what *I* like.

EROSTA

What about what *I* like?

NARCISSUS

(*Lewdly*)
What do you like?
(*Seductively, without moving*)
What do you like?

EROSTA

(*Gasping*)
I don't know—
(*She clutches her throat. A stream of blood trickles out of her mouth.*)
Accch—ahhhhhhhhhhhhhhhh.

NARCISSUS

(*Savage*)
You know so well what you don't like
That you've never had much time
To decide what you do like.

(The following speech is said without hate or anger. It has a bored tone to it as if it were a masturbation ritual. EROSTA *falls to her knees, freezes in* Niobe *pose. Her death rattle continues throughout his whole speech.)*
You've never taken leave of criticism
For long enough to find out what you do desire—
There's a lot that *can* be given, a lot that *can* be taken,
But you've carved pigeonholes in your brain
That stop the flow of seeing—
Your thoughts have murdered your perceptions
And that's true murder . . .
You taste meat loaf only because you know it's a miracle
And you've learned to love orange
Because you know that it is the color orange
And the color orange alone
That proves there is a God.
It takes four boxes of Mars bars
To put you to sleep at night
And you can't go out until
You've counted all the cracks in your hate.
Each day you push on mink counters
And into resorts
Bumble up stock markets
And barge down aisles
Before curtain calls are over—

> Erosta, you've told me that you are
> The only whore in the history of history
> Who doesn't have a Golden Heart . . .

I know more—I know more—I know more.

I know all your secrets for my name's Narcissus.
I love my reflection and it will never go away.
So I can see you and your loss of reflection.
When you pass mirrors they blur.
You only know what you *don't* like.

You're frightened because
I asked you what you liked and you don't know.
(EROSTA *gags.*)

You're choking on your own preconceptions.
Let them go—let them go—let them go!
(*Marbles fall out of her mouth.*)

EROSTA

(*Softly*)
Kiss me. . . .

NARCISSUS

My name is Narcissus——

EROSTA

I don't give a damn what your name is, kiss me!

NARCISSUS

My name's Narcissus—I love my reflection——

EROSTA

(*Threateningly yet gently*)
Look into my—look into my eyes, Narcissus,
and say that——

NARCISSUS

(*Without malice*)
If I looked into your eyes, all I'd see
would be *my reflection.*

EROSTA

(*Screams*)
Jew!

NARCISSUS

(*Smiling*)
I was just about to accuse you of that.

EROSTA

I shoulda known—just another
pretty face. I shoulda known you just
wanted to be alone with that—that—
(*Points to* DOVE)
that *faggot!*

NARCISSUS

That isn't a faggot, it's a dove.

EROSTA

(*Exiting*)
They're the worst kind!
(GENTLE TINKLING MUSIC up)

DOVE

(*Waking up*)
Oh dear—oh dear——

NARCISSUS

Why are you so fey?

DOVE

As a very young dove I suffered
quite frequently from the vapors—
it's the dread disease of the delicate.

NARCISSUS

Is there no cure from it?

DOVE

Some people go to gyms, some people
dress only in leather, some marry *many* times,
some even drive trucks. But you can
never get rid of it, you can only suffer
from it—vapors are vapors.
(*Bravely, with a twig in his beak*)
It's my tiny cross.

NARCISSUS

We almost had a conflict——

DOVE

(*Bitchy*)
You and your reflection?
Does your reflection want to call it quits?

NARCISSUS

No—birdbrain!

DOVE
(*Hurt*)
Birds have extremely large brains.
(*In a titter*)
You myths certainly have a *nuance* problem.

NARCISSUS
Forget it.

DOVE
Please tell me about "your" conflict.
They're really almost as rare as "real" problems.

NARCISSUS
You know the one that has the razor blade
for a vagina—well, she asked me to look into
her eyes!

DOVE
What did you see in them?

NARCISSUS
My own reflection!
(NARCISSUS *laughs.* DOVE *giggles.*)

(THEME MUSIC *up—opening of* "Das Lied von der Erde." *Lights become fantastic.*)

NARCISSUS
(*Looking about*)
Color is here.

DOVE
Thank God for small *feathers*.

NARCISSUS
They say that colors can only be adjectives.
Isn't it strange that colors cannot be spoken of
without mentioning an object?

DOVE
(*Prissy*)
Don't believe them; poppycock seems to be
a very scholarly pursuit these days!

Don't you believe them.
(*Shyly*)
Narcissus, I have an extremely strange request
to make of you.

NARCISSUS

What invasion of privacy does it involve?

DOVE

(*Speaks quickly without inflection*)
Will you be the shoulder that joins me in eternal life?

NARCISSUS

Do you have a speech problem?

DOVE

No, I'm just lonely.

NARCISSUS

Well, then, don't be so beak-tied,
Say what you said and say it clearly!

DOVE

(*As if at school recital*)
Dear Narcissus
Gentle myth
I know you love your reflection
And see all things through it
But as you know I'm a bird
And not a housewrecker.
I'm just a little dove and lonely.
I suffer from the vapors and only
can exist if there's a shoulder
For me to live on.

Saint Isabel,
The patron saint of feathered things,
Is often doing social work on Park Avenue
So I'm almost often alone and always hungry.

Could I—
Would you—

May I—
Sit on your shoulder for all eternity?

Will you allow your shoulder to join me
In eternal life?

NARCISSUS
(*Smiles as if about to say yes. The little* DOVE *becomes ecstatic until* NARCISSUS *speaks.*)
(*Gently*)
No!
(*Firmly*)
No!
(*He seems to withdraw all his concentration into himself.*)
(*Haunted*)
No!

DOVE
(*In a feathered fury*)
Wicked myth.
(*Waits for an answer*)
Naughty myth.
(*Waits for an answer*)
Greek myth!
(*Waits for an answer*)
Ancient myth!
(*Waits for an answer. Struts, preening*)
I can fly, you can't.
I can also talk to parrots and goldfish.
(*Embarrassed*)
I'm behaving like a peacock.
(NARCISSUS *remains frozen, his eyes closed, a golden light upon him.*)
I just thought that it might be possible—
Since men can never love men—
That perhaps a dove might.

I hope your reflection isn't angry,
It certainly must understand my torturedness.
(*Crying out*)
One gets so lonely.

That it's almost worth
Turning into salt or paste.

I've been a feathered friend
For so long that I've let my birdbrain go dry.

ONE GETS SO LONELY
And the glamour of tragedy wears off.

> Your shoulder would have made a groovy nest,
> I could have framed your face with my wings
> When you made love to your reflection—
> I could have stolen jewels and woven them
> In a nest of your dark wavy hair.

I could have—could have—could have—

The Audubon Society has told a dreadful lie,
Bird watchers are not voyeurs.

So many "could haves"
Had I for you—
Did you know that a slap and a kiss
Can mean the same thing
And often people are rude and rough and butch
Because they think that love and gentleness
Are *gauche?*

I could have twittered with your reflection
Through all reflections reflected in reflectors
Everywhere.

I'm a much wiser dove now—I have a *fact*
Though I'm not German—I have a *fact*—
One fact but it's enough. This thing called
Reality is anything that offers resistance
To gossamer and fantasy.
(*Slowly exiting backward*)
Twitter—twitter—
Sweet . . . sweet myth—
Goodbye, dear Narcissus.
(*Puts twig in his mouth after looking at it*)
I have my tiny cross to bear!

(*Silently, in the shadow, all of the creatures have lined up:* HARLOW, COBRA PRIEST, *and* EROSTA *on stage right, the* THREE WITCHES *on stage left. The* DOVE *freezes, twig in mouth.*)

DOVE
(*Fear*)
Twitter . . . twitter.

EROSTA
(*Points at* DOVE)
That's him.
(DRUM MUSIC *up, as if for marching troops or guillotine*)

EROSTA
We know who you are!

ALL EXCEPT NARCISSUS
(*Echoing*)
We know who you are! Know—know——

EROSTA
We should have known with all that sweetness
that's so deadly!
(*They begin marching from each side of the stage.*)

DOVE
(*Runs to each corner of the stage trying to escape. At each corner he screams.*)
Twitter—
Twitter—
Twitter—
Twitter—
(*Down center straight to audience*)

EROSTA
Admit it.
(*Screams*)
CONFESSION'S GOOD—Admit who you are!

DOVE
(*Over shoulder, trying to be brave*)
I'm a—I'm a—I'm a DOVE.

COBRA PRIEST

Even the cobras have left the temple
of the cobra cult.

HARLOW

Glamour is dead.

WITCHES

Tigers' tits
And mummies' tongues,
Bubbling gall by the cauldronsful.

ALL

Meat loaf and orange,
Salvation and eternity,
Fire festivals
In the land of Baal!

EROSTA

(*Detectively*)
I *have* read the last testament . . .
I have, I have . . . where were you last seen?

DOVE

(*Over shoulder, stuttering*)
In a tree—in a tree . . .

EROSTA

I'll tell you—on John the Baptist's shoulder . . .
you were disguised as a Dove then, too.
(*Bitter*)
How does it feel to be GOD?
Do you like the looks of things?

COBRA PRIEST

Bring me my viper pit!

EROSTA

(*Hate*)
You are GOD.

ALL EXCEPT NARCISSUS

You are GOD!

(*A tremendous clash of thunder. Chaos. Blackout as they all rush at* DOVE. *Only* NARCISSUS *remains frozen.* MUSIC OF VIOLENCE AND MYSTERY: "Dies Irae" *from Verdi's* Requiem. *There is much moaning and wailing with a bit of keening as the thunder continues in the dark. When the lights come up, the characters are all forming a flower about* NARCISSUS.

The DOVE *has vanished, but high upstage center is a small dove icon with rays shining down from it onto the characters' flower formation. They are all looking up toward it.*

RITUAL MUSIC *up. The characters begin circling* NARCISSUS. *They wrap a golden mantle about him and place jewels in his hair. They do a warped dance, a choreography of the crippled, the sad, the yearning. All of the shapes generally considered horrid make up this dance. They are using their handicaps to dance. They do not leave the circle they have made in front of* NARCISSUS; *they dance low as they pass him so that the audience can see him to the waist.*)

NARCISSUS

(*To dove icon*)
Meat loaf and orange—
Henny Penny prophecies—
Tender tidings and small burdens—
Loss of all that was once a gift.

HARLOW

Still we weave our gossamer lives
Across the abyss
Not much and liable to break
But enough to make sleep less frightening
And firm enough to dream about.

NARCISSUS

Tidy passions
Protect us from the sea and wind.
(*The kaleidoscope set starts to turn.*)

EROSTA

Change and moving sifting sorrows,
Life's kaleidoscope turns clichés to gold.
Clichés come alive
Turning into new loves and fears.

Meat loaf and orange—
Henny Penny prophecies—
Tender tidings and small burdens—
Loss of all that was once a gift.
(*Music is up full now. Colors are exciting and exotic.*)

NARCISSUS

Tidy passions
Protect us from the sea and wind
That dust the cubbyholes of our mind.
Life's kaleidoscope turns clichés to gold.

(*Sad curtain*)

GEORGIE PORGIE

by George Birimisa

GEORGIE PORGIE was originally produced at Eugenia's Cooper Square Arts Theater on November 20, 1968. It was directed by the author with the following cast:

MOM, INA, and GRACE	Carole Getzoff
GEORGE	Claude Barbazon
MARV, THE STROLLER, JACK, RUFUS	Dan Leach
STEVE AND SKYLAR	Ron Schermer
THE MAN AND JIM	Barry Kael
MR. FINLEY	George Birimisa
GROVER SMITH	Lloyd Carson
TONY	Al Barino
CHORUS	Claude Barbazon
	Lloyd Carson
	Carole Getzoff
	Dan Leach
	Barry Kael
	Ron Schermer

GEORGE BIRIMISA was born in Santa Cruz, California, on February 21, 1924. His first play, *Degrees,* was produced at Theatre Genesis in New York in February, 1966. *Daddy Violet* opened at the Troupe Theater Club, moved to the Caffe Cino, and then toured the United States and Canada. *Mister Jello* opened at the Playbox in April, 1968, and was subsequently produced in London; the Rockefeller Foundation gave the author a travel grant to attend rehearsals. Other plays are *How Come You Don't Dig Chicks?* and *17 Loves and 17 Kisses*. In 1969 Birimisa moved to Hollywood, where he wrote a screenplay, *You're Beautiful,* and he now lives in a rural commune in Pennsylvania. He is at work on a new play.

ACT I

SCENE 1

(*As the play begins the* CHORUS *is seated in the audience. All the houselights are on.*)

ACTOR ONE: CLAUDE

(*Stands*)

The great men who in France prepared men's minds for the coming revolution were themselves extreme revolutionists!

ACTOR TWO: LLOYD, *a black actor*

They recognized no external authority of any kind whatever!

ACTOR THREE: CAROLE

Religion!

ACTOR FOUR: BARRY

Natural science!

ACTOR FIVE: DAN

Society!

ACTOR SIX: RON

Political institutions!

CLAUDE

Everything was subjected to the most unsparing criticism!

LLOYD

Everything must justify its existence before the judgment seat of history or give up existence!

CAROLE

Reason became the sole measure of everything!

DAN

I beg your pardon?

ALL

Reason became the sole measure of everything!

DAN

Everything?

ALL

Everything!

BARRY

(*Gets on stage and looks at audience*)
Good evening!

CAROLE

It was the time when, as Hegel says, the world stood upon its head—first in the sense that the human head, and the principles arrived at by its thought, claimed to be the basis of all human action and association; but by and by also in the wider sense that the reality that was in contradiction to these principles had, in fact, to be turned upside down.

ALL

Upside down?

CAROLE

Yes, upside down!

CLAUDE

Every form of society and government then existing . . .

LLOYD

Every old traditional action was flung into the lumber room as irrational!

CAROLE

The world had hitherto allowed itself to be led solely by prejudice!

BARRY

Everything in the past deserved only pity and contempt!

DAN

The kingdom of reason.

RON

Henceforth—

CLAUDE
Injustice!

LLOYD
Privilege!

CAROLE
Oppression!

BARRY
Were to be superseded by . . .

DAN
Eternal truth!

RON
Eternal right!

LLOYD
Equality based on nature and the inalienable rights of man!

ALL
Inalienable what?

LLOYD
The inalienable rights of man!

(*End of* CHORUS. CLAUDE *and* CAROLE *move to the stage that is set up for the first scene.* CAROLE *puts on robe and sits.* CLAUDE *has martini and paddle with a rubber ball attached. Lights up onstage.*)

MOM
There's food in the fridge, dear!

GEORGE
What?

MOM
I'll get you something to eat!

GEORGE
I'm not hungry, Mother!

MOM

But you said that yesterday!

GEORGE

Did I, Mother?
(MOM *goes backstage and comes back with a loaf of bread in a pan.*)

MOM

Just a nibble, dear?

SON

No!

MOM

If you'll just smell it, I'm sure it'll get to your appetite buds!

SON

It looks like Wonder Bread. Don't you understand that the wonder years have passed me by, Mother? I'm old—old and gray!

MOM

But it's homemade!

SON

Ugh . . . it's . . . it's spongy and white . . . white . . . just like you . . . like all of you. I want to watch my movies!

MOM

I baked it early this morning, Georgie.

GEORGE

The name is George!

MOM

Don't you remember, dear? I used to bake it every Saturday morning!

GEORGE

George, Mother!

MOM

Remember the deviled-ham sandwiches?

GEORGE

I'm thirty-eight years old!

MOM

You were so good, so good.

GEORGE

Georgie, at my age!

MOM

What, Georgie?

SON

Nothing, nothing, nothing!

MOM

You're young . . . why, in this day and age forty-four is very young!

GEORGE

Will you go away so I can watch my movies?

MOM

What, dear?

GEORGE

I've got a brand-new one. Wild, Mummy, wild!

MOM

Yes, you always gave your deviled-ham sandwiches to that sweet little pickaninny who had her kinky hair in six little braids. What was her name, dear?

GEORGE

What on earth are you talking about?

MOM

Ah—Alice—Alice Smallwood!

GEORGE

Alice Smallwood? How utterly quaint. I gave them to her because I couldn't stand Underwood Deviled Ham sandwiches then and I can't stand them now.

MOM

I don't believe you. You love Underwood Deviled Ham!

GEORGE

There are a lot of things I've never told you. Mother?

MOM

Yes, dear?

GEORGE

Will you please listen?

MOM

I am, dear.

GEORGE

There's something very important I want to tell you!

MOM

Do you remember the carnival, dear?

GEORGE

Mother, will you please——?

MOM

It was about six months after Charlie died.

GEORGE

Charlie?

MOM

Your father. Don't you remember?

GEORGE

Your son is a faggot, Mother.

MOM

You must remember the miniature golf course?

GEORGE

I'm queer, Mother!

MOM

It was in the center of the carnival and it was surrounded by enormous chunks of emerald glass. You loved it. I wanted to take you on the ferris wheel and into the fun house but all you wanted to do was stare at the enormous chunks of glass.

GEORGE

I'm a homosexual!

MOM

That's all you wanted to . . . do.

GEORGE

A degenerate, Mother dear! Now would you leave me alone so I can watch my dirty movie?

MOM

Remember, dear?

GEORGE

(*Singing*)
It's great to be gay, yeah, yeah, yeah!

MOM

Darling?

GEORGE

Please, Mother, I have Excedrin Headache Number One!

MOM

That's because you won't eat anything, Georgie. Mmmm . . . I'll cut you a great, big, thick slice of bread and I'll toast it and I've got some scrumptious homemade blueberry preserves!

GEORGE

I'd have indigestion for a week. I don't want that kind of good, Mother. I want a *man!*

MOM

Do you remember what you said?

GEORGE

I want a man!

MOM

Of course you remember. You thought the emerald-colored glass was real and you said . . . ? And you said . . . ?

GEORGE

When I grow up and become rich and famous, I'm going to buy you a dress made of emeralds and diamonds. Look, Mother, would you like me to tape that crummy little speech and give it to you for Mother's Day?

MOM

After we left the miniature golf course, we went to the fat-lady concession and the nice man let us in free, and when we came out he filled your pockets with nickels and dimes and——

GEORGE

It was pennies!

MOM

What about the red candy apple?

SON

It had a worm in it. Reminds me of one of my rough-trade tricks.

MOM

Would you care for a couple of aspirin?

GEORGE

In this day and age, Mother? You must be shining me on!

MOM

Doing what, Georgie?

GEORGE

Joshing, Mother, joshing!
(*From pillbox he takes a pill and downs it with his martini.*)
These are the only kind of pills I love, Mother. Now, you just give your little Georgie Porgie a few minutes and she'll—ah—he'll feel absolutely stunning!

MOM

Compoz or Cope?

GEORGE

Oh, just a smidgeon of compressed happiness to get me over the fact that I'm old and gray and—and—also—yes, Mother, to get me over that excruciatingly nice man who ran the fat-lady concession. Do you honestly remember him, Mother, the way he really was—after a hot piece of ass?

MOM

I don't know what you mean, dear.

GEORGE

Vulva? Pussy? Cunt!

MOM

Let me fix you something to eat, dear, you are not——

GEORGE

What about the next day?

MOM

What next day, dear?

GEORGE

When Mister Fat Lady Concession came acallin' for the payoff! He had a pointed nose with curlicues of hair coming out of his nostrils that were covered with seaweed-colored snot. We were living in that lice-infested railroad flat on Eddy Street. . . . All the time he was there, I stared out the window at the stupid cable cars. I could hear the two of you like pigs in heat.

MOM

If you'd stop filling your body with chemicals and liquor you might begin to see what really happened and remember it. Yes, Georgie, he did come over the next day. He knocked on the door but I didn't answer. He kept knocking and calling out. But we were very, very quiet. I was holding you in my arms and kissing you and finally he went away and you were so happy . . . so happy . . . and we took the money he had filled your pockets with and we went to Fisherman's Wharf and had a huge shrimp salad and later we watched the fishing boats bobbing up and down in the harbor. Just us, Georgie.

GEORGE

Bullshit! Next you'll be telling me I'm an Immaculate Conception.

MOM

It wasn't easy—a woman all alone!

GEORGE

All alone? You were even fucking around when Daddy was alive. What about that music professor who was always jerking off over Shicklgruber?

MOM

He was a kindly old gentleman who gave you trombone lessons for free, son.

GEORGE

He took it out in trade!

MOM

He gave them free because we were so poor!

GEORGE

Yes, Mother. But at the moment it really doesn't matter. I'm beginning to feel nice and cozy and in the best of all possible worlds. (*Sips his martini and then toasts* MOTHER)
Mmmmm. How lovely . . . mother and daughter . . . reminiscing . . .

MOM

Mother and son, Georgie.

GEORGE

I'm getting horny, Mother. Since you dig anything in pants, why don't you stay and watch my dirty movie? Two gorgeous weight lifters, Mummy.

MOM

I'll fix you a delicious deviled-ham sandwich, dear, and then I have to go to work. We must pay the rent, you know. . . .

GEORGE

Oh, Mother . . . .

(*Lights out onstage.* MOM *and* GEORGE *freeze. Lights up on* CHORUS. *As in previous* CHORUS, *they stand up and deliver their lines.*)

LLOYD

We know today that this kingdom of reason was nothing more than the idealized kingdom of the bourgeoisie!

BARRY

That this eternal right found its realization in bourgeois justice!

DAN

That this equality reduced itself to bourgeois equality before the law.

RON

That bourgeois property was proclaimed as one of the essential rights of man.

DAN

Did you say property?

RON

Yes, property. It became a natural law.

DAN

I see. Property was proclaimed as one of the essential rights of man.

ALL

Life, liberty, and the pursuit of property.

SCENE 2

(Lights on audience stay up as CHORUS *changes set for* SCENE 2. *All the lights go out. When they come up,* MARV *is seated in living room.* BLACK ACTOR *who plays statue is standing on a red box upstage. He is totally naked with a spotlight on him.* STEVE *comes dancing down center aisle, dances onto the stage, and stops in front of* MARV, *who has quickly picked up the Sunday* Times *and is pretending to read it.)*

STEVE
What do you think?

MARV
Hi ya!

STEVE
Hi! What do you think?

MARV
About what?

STEVE
My dancing . . . better, huh?

MARV
I didn't pay that much attention.
(*Goes back to paper*)

STEVE
Really hot out, you know?
(*No answer*)
I said it's really hot out!

MARV
. . . Supposed to rain.

STEVE
Marv?

MARV
What?

STEVE

You want me to do it again?

MARV

Oh, I'm sorry, I wasn't——

STEVE

Wasn't *what?*

MARV

I wasn't watching . . . that's all!

STEVE

Come on, Marvie!

MARV

All right, what is it now, Steve?

STEVE

Shit, such fucking innocence! Who the hell do you think you're kidding, Marv, huh? Come on—tell me! It's four o'clock in the morning and you're sitting there like—well, shit, man, you know you're just sitting there waiting!

MARV

Waiting?

STEVE

Yeah, waiting to see what time I come in. It's exactly four seventeen. Now, does that make you happy?

MARV

Steve, I'm not in the mood for an argument!

STEVE

So why aren't you in bed?

MARV

For the very simple reason that I couldn't sleep.

STEVE

Why is it that every time I go out you just happen to be up waiting for me? Come on, answer that one!

MARV
I am?

STEVE
Yes, you are and you know it.
(*Exits to backstage area and gets a Coke*)

MARV
You want to talk about it? Okay! Did you have a good time?

STEVE
It was okay.

MARV
What was *he* like?

STEVE
Oh, brother, here we go!

MARV
Oh, I get it. Now you're going to tell me you went to a bar and didn't pick up anyone. Right?

STEVE
You really want to know?

MARV
No, I don't.

STEVE
Okay, I'll tell you then.

MARV
Look, just forget it!

STEVE
No, I won't forget it. I'm going to tell you the truth—what you're scared to death to hear!

MARV
Look who's talking about the truth!

STEVE

(*Comes running in from backstage. Leans over chair and shouts*)
He was a nigger!

MARV

That's all you dig, isn't it? Isn't it, Steve?

STEVE

That's right, that's all I dig! Black and beautiful. You should've
seen him, Marvie. Wowie! What a groove. Seven feet one and
twelve inches. Now, does that make you feel any better?

MARV

Yeah, I feel great. You feel good now that you've had your king-
sized pacifier?

STEVE

Yeah, I feel just great.
(STEVE *goes into a wild dance across the stage and ends up kissing
the rear end of the* LIVING STATUE.)

MARV

Very funny.
(*Pause*)
I have to be up at eight!

STEVE

So go to bed!

MARV

We just can't go on like this, Steve!

STEVE

We just can't go on like this, Steve. Shit, Marv, like what?

MARV

We're going to have to settle this once and for all and—and it
might as well be now!

STEVE

You really got a fantasy going, don't you? You really do want to
believe that I'm fucking around every time I go out, don't you?

MARV

Yes, I'm afraid I do.

STEVE

You really believe that?

MARV

I didn't for a long time, Steve, but I know you—now!

STEVE

Yeah . . . yeah . . . I know it doesn't make any difference to you but—what the hell is this, Marv, a marriage out of Peyton Place? Huh? So I was down in the Village at the club near the docks and I had a few beers—but that's all, believe me! I was just enjoying myself—wasn't thinking about sex at all. I saw this one guy that I wasn't attracted to at all. Oooh, he had a long, long orange beard and his nose was pointed and his mouth—ooooh—I went over and talked to him. Ended up giving him my beads and——

MARV

So I noticed.

STEVE

He's a poet from Egypt . . . ugly as hell. I wanted to invite him over for dinner so he could meet you. I know you'd groove on his mind.

MARV

Oh?

STEVE

Christ, does everything have to be sex?

MARV

Yes, for you it does! Absolutely everything!

STEVE

Oh, I see. Everything!

MARV

If you'd read a book once in a while, you might stop being so compulsive!

STEVE

That's your answer to life. Read a book!

MARV

I didn't say that!

STEVE

I've got his phone number right here. You want to call him?

MARV

Right away, Steve. I'll call him at five in the morning and ask him if he's making it with you!

STEVE

So call him tomorrow.

MARV

What difference does it make? You're out every night!

STEVE

I was home last night! I made dinner for both of us.

MARV

Practically every night. But what really bugs me is your bringing all these different guys around. You tell me you're not making it with them but it always turns out that you are. I don't care. If only you were honest about it, it wouldn't be so——

STEVE

You don't care? That's hilarious! Why do you think I lie to you? Huh? Why?

MARV

This is going to be a beauty. Why?

STEVE

Because you're so damned jealous. Hell, all we did was——

MARV

Forget it. I'm going to bed—*alone!*
(*He moves stage left.*)

STEVE

Marv?

(*Runs after him*)

I have to sleep on the couch, huh?

MARV

That's the general idea.

STEVE

Okay, Marv! Let's have it out—right now!

MARV

So tell the truth!

STEVE

I know how you feel, Marv, but I am telling the truth. I really am—even if it's for the first time. Marv?

MARV

What?

STEVE

(*Moves away*)

You know, it might be a good idea if I split for a couple of months.

MARV

Are you naïve! You think that'll change anything?

(*No answer*)

What are you going to do, go home to Mommy and Daddy?

STEVE

Why not?

MARV

But it's no solution. You did the same thing last year!

STEVE

So maybe it'll be different this time!

MARV

It just isn't going to happen, Steve. You'll go out to the Coast but when you get back it'll be great for a couple of months and then, boom! Out cruising every goddamned night!

STEVE

You're saying something. I'm not quite sure what!

MARV

I've reached the point—well—I don't believe anything you say any more—not a word that comes out of your mouth!

STEVE

I see . . . I see . . . you want me to cut out—for good?

MARV

Can you think of another solution?

STEVE

I just did!

MARV

But it's no solution!

STEVE

How do you know it isn't? I want to change! I want to stay home and read a book or watch television but I've just got to keep going! I just got this thing inside me—it's not when I'm in the bar or anything like that. It's going there and leaving. That's when I'm the happiest—when I'm moving, rushing, really going somewhere, and I don't care where it is or what. I just can't sit and read and watch television. It's stupid. I'm not like that, Marv.

MARV

That's crap and you know it!

STEVE

I—ah—Marv, don't you know . . . .
(*He moves to him now . . . close . . . and on these lines tries to kiss him.*)
. . . you're the only one I've ever cared for? I never thought I could care for anyone. You're the only one I've ever loved in my whole life and——

MARV

Just *cut* it. Next I'll get the tears. I'm not falling for that crap any more!

STEVE

My feelings are crap, huh? Okay, Marvin, I'll leave right now!

MARV

What?

STEVE

Right this second!
(*Looks at watch*)
At four forty-three. That's right now.
(*Quickly he is putting on his boots and his shirt, getting ready to leave.*)

MARV

Well—if that's the way you want it!

STEVE

It's the way you want it and you know it! I'll pick up my things in the morning.

MARV

So we can have another big scene?

STEVE

I'll come when you're at work!

MARV

(*Pointing at* LIVING BLACK STATUE)
Don't forget to take that!

STEVE

Larry gave it to both of us. It's half yours!

MARV

I don't want it!

STEVE

So I'll take it tomorrow!

MARV

Take it now!

STEVE
NOW?

MARV
That's what I said, now!

STEVE
Wow!
(*He begins to laugh wildly.*)

MARV
What's so funny?

STEVE
Oh, do you have a *thing*, baby!

MARV
Oh, I see some brilliant truth is about to emerge from the mouth of the ignorant one!

STEVE
Are you middle class! Yeah . . . you're a WASP. Yoweeeee!

MARV
Yes, I am. So what?

STEVE
So *what?* Man, I just figured it out. I really did and I don't have a book . . . I did it all by myself. Now—listen—if I dug middle-class faggots who worked on Madison Avenue you wouldn't be uptight. That statue bugs the living shit out of you because it's black . . . that's all. All right, now I'm going to give you the absolute truth. Yeah, I did talk to an Egyptian poet tonight . . . interesting guy but I didn't tell you what happened afterward. I was out with a beautiful jig. Wowie! I just left him and I've got his smell on me. It's wild, Marvie baby, just wild. Here, you want a sniff?

MARV
The filth is finally coming out! All this—you think you have to degrade yourself with a colored guy because——

STEVE

Colored? What color, Marvie? Green, purple, blue?

MARV

Because you're loaded with guilt!

STEVE

That's profound! Yeah. Guilt. Tell me, Marvie baby, do you know any faggot who isn't loaded with guilt? Do you know any human being who isn't? What about you, baby? Why don't you ever hit the sack with a black man? You scared it might rub off?

MARV

I think you better leave!

STEVE

I'm going—right now!

MARV

You can find some other middle-class sucker to support you.

STEVE

I was waiting for that!

MARV

So, you're interested in the truth. I'll give you the truth, Steve! Truth Number One—I pay the rent, the gas, the electricity, and I buy all the food. Truth Number Two—you've got more cash than I do from your unemployment check. Truth Number Three—I'm supposed to support you while you bend over for every guy in the city!

STEVE

It's with any black man with a big cock!

MARV

And that's the truth!

STEVE

Gloriosky! We've finally found the truth!
(*Lights go out on* STEVE *and* MARV. *The only light in theater is a spot on the* LIVING BLACK STATUE. *The* CHORUS *delivers its lines while seated.*)

LLOYD

The demand for equality was no longer limited to political rights!

CAROLE

It was extended also to the social conditions of individuals!

BARRY

It was not simply class privileges that were to be abolished, but class distinctions themselves!

CLAUDE

A communism, ascetic, denouncing all the pleasures of life, Spartan, was the first form of the new teaching!

LLOYD

Then came the three great Utopians!

CAROLE

Saint-Simon!

BARRY

Fourier!

CLAUDE

And . . . Owen!

CAROLE

They do not claim to emancipate a particular class to begin with but all humanity at once!

BARRY

They wish to bring in the kingdom of reason and eternal justice!

LLOYD

Groovy, man, groovy!

ALL

Eternal justice?

LLOYD

That's what the honkies say!

SCENE 3

(The ACTORS *clear the stage. It is bare. Lights up onstage.* INA *is playing hopscotch.* GEORGE *comes down center aisle. He has a bubble kit and is making and blowing bubbles. He makes them go over the heads of the audience. He moves down aisle. Now he begins to sing.)*

GEORGE

There is nothing fina, in the state of Carolina, than Ina, my Ina Lee! *(He moves onstage and covers the stage with bubbles.* INA *stops playing hopscotch and plays with the bubbles.)*

INA

Let me do it, Georgie!

GEORGE

I want to blow some more!

INA

They're beautiful!

GEORGE

Here, I'll blow a big one!
(He does.)

INA

I'll bet I can blow a bigger one!

GEORGE

Okay. Here.
(He hands her the bubble kit.)
Go on.

INA

Just a second, Georgie!
(She tries to blow a bubble and fails.)

GEORGE

You don't know how to do it!

INA

I do, too.

GEORGE
You do not!

INA
(*She tries again*)
They're very silly! I don't——

GEORGE
You're just mad because you can't do it. Oh, Ina, let me show you the dance I learned in dancing school. It's the Mexican hat dance! (*He puts his hands on his hips and demonstrates.*)

INA
You're a sissy show-off. Just because your mother sends you to dancing school!

GEORGE
What are you doing here all by yourself?

INA
What do you think I'm doing?

GEORGE
All by yourself?

INA
What are you doing?

GEORGE
Blowing bubbles, Ina.

INA
You're up to something!

GEORGE
I am not!

INA
This isn't the way you go home!

GEORGE
I like to go home different ways!

INA
So go!

GEORGE
I can sit here if I want to. It's a free country!

INA
That's how much you know!

GEORGE
I'll sit here as long as I want to!

INA
Why?

GEORGE
Because. That's why!

INA
That's no reason. You're silly!

GEORGE
I am not!

INA
You're a liar, Georgie!

GEORGE
I am not!

INA
You know you came here to see me!

GEORGE
Why would I want to see you . . . you're ugly!

INA
I am not! Come on, play hopscotch with me!

GEORGE
That's a sissy game—for girls!

INA
You know I'll beat you!

GEORGE

Does Joe play it with you?

INA

None of your bee's wax, Georgie!

GEORGE

Come on—does he?

INA

I said, none of your bee's wax!

GEORGE

I'll bet that isn't all he plays with you!

INA

What do you mean by that?

GEORGE

You know what I mean!

INA

You better tell me, Georgie!

GEORGE

Come here, Ina. Pussy. Here, pussy. Here, pussy. Pussy! Pussy! Pussy!

INA

You just stop that or . . . .

GEORGE

Meooow! Meooow! Meooow! Let me see your pussy! Let me see it, Ina!
(*He grabs her and tries to lift her dress. They fight. She pulls away and slaps him and runs to stage right.*)

INA

You're . . . you're . . . .

GEORGE

Let's do it, too, Ina!

INA
Do what?

GEORGE
You know!

INA
No, I don't know!

GEORGE
You do, too!

INA
You want a kiss?

GEORGE
That's kid stuff. I want to do what Joe did to you!

INA
He didn't do anything to me!

GEORGE
He did, too!

INA
He did not!

GEORGE
Let me put my finger in, then!

INA
You're nasty!

GEORGE
You got one of those dirty books?

INA
I don't know what you're talking about.

GEORGE
Joe told me about the one you showed him, Ina!

INA
You're lying!

GEORGE

I am not. He showed it to me. The one where Superman is fucking Lois Lane with a fifty-foot peter!

INA

All right, all right . . . But why should I show it to you? You couldn't do anything, anyway. You're a sissy. Go back to your dancing class!

GEORGE

Joe does it to you, doesn't he?

INA

Joe does it to you, doesn't he?
(*Mimics him*)
Georgie Porgie wants to do it with a girl. That's a twist . . . yes . . . Now let me tell you something, Georgie Porgie . . . what Joe told me. What Joe told me about you!

GEORGE

He didn't tell you anything!

INA

He did, too. He told me all about you, Georgie Porgie. How you tried to play with him! He told everyone. We all know about Georgie Porgie, don't we, girls?
(*She moves in on him. She lifts her skirt up high.*)
Get a good look at it, Georgie Porgie. You'd be scared to put your finger in it. Girls? Girls? Girls?
(*The* ACTORS *in the audience run up onstage. They grab* GEORGE *and drag him center stage.*)

LLOYD

Georgie Porgie!

DAN

Puddnin pie!

BARRY

Kissed the girls and made them cry . . .

RON

When the girls came out to play . . .

LLOYD

Georgie Porgie ran away.
(*Now they form a circle around him and they take each other's hands and skip around him.*)

ALL

Georgie Porgie, puddnin pie, kissed the girls and made them cry. When the girls came out to play, Georgie Porgie ran away!
(*They repeat this a couple of times. Then they come downstage of* GEORGE, *hiding him from the audience.* INA *gets a red shawl and a large picture hat and puts it on* GEORGE. *Then the* ACTORS *part and* GEORGE *is sitting with hat, etc.*)

INA

(*Shouting*)
Joe?????? Joe?????? Come and see the pretty little girl. Oh, Joe, she's very pretty. Joe???? Joe????????
(*Now* LLOYD *comes downstage. The* ACTORS *will form a line facing the audience. This* CHORUS *is done very precisely and fast.*)

LLOYD

Yes, Fourier!

DAN

(*Moving quickly downstage*)
Fourier on the position of woman in bourgeois society!

RON

(*Next to him*)
Fourier was the first to declare that in any given society the degree of woman's emancipation is the natural measure of the general emancipation!

BARRY

As Kant introduces into natural science the idea of the ultimate destruction of the earth, Fourier introduced into historical science that of the ultimate destruction of the human race.
(CLAUDE *moves downstage in woman's hat. He stamps his foot on the floor.*)

ALL

The ultimate destruction of the human race!

SCENE 4

(The MAN *stays onstage. All the other* ACTORS *go back to their seats. The* STROLLER *moves slowly up the aisle lighting a cigarette. The* MAN *leans against the wall. He is wearing very tight blue jeans and he is obviously well-endowed. The* STROLLER *looks him up and down, his eyes concentrating on the bulge in his pants. Finally he moves onstage.)*

STROLLER

Hiya! How's it going?

MAN

Okay, I guess. You got an extra cigarette on you?

STROLLER

Ah . . . they're Virginia Slims!

MAN

That's all right!

STROLLER

I'll bet you smoke Camels.

MAN

Yeah.

STROLLER

Mmmm.

MAN

Damned hot, huh?

STROLLER

Me?

MAN

I was talking about the weather!

STROLLER

Oh? Stoned, I guess . . . a little fuzzy right now!

MAN

Grass?

STROLLER
Scotch!

MAN
Oh?

STROLLER
So what are you doing?

MAN
I've got a couple of hours to kill.

STROLLER
Oh . . . really?

MAN
What time you got?

STROLLER
All the time in the world.
(*He looks at clock on 42nd Street*)
Ah—it's two.

MAN
A stinking hour and a half to wait on the goddamned bus.

STROLLER
Port Authority, huh?

MAN
Yeah, four ten.

STROLLER
You've got two hours and ten minutes to kill!

MAN
That's about it.

STROLLER
You in the service?

MAN
Stationed in Norfolk!

STROLLER

Oh, yeah? I was down there a few years back. They call it the *asshole* of the Navy!

MAN

Still is!

STROLLER

Where you from?

MAN

The Bronx.

STROLLER

Oh . . . you really must know the city, huh?

MAN

Things change damned fast!

STROLLER

Ah . . . did you make out this weekend?

MAN

Didn't try! Spent my time with the family.

STROLLER

Oh, I see . . . you're a married man?

MAN

Not that stupid. With my parents.

STROLLER

Oh . . .

MAN

You pimping?

STROLLER

What?

MAN

Maybe you got a couple of Harlem hookers?

STROLLER

You're kidding!

MAN

It's either that or the other!

STROLLER

Well . . . ah . . .

MAN

You a little gay, huh?

STROLLER

I guess that's the general idea.

MAN

So?

STROLLER

My apartment's not far from here and—I've got plenty of liquor.

MAN

You got any grass?

STROLLER

I didn't know servicemen turned on. I—

MAN

Are you kidding? Half the guys in Vietnam turn on.

STROLLER

I—ah—I——

MAN

I'd love to turn on right now.

STROLLER

I don't have any.

MAN

Don't you have a buddy who has some?

STROLLER

Well . . . yeah . . . but he's out of town!

MAN

That's the end of that, huh? You got any beer?

STROLLER

We can stop at the deli.

MAN

I really wanted to turn on and I only have a couple of hours.

STROLLER

We can grab a cab—only about twenty blocks!

MAN

Naw . . . forget it!

STROLLER

We're wasting all this time talking!

MAN

But—shit, man, I'm not queer!

STROLLER

That's why I'm talking to you. I could have all the fags I want!

MAN

So what do you dig?

STROLLER

Ah . . .

MAN

What do you dig?

STROLLER

Real men!

MAN

Ah . . . what do you—you know. . . .

STROLLER

Well . . . I . . . ah . . . I'd like you to be top man!

MAN

That could mean a lot of things!

STROLLER

So come down and have a drink!

MAN

(*Starts to walk away*)
Forget it!

STROLLER

You don't have to do anything!

MAN

Then what the hell do you want me to come down there for?

STROLLER

You know what I mean!

MAN

I *don't* know what you mean!

STROLLER

You want a blueprint?

MAN

(*Really walks away*)
Forget it. I'll see you around!

STROLLER

Hell, all you have to do is lie back and I'll do the rest!

MAN

On my stomach or on my back?

STROLLER

Come on! This is damned stupid, you know? Hell, you're a real rugged-looking guy and I wouldn't want you to be queer. Hell, I'm sure a lot of your buddies get a blow job when they're hard up!

MAN

You want to suck my cock?

STROLLER

That's the general idea.

(*From his coat the* MAN *pulls out a wallet. He opens it up. There is a badge in it. He shows it to* STROLLER.)

MAN

All right, let's go!

STROLLER

(*Pulls away in shock*)
I—ah——

MAN

Let's go!
(STROLLER *pulls away further.* MAN *kicks him in balls.* STROLLER *doubles over and* MAN *gives him a karate chop to the back of his neck.* STROLLER *falls.* MAN *gets on top of him and begins to beat his head against the floor. Lights out on stage and then up on audience.*)

LLOYD

The development of industry upon a capitalistic basis made poverty and misery of the working masses conditions of existence of society.

CAROLE

Cash payment became more and more, in Carlyle's phrase, the sole nexus between man and man!

RON

Formerly, the feudal vices had openly stalked about in broad daylight!

CLAUDE

Though not eradicated, they were now at any rate thrust into the background!

LLOYD

In their stead, the bourgeois vices, hitherto practiced in secret, began to blossom all the more luxuriantly!

CAROLE

Trade became to a greater and greater extent cheating!

RON

Oppression by force was replaced by corruption!

CLAUDE

The sword, as the first social lever, by gold!

LLOYD

Gold, baby?

ALL

Yeah . . . yeah . . . yeah. . . .

SCENE 5

(Now all the lights come up on the stage and in the theater. We are in a courtroom. The MAN *gets a chair and places it downstage. He walks offstage and then enters. He holds up his hand.)*

LLOYD
(From where he is seated in audience)
Do you swear to tell the truth, the whole truth, and nothing but the truth, so help you God?

MAN
I do.

LLOYD
Be seated!

MAN
(He sits.)
Yes, surely, in my own words.

CAROLE
(From her chair)
Will you speak up so the court can hear you!

MAN
Yes, surely, in my own words. Ah—first I'd like to say that I do feel embarrassed about the language used by the defendant, but ah—well, I realize that for justice to be done, I must say it as it is. Well, I was standing on the southwest corner of 41st Street and Eighth Avenue at exactly one fifty-eight of the morning of August 17th, 1968. I was waiting for Detective O'Connor, who was checking out the men's room at the Port Authority bus terminal. You see, the bus terminal and the seedy bars in the area are hangouts for homosexuals who prey on the servicemen. My job on the vice squad is to check the bars immediately across the street from the terminal for degenerates. I would like to describe the bar where I first met the defendant. It is well-known by the police. The graffiti in the men's room is disgusting and the walls are covered with sperm where the degenerates have masturbated. It is not unusual to find one of them in the men's room having oral copulation with a serviceman. They ply these young men with drinks and money.

Well, Your Honor, I was making use of a urinal in this homosexual hangout when the defendant entered. He stood next to me and kept looking down at my penis and licking his lips. I left immediately and he followed me. Well, Your Honor, this is the part that I dislike speaking about in an open court, but I do realize it is my duty. The defendant said . . .

(*He looks into little black book.*)

. . . quote, "Hello. It's hot out. I'll bet you feel the same." I answered, "Oh?" He said, quote, "Would you like a blow job? I'm the best cocksucker in town!" I have only been on the vice squad for a few months and I was shocked. However, I answered, "Is that all you do?" He said, "Anything and everything. Would you like to shove it up my ass?" That's when I took out my badge and put the defendant under arrest, Your Honor. He resisted, but I subdued him in the manner taught at the police academy and he was not injured. On the way to the station, the defendant tried to bribe me in the presence of Detective O'Connor. Of course, I refused his bribe.

JUDGE

(*He stands and looks at the* STROLLER *who is back in his seat.*)
Will you rise for sentencing?

STROLLER
Yes, Your Honor!

JUDGE
You have been found guilty on two counts, One, of lewd language in public. Two, of trying to bribe an officer of the law. On count one, thirty days or one hundred dollars. On count two, six months in the county jail. The sentences will *not* run concurrently.

LLOYD

(*This is the* CHORUS *now.*)
Compared with the splendid promises of the philosophers, the social and political institutions born of the "triumph of reason" were bitterly disappointing caricatures.

STROLLER (DAN)
Society presented nothing but wrongs.

CAROLE
To remove these was the task of reason.

DAN

To remove these was the task of reason!

RON

It was necessary, then, to discover a new and more perfect system of social order.

CAROLE

What?

LLOYD

(*To* JUDGE)
Social order, Whitey, social order.
(*Now the* BLACK ACTOR [LLOYD] *goes stage center. He looks at the audience.*)
There will be a ten-minute intermission.

ACT II

SCENE 1

(*The lights come up.* GEORGE *is lying on the bed in his shorts.* GRACE *enters down center aisle. She is singing.*)

GRACE

Where have all the young men gone . . . la da . . . da . . . da. . . .
(*She takes off coat and kisses* GEORGE.)
Hi, honey! Just get home?

GEORGE

'Bout an hour. How'd it go?

GRACE

The neo-fascists were out in force; you know, the rotten-egg syndrome? It was truly inspiring, though. Two hundred fifty thousand peace marchers.

GEORGE

The radio said a hundred thousand.

GRACE

When I left the UN Plaza twenty minutes ago, they were still streaming in! Of course, the *News* will say forty thousand, the *Nation* one hundred and fifty, and the *National Guardian* will give the actual figure.

GEORGE

Which is yours, right?
(*He pulls her down onto the bed and kisses her.*)

GRACE

I didn't say that. By the way, Tom was beautiful!

GEORGE

Oh?

GRACE

Tom doesn't have a hostile bone in his body! He just kept smiling away even with the egg yolk on his chin! He said it was great for the skin.

GEORGE

Tom *Seymour?*

GRACE

(*Opens her bag*)
Oh, the Dubois Club handed out free copies of the *Guardian*. A
fascinating article by Burchett! Did you know he's in Hanoi?

GEORGE

No, I didn't, Grace.

GRACE

Listen to this, Georgie . . .
(*She looks through* Guardian.)
. . . Where is it? Ah! Let's see—he writes about a leprosarium near
Hanoi that was attacked by American planes. Thirteen attacks and
over one hundred buildings destroyed. Ah! Listen—
(*She reads.*)
"Lepers who were buried after the first attacks were bombed out
of their graves in subsequent attacks; some of the buried were
exhumed by bombs several times."

GEORGE

The resurrection, huh?

GRACE

That's not funny . . . ah, honey?

GEORGE

Yeah, Grace?

GRACE

When are you going to see *Salt of the Earth?*

GEORGE

I dunno . . . one of these days, I guess.

GRACE

I'll go with you. I want to see it again!

GEORGE

Well. . . .

GRACE

How 'bout tomorrow?

GEORGE

I'm going to the poetry reading at Theatre Genesis.

GRACE

That's in the evening, isn't it?

GEORGE

Yeah, but I want to rewrite one of them.

GRACE

I could see that movie twenty times!

GEORGE

(*Laughing*)
Twenty times? Really, Grace!

GRACE

It's Brecht without irony. At first I assumed it would be a simple
tale of the working man fighting the dirty capitalists, but it isn't
that at all. The Mexican women have the status of beasts of burden—the men actually treat them like farm animals. The strike is
progressing and then the mine company gets an injunction against
the men—they can no longer picket on mine property, and since
the town and their very homes belong to the company, it looks
as if the strike is doomed. However, the injunction says nothing
about women picketing on mine property. So the women picket
and the police throw them in jail. This changes everything—the
catalytic event——

GEORGE

Catalytic event, Grace?

GRACE

Yes, the catalytic event redefines the man-woman relationship.
The husbands begin to see their wives as human beings and consequently equal. The movie really says that all human beings have
to love before there can be any historical progress.

GEORGE

Oh, Grace, it sounds pretty pat to me!
(*He pulls her flat on the bed and gets on top of her.*)

GRACE

Pretty what?

GEORGE

Pat—and very dull!

GRACE

That's because you have no social consciousness!

GEORGE

And . . . you have no human consciousness.

GRACE

I'm not in the mood for arguing . . . you're not going to bring me down . . . I feel great.

GEORGE

(*Kisses her neck*)
Mmmmmm.

GRACE

You hungry?

GEORGE

No, Grace, I'm not. I was trying to write.

GRACE

You feel like a goodie?

GEORGE

Yes, I do.
(*He lifts her blouse and kisses her on the stomach.*)

GRACE

(*Quickly getting up*)
Let's go to Schrafft's.

GEORGE

You know I can't stand that place.

GRACE

They have pure cream in their coffee.

GEORGE

Big deal. Aren't you exhausted from all that marching?

GRACE

No, I'm full of energy.

GEORGE

(*Gets poem from stack on floor next to bed.*)
I finished a new poem.

GRACE

Oh?

GEORGE

You want to read it?

GRACE

I'll read it in the morning!

GEORGE

Read it now, Grace, it isn't very long!

GRACE

I'm just not in the mood right now . . . that's all.

GEORGE

Grace, can I ask you a question?

GRACE

Help yourself.

GEORGE

How come you're always slobbering at the mouth to read Tom
Seymour's stuff? Why is that, Grace?

GRACE

Here we go . . . off and running!

GEORGE

Why is that?

GRACE

You're being infantile, Georgie!

GEORGE

Why is it that every time you try to put me down you call me Georgie? You'd flip out if I called you Gracie. Come on, tell me!

GRACE

Which question would you like me to answer, *George?*

GEORGE

Be my guest, *Gracie!*

GRACE

I'm going to Schrafft's!
(*She gets off edge of bed and moves to chair. She takes off her skirt and starts putting on another one.*)

GEORGE

(*Kneeling on bed*)
Tom Seymour's writing has a Brechtian quality. Tom Seymour is on the verge of greatness! Tom Seymour leads an existential existence with egg yolk on his face!

GRACE

Will you stick to the issue, George? Do you really believe it will make any difference in *your* writing if Tom's a great writer or a lousy hack? Georgie, it's not the——

GEORGE

George, goddamn it!

GRACE

You set yourself up as a Georgie and then you want people to call you George. Very interesting!

GEORGE

I'm glad you think so.

GRACE

It's what's inside you that counts—what you can produce honestly —as an artist!

GEORGE

Maybe if my wife had a little confidence in me I might be a great writer!

GRACE

You want blind loyalty? I can't give you that! That's why I want you to see that movie, George. You'd never be any good if I gave you that. Don't you understand? Do you remember when you walked out of that creative-writing class at the New School because they criticized one of your poems? You don't want to face what's going on inside—your feelings. All you want is praise!

GEORGE

You're twisting the truth as per usual. Do you know what you are, Gracie, dear? Would you like a bit of unvarnished criticism about you?

GRACE

I've never said you don't have potential. Why, hell, you're ten times the writer you were when I met you.

GEORGE

Thanks a lot!

GRACE

You're welcome a lot. Evidently you've forgotten how it was when we first met. How terrified you were of me. And—and it was because I'm a woman. When we met, you were emotionally cut off from over half the human race. Then you began to flower!

GEORGE

Yeah, yeah, yeah! Gracie brought Georgie Porgie out of his shell and now Grace is wearing two (*makes a motion to her breasts*) gold stars for merit beyond the call of duty!

GRACE

Your phony cynicism can't hide the truth!

GEORGE

Did the heroine turn the faggot into a skirt-chasing, hairy-chested hetero?

GRACE

(*She laughs.*)
I'm afraid not!

GEORGE

We really have the truth, don't we? Grace, why did you demonstrate today? Was it for peace in Vietnam or was it for Tom Seymour?

GRACE

You are something! Would you like me to keep my eyes cast down at all times and not speak to any man, not even the milkman? Is that what you want—a piece of property instead of a wife?

GEORGE

You went to his apartment after, didn't you? Didn't you, Grace?

GRACE

Vomit it out, Georgie Porgie!

GEORGE

Tom Seymour—the uptight, cop-out artist! You talk about me and yet you just won't give me a chance. Christ, you don't want to see anything, do you, Grace? What about Tom's latent homosexuality? It's dripping out of his ears!

GRACE

It just kills you because Tom is a real man, doesn't it? To you, everyone has to be a faggot! Is that the only way you can survive?

GEORGE

Yeah, it's the only way, Gracie, dear. When Tom was over here a few weeks ago, I was in my shorts and he couldn't keep his eyes off me. He said——

GRACE

(*She laughs*)
Oh. . . .

GEORGE

He couldn't keep his eyes off me! He said, "What have you got in those shorts, Georgie, a Pepsi bottle?"

GRACE

(*Laughing harder*)
I don't——

GEORGE

That's exactly what he said, Grace!

GRACE

All right . . . I give in! I've been wrong all along. The whole world is queer. Heterosexuality has gone down the tube of history. Andy Warhol and the fags of Madison Avenue have taken over the world. Does that make you feel nice and warm?

GEORGE

Okay . . . okay . . . Grace, why is it that the moment I start making love to you, you turn off? When I'm hard you want me to be soft? Soft and spongy and cuddly . . . is Tom like that, Grace? Is he? Is that why you dig him?

GRACE

You're disgusting!

GEORGE

Am I, Grace? You want me to put on my Max Factor and my high heels? Grace, wouldn't it be a lot simpler for you to go out and get yourself a nice chick?

GRACE

You're sick—you're——

GEORGE

I'll give you my pants and my cock. Ah—correction, you already have them!

GRACE

Oh, now it's me, too? I guess there's no one left who isn't queer or latent. You just don't want to understand anything, do you? You wonder why I cut you off the other night? Are you really that desensitized by your faggotry? What on earth do you think a woman is? Do you—what do you think I am? Dear God, love is more than an erection! I'm not a hole. I'm a woman, George. I'm not one of your faggots who thinks a penis is a weapon!

GEORGE

What difference does it make? Can't you see how everything is completely and totally fucked up?

GRACE

What difference does it make? If you haven't found the answer to that question—well, I can't tell you! Did you ever hear of a such a thing as a man and a woman being in love? I'm talking of really caring for each other—of giving and taking and having children and being part of the pattern of life. Love, George, love! It may sound square and perverted to your inverted mind but it's what makes the world go round. It's what gives reason to all of this. You might call it a group, a universal consciousness. And—heterosexual love just happens to be the way things are on the planet Earth!

GEORGE

Maybe I should pack my bags and take off for the moon!

GRACE

Oh, George! It's——

GEORGE

Maybe the UN should create an enclave up there for faggots! Would you like that, Grace? You want social consciousness? You're the one who's prejudiced. Despite all your pretensions to being a revolutionary, you're—plain middle class! Your attitude toward homosexuals is middle-class bullshit! You're a complete victim of the power structure—that's what's so ironic. You play right into their hands, Gracie dear!

GRACE

It's so simple—simple—simple—simple! Why can't you see it? You want to wallow in your infantile dream world—playing with boys instead of acting up to the responsibility of being a man. That's where it's at, George, being a man and accepting the horrors and terrors of that position in this world. Don't you know that being a faggot is the big cop-out? Don't you know where it leads to? Fascism, George! When people are cut off from the mainstream of life, when they're alienated from nature, when they're fighting it, what else can they be? Their reality is all twisted. I feel sorry for you—sorry! Sorry! Sorry! Sorry! Sorry!

GEORGE

(*Absolute rage. Both are screaming and hysterical.*)
You feel sorry for me?
(*He grabs her and presses her against the wall. She has her coat and her purse and is trying to leave.*)
Grace, do you know what a fag hag is? Do you? Well, I'll tell you! *You,* dear! It's a woman who's afraid of a real man. It's a woman who really wants another woman, but she's too frightened to admit she's queer so she picks on a faggot like me or a potential one like Tom Seymour! Baby, the fascists of this world are people like you who don't know where they're at, who are too terrified to admit what they really dig! The sick latents are the ones who go out and make the wars, Gracie dear. And that's you, baby, a fag hag—all the way down the line! Fag hag! Fag hag! Fag hag! Fag hag!
(*Stage lights go down quickly and houselights come up.*)

ACTOR TWO: LLOYD

It is just as impossible to determine absolutely the moment of death, for physiology proves that death is not an instantaneous, momentary phenomenon, but a very protracted process.

ACTOR FIVE: DAN

In like manner every organized being is every moment the same and not the same; every moment he assimilates matter supplied from without, and gets rid of other matter; every moment some cells of his body die and others build themselves anew; in a longer or shorter time, the matter of his body is completely renewed and is replaced by other molecules of matter, so that every organized being is always himself and yet something other than himself.

ALL

. . . So that every organized being is always himself, and yet something other than himself.

SCENE 2

(*An apartment on Sutton Place.* MR. FINLEY *is seated. He sips a martini. We hear a flushing toilet.* JIM *enters. He is wearing blue jeans. He looks at* FINLEY *and buttons his fly.*)

MR. FINLEY

Would you care for a drink, ah—ah——

JIM

(*Reaches in* FINLEY's *shirt pocket and takes a cigarette. He lights it and throws the pack on coffee table.*)
Jim! Jim Kelly!

MR. FINLEY

Irish, huh?

JIM

(*Throws match on floor.* MR. FINLEY *eyes it.*)
Part.

MR. FINLEY

Scotch?
(*Picks up match and puts it in ashtray.*)
Vodka? Bourbon?

JIM

No, thanks.

MR. FINLEY

How about a cool gin and tonic?

JIM

(*Puts his feet on the coffee table and begins to shake it slowly.*)
You got any Bud?

FINLEY

Any *what?*

JIM

Budweiser—you know, *beer?*
(*He is shaking the table very hard. A wine bottle is shaking.* MR. FINLEY *takes the wine bottle and moves it to another table.*)

FINLEY

I'll call the delicatessen. They'll deliver it right away.

JIM

Forget it!

FINLEY

No bother at all . . . just a phone call!

JIM

Fuck it!
(*He is still shaking the table.*)

FINLEY

(*Trying at humor*)
That would be a neat trick—if you could do it.
(JIM *just looks at him.*)
Ah . . . why did you ask for it if you didn't want it?

JIM

Better than nothing!

FINLEY

I'm sorry, you've lost me!

JIM

It figures. I'm a head, man!

FINLEY

(*Places his martini on the other table.*)
Oooh? Ahead of what?

JIM

H-E-A-D! Head. I don't drink. I turn on.

FINLEY

Marijuana?

JIM

Acapulco gold, THC, pure sunshine acid, STP. You name it!

FINLEY

Well, it's rather obvious that I'm from another generation!

JIM

Yeah, great, man, great. My generation calls it straight!

FINLEY

Me straight? Hardly!

JIM

You've got status quo written all over you. You got anything to eat?

FINLEY

I presume you're talking about regular food?

JIM

(*Slaps his leg.*)
You're right with it, man! Right here in the twentieth century. As Mel Allen would say, how about that?

FINLEY

(*Stands up and moves stage left.*)
I'll have a look-see!
(*He goes offstage.*)
Caviar? Artichoke hearts?

JIM

How about a sandwich?

FINLEY

There is some Genoa salami!

JIM

Forget it. That's for the greasy dagos!

FINLEY

Well . . . ah . . . a chicken leg? Will that do, *Mister* Kelly?

JIM

That's okay!

FINLEY

Let's see . . . a knife and a fork and . . . .

JIM

Just hand it to me!

(MR. FINLEY *enters. He has the chicken leg on two napkins. He places it on coffee table next to* JIM. JIM *picks up chicken leg in bare hand.*)

FINLEY

Tom Jones, huh?

JIM

Yeah, I may be Tom Jones but you ain't the sexy bitch!
(*He takes a bite of the chicken. He spits some of it on the floor.* FINLEY *picks up a piece of it and deposits it in the ashtray.*)
What do you think of Nietzsche?

FINLEY

Ah . . .

JIM

Huh?

FINLEY

I beg your pardon?

JIM

The German philosopher.

FINLEY

Oh! Ah . . .
(JIM *grinds his cigarette out on the floor and holds his foot on it for a moment. Then he takes it off.* FINLEY *picks up the butt.*)
Well . . . his theory of the innate superiority of man over women is quite interesting.

JIM

That's an oversimplification. Leave it to you to latch onto that!

FINLEY

I'm not quite sure that I——

JIM

You dig him?

FINLEY

Well, ah—actually I don't consider him my favorite philosopher.

JIM

Who the fuck do you dig?

FINLEY

I must say—I'm not particularly in the mood to discuss philosophy —to put it mildly!

JIM

You groove on Spinoza?

FINLEY

Really!

JIM

(*Imitating him*)
Really! Answer me!

FINLEY

Well—ah—to be quite honest about it, young man, I don't re-member too much about him—a rather vague memory from college!

JIM

You don't remember much about anything, do you?
(*Now* JIM *is sitting on the back of the chair with his feet on the seat.*)

FINLEY

Now, look, young man, I——

JIM

Okay, relax. What about Ginsberg?

· FINLEY

Allen Ginsberg? Ugh . . . rather untidy!

JIM

Did you read *Howl?*

FINLEY

I'm afraid not!

JIM

What 'bout Gurdjieff?

FINLEY

What is this, the Inquisition?

JIM

Just wondering where you're at, that's all.

FINLEY

Ah . . . where did you go to college?

JIM

I didn't. That's Establishment bullshit!

FINLEY

Oh! A diamond in the rough. A Jack London! How fascinating!

JIM

You're a condescending motherfucker!

FINLEY

I don't mean to insult you but you just don't quite strike me as the type of young man who would be interested in the aesthetic side of life . . . you look quite elemental!
(JIM *moves in on* FINLEY. *He is behind* FINLEY, *who is seated.*)

JIM

You want to know something, Mr. Finley?

FINLEY

Let's say that at the moment I'm not interested in a learned discussion on the relative merits of Nietzsche and/or Spinoza.
(JIM *grabs* FINLEY *by the hair and jerks his head backwards, holding it.*)

JIM

You want to know something, Mr. Finley?

FINLEY

(*Finally pulls away and runs to other side of room.*)
You're repeating yourself, young man!

JIM

I've got something else to say!

FINLEY

Bravo!

JIM

All you faggots are alike!
(*He is following* FINLEY *around room.* FINLEY *finally sits in chair.*)

FINLEY

That's very profound.

JIM

You're a fucking drag!

FINLEY

Sorry to disappoint you, young man, but I've never been in drag. I don't particularly go for that fantasy!

JIM

But there's a lot of others you go for, right?

FINLEY

I don't quite. . . .

JIM

(*Moves in on* FINLEY)
Fantasies, Mr. Finley! Like the real ultimate. Did you ever blow a guy in a subway john, huh?

FINLEY

That's enough, young man. I——

JIM

You've dreamt about doing it, haven't you? Come on—and the fuzz catch you while you're doing it. The ultimate in degradation and humiliation. Right, Mr. Finley?

FINLEY

All right, that's it! That's it. Out! Out! This has gone beyond reason! Out!

JIM

(*Now he takes off his jacket. He is grinning.*)
Goddamn! You really are something! Yeah! A fucking sniveling faggot standing up to me! It's simple and very uncomplicated, Mr. Finley. Jim here ain't fitting into Mr. Finley's fantasy world.

(FINLEY *is back in chair.* JIM *is next to him.*)
Does Jim know too much? Okay, you want the animal, right? Ah. . . .
(*He shoves his rear end in* FINLEY's *face. He strains.*)
Goddamn I can't let go with one right now! We got to build up to
that fantasy—animal, man, animal. Oh . . .
(*He outlines his penis in his blue jeans.*)
. . . that turn you on, Mr. Finley?

FINLEY

Believe me, you're only a small variation of Stanley Kowalski!

JIM

I'll bet you really grooved when Brando did it, huh? Those old
fantasies really took over, didn't they, huh?

FINLEY

I do realize it's rather difficult for a Neanderthal man like you to
comprehend a civilized human being, but if you'll just walk to the
door and turn the knob you'll find yourself on Sutton Place. I'll be
more than glad to give you the cab fare so you can go to your
little furnished hovel. Just ask Henderson, the doorman, to blow his
little whistle. Do you think you can do that?

JIM

Goddamn!
(*He slaps* FINLEY *across the face.*)
It's all coming out . . . all the shit! I never yet met a faggot who
didn't try to deball me. You're jealous, baby, because you can't
groove—because you're not a man. Wow!

FINLEY

You better leave right now or—or——

JIM

Or what, *fag?*

FINLEY

Or I'll call the police!

JIM

You fruit square—you really think they're on your side? You really
want the nails in your hands, don't you? Hey, let's crucify the faggot—groove, huh?

FINLEY

I can't quite believe what I'm seeing and hearing!

JIM

(*Slaps him hard.*)
You better believe it, faggot. I haven't even started yet!

FINLEY

The ape thinks he's a higher form!

JIM

Where's the fucking phone?

FINLEY

You better leave if you know what's good for you!
(JIM *dials a number.*)

JIM

(*Into phone*)
Sue, baby? How's it going? Yeah, I'm coming right over. I got a hard on!

FINLEY

Get out of my apartment—you're disgusting!

JIM

Throw on a steak. . . .

FINLEY

Disgusting! Disgusting!

JIM

What, Sue? No . . . no . . . just some middle-aged faggot who's dying to have his face smashed in. You ought to see him, Sue. A miserable-looking cocksucker. Losing his hair . . . frightened to death of dying. Are you kidding, Sue? Shit, baby, I wouldn't let him lick the sweat off my balls. Yeah . . . and heavy on the onions . . . yeah . . . be right over!
(*He hangs up.*)

FINLEY

You—you are the typical American male—absolutely—ab—completely prejudiced against the homosexual because you are terrified—terrified of what's in you!

JIM

You've got the platitudes up your ass, man. Okay . . . I see . . .
you're a homosexual!
(*Now he lets him have it.*)
I thought you were a fucking faggot cocksucker!

FINLEY

(*He is beginning to cry.*)
How dare you talk to me like this? Do you know who I am? I made
a hundred thousand a year!

JIM

Great, just great! But I don't give a shit if you're Mao Tse-tung—
you're a miserable queer, Mr. Finley. Your life is just plain shitty
and I ain't speaking figuratively. What's this bit of licking assholes
and sucking cock? Just look at you! Goddamned hungry eyes . . . .
(*He is holding* FINLEY *by the jaw, making him look at himself.*)
. . . sick eyes—fantasy eyes—seeking a constant faggot fantasy!

FINLEY

(*He is crying.*)
Please stop . . . please . . .

JIM

I haven't even started, motherfucker. Hey, how about that! How
about your mother? You ever thought of screwing her? You think
maybe that's where it's at? Or maybe you think you are your
mother . . . wowie!
(*He is laughing.*)

FINLEY

I'm warning you, you hate-filled man—you—you—

JIM

You're warning me? Hey, why don't you try being a man for a
change? Come on, come on . . .
(*He slaps* FINLEY *a couple of times and then he stands, waiting.*)

FINLEY

(*Jumps up and runs to phone*)
I'm going to call them—I'm going to call them!
(JIM *grabs him and hits him, knocking him across the room.* FIN-
LEY *falls to the floor, sobbing.*)

JIM

Motherfucking French phone!
(*He takes it and throws it upstage. He turns to* FINLEY *and moves center stage.*)
Come on! Come on! Stand up and fight like a man!

FINLEY

I'll kill you—you monster!
(*He attacks* JIM, *throwing punches wildly.* JIM *grabs his arm and then slaps him hard until* FINLEY *is on the floor at his feet.* JIM *is on top of him, hitting him, slapping him harder and harder.* FINLEY *is screaming and crying.*)

JIM

Hey, Mr. Powder Puff! Did you play jacks with the girls?

FINLEY

Oh, Jimmy, don't . . . don't . . .

JIM

(*Hits him harder and harder.*)
Cry, you miserable faggot, and maybe you'll find out where it's at with you!
(*He continues to hit* FINLEY.)

FINLEY

Oh, Jimmy, Jimmy!

JIM

(*Now he is standing over* FINLEY.)
You think you're worthy to touch this? You know what this is for? It's for a real woman—Sue.

FINLEY

Oh, Jimmy, please . . . don't . . .

JIM

You sniveling fucking crybaby!

FINLEY

Oh, Jimmy, Jimmy!
(*Now* FINLEY *is pressing his body against* JIM's *boot. He is moaning and groaning wildly.*)

JIM

The name is Jim.

FINLEY

Oh, Jim! Jim! Jim!

JIM

(*He grabs* FINLEY's *face. Then very deliberately he spits in his face.*)
I wouldn't piss on you!
(*He spits on his face again.*)
I wouldn't piss on you! I wouldn't piss on you! I wouldn't piss on you!

FINLEY

Oh, Jim, Jim, Jim! My God——
(*He is gyrating his body wildly against* JIM's *boot. Finally he has his orgasm and collapses as* JIM *moves calmly away and sits in the chair. Finally* MR. FINLEY *sits up. His hand goes to his face. He feels the spittle on his face. He touches it almost lovingly. Slowly he gets up. He sees a cigarette butt that* JIM *has dropped. He picks it up and puts it in ashtray. He has checkbook on table. He writes out a check. He moves over to* JIM. *He kisses him on head and hands him the check.*)
Here we go, son!

JIM

Thanks, Mr. Finley!
(JIM *stands up.* FINLEY *helps him into his jacket and then holds him close, very close.*)

FINLEY

You're absolutely incredible, Jim. Oh, by the way, the wife and I are flying to London in the morning. I'll be back at the end of the month. I'd like to see you then.

JIM

Fine, Mr. Finley.

FINLEY

And give my best to Sue!

JIM

What?

FINLEY

Your girl friend!

JIM

Yeah. You taking the kids with you?

FINLEY

No . . . they're in summer camp!

JIM

Well . . . I'll see you at the end of the month.

FINLEY

And . . . thank you . . . I feel great . . . .
(*Lights out onstage and up on audience*)

LLOYD

Then it was seen that all past history, with the exception of its primitive stages, was the history of class struggles.

CAROLE

That these warring classes of society are always the products of the modes of production and of exchange.

DAN

In a word . . .

RON

Of the economic conditions of their time . . .

LLOYD

That the economic structure of society always furnishes the real basis, starting from which we can alone work out the ultimate explanation of the whole superstructure of juridical and political institutions as well as of the religious, philosophical, and other ideas of a given historical period.

ALL

Of a given historical period.

SCENE 3

(The scene is GEORGE *and* MOM'S *apartment. As the lights go up onstage,* GEORGE *and* GROVER *are walking down center aisle.* GROVER *is black.* GEORGE *is tipsy.)*

GEORGE

Just right down here ... come on.
(The moment he gets onstage the phone begins to ring.)
Excuse me ... have a seat!
*(*GEORGE *picks up phone.)*
Hello? What? Look, Mother, I'm busy. What? Oh, I went for a walk. Oh, please ... Well, why didn't you take it out of the freezer before you went to work? I don't feel like talking!
(He hangs up.)
May I take your coat?

GROVER

No, thanks. Ah ... you read a lot?

GEORGE

Not any more! Want a drink?

GROVER

No, thanks.

GEORGE

Please sit ... you're making me nervous.
*(*GROVER *sits.)*
I'm sorry ... I think I'll have one ... those stairs are really exhausting ....
(He moves to stage left and fixes drink.)
You're not even breathing heavy. I'll bet you're an athlete?

GROVER

No ... no, I'm not.

GEORGE

I'm sorry ... but for the life of me I can't remember your name.

GROVER

Grover!

GEORGE
I'm George.

GROVER
I know. Well?

GEORGE
Well what?

GROVER
Come on, baby!

GEORGE
You'll have to forgive me. I'm a bit unsteady. I—I——

GROVER
So?

GEORGE
Well . . . I've never done anything like this before.

GROVER
Like what?

GEORGE
I've never paid anyone.

GROVER
You're kidding?

GEORGE
No, I certainly am not.

GROVER
So?
(GEORGE *walks stage left to cookie jar. He rummages around in it.*)

GEORGE
Ah—I think I can give you five!

GROVER
Make it ten!

GEORGE

I'm ah—sorry, I don't have it!

GROVER

Aw—come on, baby!

GEORGE

Well—I can give you seven.

GROVER

Okay, it's a deal. I'll have that drink now.

GEORGE

It's gin.

GROVER

Fine, baby, fine.

GEORGE

(*Fixes him drink and moves toward him*)
Are you from New York?

GROVER

Been here 'bout ten years.

GEORGE

Where you from originally?

GROVER

A small town in Alabama, baby!

GEORGE

What do you do?

GROVER

Not working right now. I was driving a truck.

GEORGE

Oh? A truckdriver. Ah . . . are you married?

GROVER

Yes.

GEORGE

Any children?

GROVER

Two lovely children.

GEORGE

I see. Ah . . . it must be pretty rough.

GROVER

It always has been, baby!

GEORGE

Ah . . . you're very virile looking. You ah—twenty-four—twenty-three?

GROVER

Twenty-five.

GEORGE

You must've married young.

GROVER

Eighteen.

GEORGE

(*Moves toward him. He is behind him.* GROVER *is seated. He runs his hands over his shoulders and feels his arms.*)
Nice arms.
(*He lifts his shirt and feels his chest and then starts down toward his crotch.* GROVER *stands up.*)

GROVER

I've worked hard all my life, baby!

GEORGE

(*Stands for a moment and then makes up his mind. He moves to the cookie jar and takes out a bill.*)
Ah—let me see.
(*He moves to* GROVER *and hands it to him after folding it.*)

GROVER

Ten?
(*He puts it in his pocket.*)

GEORGE

I guess you need it more than I do.

GROVER

Thanks, baby. What do you dig?

GEORGE

It's all right—you don't have to do anything.
(*Pause*)
I'm ah—sorry.

GROVER

(*Sarcastic*)
You mean you're just giving me this money?

GEORGE

Yes, I am.

GROVER

What are you so sorry about?

GEORGE

Well . . . ah . . . taking advantage of you.
(GROVER *stretches out in chair, spreading his legs wide.*)

GROVER

Come here, baby!

GEORGE

I—ah—I changed my mind.

GROVER

(*Puts his hand on his crotch.*)
You want it, baby?
(*Slowly he gets up. He moves to* GEORGE. *He takes off his glasses, takes the cigarette out of his mouth.*)
You want that, baby?

GEORGE

You don't have to do anything.

GROVER

Oh, but let me warn you, baby, I ain't got twelve inches.

GEORGE

Oh . . . ah . . . ah . . .

(GROVER *takes* GEORGE's *hand and puts it on his crotch.* GROVER *is facing upstage so none of this can be seen directly.*)

GROVER

Grover. Grover Smith from Tuskale, Alabama!

(*Finally* GEORGE *puts his arms around* GROVER's *legs.* GROVER *is pushing forward.*

GROVER *quickly pulls away. He moves to where his drink is; he picks it up.*)

Goddamn! I forgot my drink. That's pretty good liquor you got there.

(GEORGE *starts to stand.*)

Just stay there. Don't get up, George!

GEORGE

I feel sort of silly!

GROVER

You do? I wonder why? You've got a pretty big bill to pay, you know that, don't you?

GEORGE

I'm afraid I'm not . . .

GROVER

You're afraid, all right.

GEORGE

Did I say something wrong?

GROVER

(*He pulls out ten-dollar bill. He holds it out to* GEORGE.)

Here's your bread. I don't want it.

GEORGE

I—I don't understand.

GROVER

(*He throws the ten dollars on the floor.*)

You will, baby, you will. Let's start from the beginning. I'm not a truckdriver.

GEORGE

Then why did you say you were?

GROVER

Because you wanted me to!

GEORGE

I did?

GROVER

Yes, you did, baby!
(GROVER *gets bottle of gin and holds it as if he were going to hit*
GEORGE *over the head with it.*)
I'm not married, either.

GEORGE

I—I really don't care, Grover!

GROVER

(*Moves in on him, screaming.*)
Bullshit, baby, shit! Shit! Shit! You loved it . . . you were eating
it up!
(*Now he moves center stage.*)
I'm a dancer. I've worked with Merce Cunningham and Martha
Graham.

GEORGE

Why do you . . . ah . . . I need another drink.

GROVER

Oh?
(*From the threatening position with the bottle, he now pours* GEORGE
a drink.)
You need more than a drink.
(*Pause*)
By the way, I'm gay.
(*He sits on red box upstage. He pretends that he is crying.*)
I—I had my first experience with a white man in a choir loft who
came to fix our broken-down organ pipes and ended up sucking me
off. He thought I was a black stud, too.
(*Angry*)
Just like you do, baby!

GEORGE

Would you please——?

GROVER

Please what?

GEORGE

I just don't know.

GROVER

Stop telling you the truth? I'm not going to do that. By the way, I live with a very white guy in a penthouse on the east side. He thinks I'm a black stud, too.

GEORGE

But—you are rugged looking!

GROVER

Am I, really?
(*He stands on red box. He pulls his coat down over his shoulders in a very campy way.*)
Ooooooooooh!

GEORGE

Just stop it!

GROVER

Stop what, Georgette?

GEORGE

You know you're just trying to put me on!

GROVER

(*Swishes downstage.*)
Really, oh, sweetie, what I really dig is a cock up my ass. Why, all the boys on 125th Street whistle when I go by. You should see them, honey, real studs!

GEORGE

I thought you said you lived on the east side?

GROVER

I do, honey. I just go up there, that's all!

GEORGE

I'm sorry, my mother's coming home in a few minutes!

GROVER

You live with your Mummy?
(*He picks up picture of* MOM *and looks at it. Then he rubs it on his crotch and on his ass. Then he throws it at* GEORGE.)
How sw—eet!

GEORGE

Just get the hell out of here! Goddamn it!

GROVER

Oh, how rugged. You're turning me on!

GEORGE

(*He stands up. Absolute rage*)
Get out of here, you—you black—ni——

GROVER

Yes?

GEORGE

Will you get out?

GROVER

I'm leaving, honey. Bye, bye!

GEORGE

I'm—I'm sorry . . . I . . . I . . .

GROVER

(*Approaches* GEORGE. *Pulls blanket over him, tucking him in.*)
Mummy will be home soon and she'll wipe away your tears.
(*He picks up bottle of gin and moves toward the aisle.*)
Take it easy. . . .
(*He moves back to* GEORGE *and into his ear he screams:*)
Whitey!
(*He moves down aisle.*)
Better luck next time!
(MOM *passes him in aisle. She moves onto the stage.*)

MOM

Hello, dear. Did you take out the chicken?
(*No answer. She puts down her shopping bag.*)
I didn't know there were Negroes in the building.
(*She sees the ten-dollar bill. She picks it up and puts it back in the cookie jar.*)

RON

(*This is the* CHORUS.)
The idea that all men, as men, have something in common, and to that extent they are equal, is of course primeval.

BARRY

In the most ancient, primitive communities, equality of rights could apply at most to members of the community.

DAN

Women, slaves, and foreigners were excluded from this equality as a matter of course.

RON

Among the Greeks and Romans the inequalities of men were of much greater importance than their equality in any respect.

CAROLE

Christianity knew only one point in which all men were equal.

RON

That all were equally born in original sin.

ALL

Did you say original sin?

RON

Yeah, original sin.

ALL

That's what we thought you said.

SCENE 4

(*The stage is bare.* TONY *is center stage. He is exercising with a hand pulley. He does an exercise, stops, and then poses, examining his muscles.* SKYLAR *comes down the center aisle. He is wearing a leopard-skin bikini, carrying a book and a carton of yogurt. He places them down on the red box and then begins a standing job. He finishes, sits and eats yogurt, watching* TONY.)

SKYLAR

Hi!
(*No answer*)
Hiya!

TONY

Hi!
(*He continues working out.*)

SKYLAR

I've never seen you here before!

TONY

I come six times a week!

SKYLAR

Oh? I only come once a week. When do you come?

TONY

When I get off work!

SKYLAR

Oh?

TONY

What's that you're eating?

SKYLAR

Yogurt. The fellow at the desk told me to eat it . . . said it would make me big and strong!

TONY

Did you see the guy at the desk?

SKYLAR

Yeah ... but ...

TONY

Just a good all-around diet . . . meat, vegetables, protein, and plenty of sleep.
(*He goes back to his exercises.*)

SKYLAR

You seem to know a lot of exercises. Maybe you can help me . . . I've got a problem.

TONY

Yeah, I can see that just by looking at you!

SKYLAR

Oh, really? My arms are like toothpicks!

TONY

You can say that again!

SKYLAR

What is that exercise you just did for?

TONY

The delts!

SKYLAR

The what?

TONY

Deltoids.
(*He shows* SKYLAR *his deltoids.*)

SKYLAR

Oh! Ah . . . could you show me an exercise for my ah . . . arms?

TONY

Biceps? Just do a regular curl.

SKYLAR

That'll really build them up, huh? Oh, by the way, I have a big house on the island, and if you want to come out some weekend, ah . . . you could have your own room!

TONY

What island?

SKYLAR

Fire Island—right near the Pines.
(*He holds out his hand.*)
Oh, my name is Skylar.

TONY

Is that really your name?

SKYLAR

I don't understand!

TONY

I thought it was Fruit Cup!

SKYLAR

What do you mean by that?

TONY

Shit, man, I've seen you here before and you know how to do a curl!

SKYLAR

So?

TONY

Do me a favor?

SKYLAR

Anything you say!

TONY

Look, I'm almost finished with my workout. In about two minutes I'm going into the steam room. You followed me in there last week. The next time you do, I'm going to bust you right in the mouth. Another thing—you happen to be on the straight side of the gym. That's out of bounds for you—
(*He pushes him to the other side.*)
You stay on the faggot side and I don't want you staring at me like a sick cow. So beat it!
(SKYLAR *grabs his yogurt and his book and retreats to edge of stage.*)

SKYLAR

Such gorgeous hostility!

TONY

Get the fuck out——

SKYLAR

If you come over to this side you'll turn into a faggot!
(TONY *moves across invisible lines.*)
You just did!
(TONY *takes skip rope and begins to jump rope à la a boxer in training. He is muttering:*)

TONY

My name is Skylar . . . Fire Island . . . shit. . . .
(JACK *enters. He sees* TONY.)

JACK

Hot damn! Tony!

TONY

Jack, baby, how the fuck are you?

JACK

Great, man, great! How the hell are you?

TONY

Just great! Goddamn! Hey, look at the mop! Where the hell you bin keeping yourself?

JACK

Out on the Coast, Tony. I just got in!

TONY

Santa Monica?

JACK

Venice, baby, Venice!

TONY

Yeah?

JACK

Great out there—and the chicks—a whole flock of them that dig body builders.

TONY

No kidding!

JACK

You look great! What did you do—knock off a few inches around the middle?

TONY

Been working out every day!

JACK

Your abs—like a fucking washboard. What you been doing for them?

TONY

Five hundred sit-ups a day, every day, including Sunday!

JACK

A weight behind your neck, Tony?

TONY

Nope . . . on the incline board—it really works if you do them every day.

JACK

Wow! Those cuts! Beautiful. Come on, pose!

TONY

(*He looks upstage.* SKYLAR *is peeking in from offstage.*)
Naw . . . the fag'll groove on me!

JACK

Aw . . . come on!
(TONY *poses, showing off his abs.*)

TONY

Come on, let Tony have one in the gut!
(JACK *hits him in the stomach.*)
Come on, harder, man, harder!

JACK

Well, goddamn, you really look great. Stand back and let me get a good look at you.

TONY

Let me get a look at you, Jack!

JACK

Let's see that bicep!

TONY

Aw . . . that creep is still watching!

JACK

Screw the fag . . . come on!
(TONY *poses.*)
Mama mia! You added a couple of inches?

TONY

Seventeen inches cold and eighteen when they're pumped!

JACK

Mine are only fifteen and a half.

TONY

You kidding?

JACK

Nope. You got me beat by an inch and a half!

TONY

You mean my biceps are bigger than yours?

JACK

That's right! Hey, man, you remember Sandra? She grooves on big biceps. She'll get one look at your arms and pass out. Why don't you come over to the pad tonight? We'll turn on—I got the new Stones album—I'll have Sandra and some other chick over. How 'bout it, Tony?

TONY

Sounds great, man. Hey, you know, you look fabulous!

JACK

You too, baby! Just great.
(*They square off. They begin punching each other. Then they end up in a clinch.*
Lights out onstage, up on audience.)

CLAUDE

Hegel had freed history from metaphysics—he had made it dialectic.

CAROLE

But his conception of history was essentially idealistic.

RON

But now idealism was driven from its last refuge.

CAROLE

He that falls is remorselessly cast aside.

CLAUDE

It is the Darwinian struggle of the individual for existence transferred from nature to society with intensified violence.

LLOYD

The conditions of existence natural to the animal appear as the final term of human development.

SCENE 5

(The record player is stage right. A movie projector is on the coffee table with its lens facing the audience. Muscle magazines are covering the floor. As the scene opens, GEORGE is fixing the projector, rewinding a movie he has just shown RUFUS. RUFUS is on the floor. He has rolled three or four joints and is now lighting one.)

GEORGE

Be ready in a second.

RUFUS

I hope it's better than the last one.

GEORGE

I wouldn't know as I haven't seen it. It's my latest present to myself. I bought it on 42nd Street this afternoon.

RUFUS

How much?

GEORGE

Twenty. It's in gorgeous color . . . mmmm. I thought the last one was very interesting.

RUFUS

Really?

GEORGE

Yes, really. I was going to show it to Mother but she had to go to work.

RUFUS

You're too much!

GEORGE

Did you get the symbolism in the beer-drinking scene?

RUFUS

Symbolism? Drinking piss is symbolism?

GEORGE

The way it was done . . . wild!

RUFUS

Baloney . . . they don't know how to act!

GEORGE

Who do you want—Steve McQueen?

RUFUS

I prefer Cornel Wilde in his prime.

GEORGE

Oh, really? Now, look, Miss 1945, I'm going to show my brand-new one. And please, no snide remarks. And I mean it. Just keep your big fag mouth shut!

RUFUS

I'll do my best!

GEORGE

I'm sure that won't be good enough. And . . . please?

RUFUS

Please, what?

GEORGE

The joint, Miss Hog!

RUFUS

Oh?
(*He hands the joint he's been smoking to* GEORGE.)

GEORGE

A whole one, please?
(GEORGE *lights his joint and leans back in the chair. He puffs away.*)
Ooooh! I'm beginning to go!

RUFUS

Don't forget your martini!

GEORGE

You're so right, honey. Just give me a few minutes and I may go all the way! All the way. Now, I don't want a word out of you because I want to go.

(RUFUS *gets up and moves to table. He takes match. There are two candles on the table. One is unlit.*)
What are you doing?

RUFUS
(*Lights the candle.*)
You bougie queen!

GEORGE
What?

RUFUS
Bougie, dear!

GEORGE
I thought I'd heard of everything! What's a bougie queen?

RUFUS
A candle queen, honey!

GEORGE
Where did you get that?

RUFUS
I was brought up in the church, honey! They have them all over the place. Now Father Howard had these huge candles——

GEORGE
Will you shut up, Miss Mudface?
(GEORGE *stands up.*)
Where are you? Ethyl? Ethyl, dear?

RUFUS
You better lay off that ethyl shit!

GEORGE
Me lay off it—you must be mad, my dear.

RUFUS
You know what Doctor Stewart said about ethyl chloride—it's a real killer!

GEORGE

(*He has bottle of ethyl and rag. He moves toward* RUFUS.)
Now, we've been friends for a long time, haven't we?

RUFUS

So?

GEORGE

(*Starts to pour some ethyl onto rag.*)
So try some!

RUFUS

I will not!

GEORGE

You're my oldest and dearest. Let's go together?

RUFUS

Let's go together? Thanks a lot. Miss Doctor Stewart says it's a real
killer and you want me to go with you. No, thanks.

GEORGE

You don't know what getting high is until you go with Ethyl!

RUFUS

Oh, well, I've had hepatitis and Miss Doctor Stewart said that I
could go into hepatic shock and also that I could get a frozen larynx.

GEORGE

Well, Miss Doctor Stewart gives me all the bennies I want!

RUFUS

She's a head—everything from DMT to THC. And you better lay
off that ethyl shit . . . it's a real killer.

GEORGE

Will you shut your yap so we can watch this gorgeous movie?

RUFUS

Okay! Okay!
(GEORGE *goes to record player and puts on a record. It is the sound
of motorcycles revving, starting and stopping, crashing into each
other, etc. Now the projector is going. He turns off the lights. Both*

of them are staring out over the audience at a fixed point. GEORGE
is starting to go. After about a minute and a half, RUFUS *begins to
pantomime the revving motorcycles as if he were on one. He starts
making the sound of the revving himself and he gets louder and
louder and louder.*)
It's hilarious!

GEORGE

Shut up, faggot!

RUFUS

It's WHEE! Yahooo!

GEORGE

Just stop!
(GEORGE *jumps up, turns on the lights, and stops the record.*)
You're a real down! You just don't understand, do you?

RUFUS

What's to understand?

GEORGE

You faggot square! You don't really see what's going on, do you?
Can't you see . . . they're playing at being so buddy-buddy and yet
they're really digging each other. If they took the camera away,
they'd be on the floor screwing each other. Whee! Really watch
and you'll see . . . you'll see what I see . . . .

RUFUS

I will?

GEORGE

(*Mimics him.*)
I will? Yes, Miss Sara Bummer, you will. You just don't want to see
anything. In fact, you're so square you remind me of my dear old
mother.

RUFUS

You're a hopeless romantic. Two stupid weight lifters who don't
even turn me on!

GEORGE

(*Really angry*)
That was not necessary! What are you trying to do to me? You son of a bitch, you!

RUFUS

Okay, okay. I'm getting the fuck out of here!

GEORGE

Is that a promise?

RUFUS

You're goddamned right it's a promise. Now you can go off—take your fucking ethyl and go all the way—but by yourself. I don't want to be in on it!

GEORGE

Oh, how terribly dramatic. I'll outlive you, honey!

RUFUS

Oh, yeah. Well, you act five and look fifty!

GEORGE

Well, I may act five and look fifty but I don't look like a woman! Now, just get out of here. And the next time you come, bring your own pot!

RUFUS

I'll do just that. And . . . do you know what I'm going to do right now? I'm going to go out and find myself the real thing, a real live man of flesh and blood!

GEORGE

Miss Bummer, you're so stupid. You don't understand anything, do you? Don't you know that it's the same thing? Haven't you figured that out yet? It's all fantasy! You won't be seeing a man—a human being—and that's because it would interfere with your dream world and that would be too painful for you, my dear. Now get out of here, you stupid bitch!

RUFUS

I'm going. And—take an extra sniff for me! Miss Malice in Wonderland!

GEORGE

I will, dearie. And when you die I'm going to write the tomb a sympathy letter!
(RUFUS *exits down center aisle.* GEORGE *mutters under his breath, sits and picks up a weight-lifter magazine. He throws it to the floor. Finally he goes to record player and selects record.*
It is Kirsten Flagstad singing "Liebestod" from Tristan and Isolde. *He puts it on and lowers the lights. During the seven minutes of the record the lights slowly dim until there is a blue-green spot on him.*
He sits in chair, sips martini, sniffs popper. Finally he takes off his shirt. His hands play with his chest. He pulls down his pants. Then he is on his knees. He reaches for the ethyl. He pours some on a rag and sniffs it.
Now the experience is changing from an orgasm to a religious one. He sniffs again and again.
Screaming)
He doesn't see . . . he doesn't see what's really going on . . . he doesn't see . . . .
(*He is on the floor now almost flat.*)
Die! Die! Die! Die woman, die man, die God! . . . . Die mankind!
(*He falls flat on the stage. Slowly his hands come up to the beam of light. His whole body pulls upward, upward, upward. As the record ends, he falls to the floor.*
In the darkness LLOYD *stands.*)

LLOYD

Man, at last the master of his own form of social organization, becomes at the same time the lord over nature, his own master, free!

ALL
Free!

LLOYD
Free.
(*Pause*)

The lines spoken by the chorus include excerpts from the book by Friedrich Engels. It is called *Anti-Duhring*. It was published in 1892.

GEORGE BIRIMISA

Good night!
(*The lights on the audience have come up.*)

ALL

(*Standing*)
Good night!
(*The* ACTORS *move to the stage and take CURTAIN CALL.*)

X
X
X
X
X

by William M. Hoffman

For Robert Kubera

X

    X

X   X

    X was first performed at the Old Reliable Theatre Tavern on August 5, 1969. It was directed by the author and produced by James K. Devlin, with set and lights by Earl Kells and Dan Thompson, sound by Jerry Bruck, music by Michelle Collison, and the following cast:

JESUS	Tom Cox and Joseph Pichette
MARY	Jean Forest
GOD, NARRATOR	Denny Leone
JOSEPH	David Adams
HOLY GHOST	Neil Flanagan

WILLIAM M. HOFFMAN was born in New York City and studied Latin at CCNY. His *Thank You, Miss Victoria* was presented at the Caffe Cino, by the La Mama Troupe under Tom O'Horgan's direction, and at the New Arts Lab in London; *Spring Play* and *Three Masked Dances* (based on American-Indian material), at La Mama; *Good Night, I Love You* and *Saturday Night at the Movies*, at the Caffe Cino; *Uptight!* (a musical revue), *Luna,* and *A Quick Nut Bread To Make Your Mouth Water*, at the Old Reliable Theatre Tavern. Hoffman has also directed and acted, and has written and published poetry, a song cycle (music by John Corigliano), rock album jackets, movie and television scripts, reviews, and other journalism. He is the former drama editor of Hill and Wang and continues to edit their *New American Plays* series.

    The play was subsequently performed by the Playhouse of the Ridiculous at Ellen Stewart's La Mama in New York, London, Amsterdam, and Brussels under the direction of John Vacarro and at the Changing Scene in Denver under the direction of Michael Smith.

SET

A painted backdrop: sky, stars, earth, plants, water—stylized; or columns of changing lights; or two hundred votive candles of various colors; or no set. In the first production at the Old Reliable Theatre Tavern, a painted backdrop of stylized rainbows was used.

MUSIC

Any combination of live and taped music. Preferably the actors should make their own music (which could sometimes blend with and fade into recorded music). If musicians, classical and rock, are available, use them.

COSTUMES

Everyone wears white or some light color. The men should wear the same clothing, say T-shirts and bells—nothing fancy such as robes.

NOTE

Mood light. Pace quick—even the "Last Words of Jesus." Never "serious." No intermission. The play should run a little over an hour depending on the "progressions" in SCENE 3 and physicalization elsewhere.

1: CHANT

(*Dim lights on stage. Maybe incense. The cast is on stage seated in a circle as the audience enters. Everyone has an instrument—tambourine, bells, flute, maracas, cymbals, etc. There could be instruments in the audience too.*)

NARRATOR

Glory be to Thee, Father.

REST

(*With instruments*)
Amen.

NARRATOR

Glory be to Thee, Word.

REST

Amen.

NARRATOR

Glory be to Thee, Grace.

REST

Amen.

NARRATOR

Glory be to Thee, Light.

REST

Amen.

NARRATOR

Glory be to Thee, Spirit.

REST

Amen.

(*Continues till audience is seated. Then each actor stands and sings in turn one of the following lines, to which the rest of the cast sings Amen.*)

I will be saved and I will save. (Amen.)
I will be freed and I will free. (Amen.)
I will be wounded and I will wound. (Amen.)
I will be begotten and I will beget. (Amen.)
I will be consumed and I will consume. (Amen.)
I will be heard and I will hear. (Amen.)
I will be known and I will know. (Amen.)
I will be washed and I will wash. (Amen.)
I will be mourned and I will mourn. (Amen.)
I will be understood and I will understand. (Amen.)
I will fly and I will stay. (Amen.)
A torch am I to all who see me. (Amen.)
A door am I to all who knock. (Amen.)
A way am I to all who pass. (Amen.)

(*When everyone is standing in a circle, a round dance begins. The chant begins again. The dance and chant should be done with ever increasing speed, coolly, and with growing intensity. At the end of the dance-chant, the cast is seated in a wide semicircle. The* NARRATOR *comes to center stage quickly.*)

2: PROLOGUE

NARRATOR

A little bit of magic. A little bit of religion. A little bit. A nickel bag. Just to let you know it's possible. Magic (*snaps his fingers—a flashbulb goes off*) and religion (JESUS *goes into a quick Jesus-on-the-Cross pose*). Magic (NARRATOR *takes off his shirt.*) and religion (*The* HOLY GHOST *starts a slow rhythmical beat on the tambourine.*) Magic—how far will I go? (*Takes off his shoes*) Tell me, you out there, how far should I go? Tell me, I'll do what you say. Give me a quicker beat, Holy Ghost. Take a bow, _____ (*name of actor playing* HOLY GHOST). Magic, I'll show you magic. Tell me, how far should I go? (*A seductive stripper*) And religion. _____ (*name of actor playing* JESUS) will give us a tune. _____ plays the son Jesus and will suffer for us tonight. I make him suffer. Give us a little bit of suffering, Jesus.

JESUS

Later with the suffering.

NARRATOR

He says later with the suffering. Okay, Jesus, give us a tune.

(*Jesus sings the melody of Bach's chorale* "O Haupt Voll Blut und Wunden" *from the St. Matthew Passion to the beat that the* HOLY GHOST *has set.* JESUS *and the* HOLY GHOST *will continue under the* NARRATOR *until it says otherwise. The tune should be slow and straight at first but can turn into jazz or rock improvs later.*)

A friend said to me a good show is tits and ass, tits and ass, or I suppose in my case, cock and ass, don't got no big tits, I got what I got—is there a cop in the house? Just checking. I suppose the big fear is that I might use what I got. Have I gone far enough? (*The light man or stage manager will yell:* Take it all off, *if no one else does. The* NARRATOR *takes off all his clothes with his back to the audience. Coming forward suddenly, he is Western Culture:*)

A definition of culture! Western Culture, mesdames et messieurs. I mean this might suddenly turn into some other culture or I might start a new one by, let's say, coming all over the first row? Or a man might come from the back with an ax and cut off my head as part of a new ritual thought up by some freak. You never know these days. I might be some kind of naked maniac. I might enjoy standing here naked in front of you (*casually caresses his body*), you know, enjoying the look in your eyes—well, at least some of you.

Taking off clothes in this culture—culture as in cars, cops, cancer, cigars, cigarettes—give me a cigarette, someone, will you? (*The music gets louder as he goes into the audience for a cigarette.*) A light? Thank you. That's culture, standing here smoking a cigarette. Slow beat, Holy Ghost. Now watch! (*Blows smoke rings*) That's magic! I mean not the smoke rings but the air around them. And on the other hand I could burn myself with the cigarette. (*Slowly brings the cigarette to his body. Music stops. All instruments on stage used for a drum-roll effect. Cymbals clash as he withdraws the cigarette. He has almost burned himself.*)

Bad luck! to talk about it. One night I might and it would throw us all into chaos. (*Cast might comment. There is a casual relationship between the* NARRATOR *and the rest of the cast.*) I mean we're playing with chaos tonight! Chaos! Good chaos, like stroking my cock (*he does so lightly*), and bad, like the cigarette. We'll try to take a stroll into chaos tonight, like Jesus did. Jesus stepped into chaos. So did Mary. _____ (*Name of actress playing* MARY) plays Mary. Her husband is played by _____ (*name of the actor playing* JOSEPH). Hello, _____. (*to actor playing* JOSEPH. *He waves to* NARRATOR.) Say hello to _____. (NARRATOR *a ventriloquist; his cock is his puppet. He is talking to* JOSEPH *still. An improvised conversation between* GOD's *cock and* JOSEPH.) Hello. How are you? I'm fine. A little warm, though.

A potent symbol, a cock, huh? (*To his cock*) Now, aren't you a potent symbol, little cock? (*Baby talk*) Hello. How are you? (*Cock answers in a deep voice:* Fuck off!) She doesn't like being called a symbol. A symbol has no personality, no past, no future. No *magic!* But the real thing, like my cock—it doesn't stand for anything— well, you know what I mean; you're real, aren't you, honey? (*Cock says:* I am real.)

(*Jesus starts singing the tune straight again.*) Religion is like that. Now there is God (*formal*) and there is that certain *je ne sais quoi*, gobs of it, all over and in between, dig? (*Formal again*) Now there is religious motivation and a lotta Bible study; there's always Billy Graham—he's against drugs and nudity in the theater and fucking and chocolate éclairs; but there are times you gotta have an éclair and that woman across the aisle on the bus or your older sister's twelve-year-old son, you wanna touch him so bad. And that's what makes you cry and carry on or just holding it together on a bummer—you end up chanting your name, there's nothing left and—never mind—it's exhausting to list my names, they come at you so fast sometimes. (*The* ACTOR *has increased his tempo.*) I'm going to sing, we're going to sing and kind of dance. We sing and then dance. And that's where we start.

(*As the* NARRATOR *puts his clothes back on, the cast stands and sings the chorale. A recorded version—full chorus—is faded in over the singing. The cast takes its place for the progression:*)

3: PROGRESSION

The physical structure of the rest of the play rests on the following movement, called a "progression,"* which can be considered as blocking basic to the play, or a dance step.

Starting from the position

X
(JOSEPH)   X (HOLY GHOST)
X   X (JESUS)
(MARY)   X (GOD *or* NARRATOR)

the HOLY GHOST, JESUS, *and* GOD *cross the stage to* MARY *and go around her once. As* JESUS *and* GOD *return to their original positions,* MARY *leads the* HOLY GHOST *some steps to the left:*

X
(JOSEPH)   X (GOD)
X   X   X (JESUS)
(MARY)   (HOLY GHOST)

Then MARY *leads the* HOLY GHOST *back to where* MARY *was originally:*

X
(MARY)   X   (JOSEPH)   X (GOD)
(HOLY GHOST) X   X (JESUS)

* I am indebted to Norman Taffel for this concept.—WMH

JOSEPH *then comes to* MARY *and the* HOLY GHOST *returns to* GOD *and* JESUS; JOSEPH *returns to his position center stage; all are back where they were at the beginning of the progression. The progression is completed.*

A: *Progression Walked Through*

When everyone is in place at the end of the PROLOGUE *(and the* NARRATOR *has his clothes back on), the cast slowly walks through the progression with the taped Bach chorale as background—like showing someone a dance step.*

B: *Progression Less Formal*

The progression is then walked through again (still with music). The actors—out of character—greet each other as they pass. Nothing important should be indicated—people are just walking.

C: *Progression Speeded Up*

The music should suddenly double time (record the chorale at twice the speed it is supposed to be). The actors walk through the progression very quickly, almost running. As they are almost back to their original places, the music suddenly changes to "Anchors Aweigh."

D: *Progression à la Gene Kelly Forties Musical*

GOD, JESUS, *and the* HOLY GHOST *put on sailor hats and become sailors.* MARY *is a port whore.* JOSEPH *marks time to the music with his back to the audience. The sailors lurch across the stage. They see* MARY *and try to pick her up.* MARY *wants the* HOLY GHOST. *The sailors fight. The* HOLY GHOST *wins, having knocked the other two back across the stage (* GOD *and* JESUS *might then cruise each other). The music then changes to a lindy and* MARY *dances off with the* HOLY GHOST *and returns with him to her apartment. Some fumbling with a key.* JOSEPH, *the irate husband, returns home to find a sailor with his wife. He slugs the startled sailor back to his place and slugs* MARY, *who says, "You didn't say May I. Go back." The progression turns into:*

E: Giant Steps

(*which is also called* Captain, May I? *or* Mother, May I?—*all the same game*). MARY *is "it." The actors are themselves doing the standard umbrella, baby, giant steps. They should also do imitations of each other or of famous people: like Richard Nixon steps or Marilyn Monroe steps—whatever might amuse a particular audience on a particular night. The object of the game is to casually fulfill the progression. Despite his constant pleading,* JOSEPH *is not allowed to take a step until the end; the* HOLY GHOST *wins the game and takes* MARY *off. Everyone might tumble back into place when the game is over.*

NOTE

Depending on the director, cast, and audience, other physicalizations might be substituted for the ones mentioned here, or added to them. All material, however, should be clearly related to the original progression.

4: MARY AND JOSEPH

(MARY *and* JOSEPH *are standing in their progression places; the rest of the cast are seated in their places.* MARY *is washing clothes.*)

MARY

I was washing clothes and thinking.

JOSEPH

I looked out the back door and my wife was washing clothes as a wife should. I was so glad she was washing clothes because she might have been doing something else. Sometimes she goes up to trees and breaks off big brown funguses and I don't know what to think so I tell her to stop and if I do that I'm afraid of the dark that night and I get into arguments with my brother and who knows how many people get killed that way so she better just wash clothes one-two one-two in that stream and not wonder where that stream leads.

MARY

I have never been able to wash clothes like other women one-two one-two. I go one-two-*three* one-two-*three*, and when I look down there's a jewel fish rubbing my heart away; I can't understand why I don't melt in water like sugar.

JOSEPH

Dogs never bark at Mary. She was washing one-two.

MARY

Three.

JOSEPH

One-*two.*

MARY

Three.

JOSEPH

At night I fuck her one-two one-two to make sure that the roof doesn't fall.

MARY

Three and the cow gives milk.

JOSEPH

Two and the roof is sure.

MARY

Three and the wheat grows high. (*Sigh*) Sometimes I think I'd do anything.

JOSEPH

(*Shouting*)
Why are you crying?

MARY

Am I crying? No, I'm not crying; I'm just washing clothes.

JOSEPH

Don't cry or it'll rain.

MARY

It's all right, dear, my thighs are shut tight.

JOSEPH

Go one-two, Mary, dear,
I have to be a carpent-er.

MARY

One second, love, a frog jumped in my hair.

JOSEPH

Hurry, please.

MARY

Right away.

JOSEPH

One-two one-two, hurry.

MARY AND JOSEPH

One-two one-two one-two one-two one-two . . .

MARY

I feel numb all over. One-two one-two, is that enough?

JOSEPH

(*Continuing*)
One-two one-two one-two . . . (*He has come.*) Yes, dear. Thank you.

MARY

I would hate that man if I knew any better. *Three, three, three!* (*She has come.*)

JOSEPH

What's that, Mary?

MARY

Nothing, dear.

NARRATOR

(*From position seated in his place*)
Then God throws whole clumps of you-know-what at Mary, and doing what she always wanted, she divests herself of herself in a flash of politeness and dreams.

5: MARY'S DANCE

Mary does a light, quick dance (like a jig) in her area of the stage. She now reveals what she has been washing: an enormous pair of pants, the pants of a giant. The music: the statement of the theme from the Gavotte II of the Third English Suite for harpsichord by Bach. The dance should last no more than thirty seconds. It ends abruptly and the music becomes once again a full marching arrangement, played loud, of "Anchors Aweigh."

6: PROGRESSION (SAILORS)

Repeat the sailors' version of the progression to the point where MARY *takes the* HOLY GHOST *to her apartment. The music cuts off mid-phrase. The* HOLY GHOST *is struggling to undress* MARY. JOSEPH, JESUS, *and* GOD *are back in their original progression positions.*

7: THE GOLDEN ROAD

(MARY *and the* HOLY GHOST *are struggling. He's trying to take off her clothes and get her to the floor.*)

MARY

You men are all alike. He was insistent and so I smiled. I didn't know him, but I smiled because he made funny jokes and said something about my eyes. You know the way you are.

NARRATOR, JESUS, JOSEPH

You know the way you are. (*These repeats are very quick.*)

NARRATOR

What did he look like?

MARY

He was some kind of man. He smelled like one, furry with a touch of tobacco, a missing button, a broken tooth. I didn't know what to do.

NARRATOR, JESUS, JOSEPH

(*In quick succession again*)
To do.

NARRATOR

He was a problem.

MARY

He was a problem. You men are a problem. (*Has gotten free of* HOLY GHOST. *She pushes him to the floor.*) I was washing clothes and thinking. (HOLY GHOST *sulks.*)

NARRATOR, JESUS, JOSEPH

Washing clothes and thinking.

NARRATOR

What were you thinking about?

MARY

I was thinking about—I won't tell you.

NARRATOR, JESUS, JOSEPH

Won't tell you.

NARRATOR

Mary, please tell us what you were thinking.

MARY

No.

NARRATOR, JESUS, JOSEPH, HOLY GHOST

No.

NARRATOR

Please?

MARY

(*Laughs*)
I was thinking—you'll think I'm silly.

NARRATOR, JESUS, JOSEPH, HOLY GHOST

Silly.

NARRATOR

Mary, Mary,
washing clothes,
tell us please
what your mind enfolds.
(*The pace, which has been quick, gets quicker.* MARY *may use the whole stage.*)

MARY

(*Softly prelude & fugue from the* SWITCHED-ON BACH *record fades in. It runs the rest of the scene in varying volumes. A dream.*)
I was thinking about the duck—you know, the white duck with the orange beak in David's pond. I told Sarah that I would wash her clothes if she would give me the white duck and let me kill. But you know Sarah. She said, "Quack, quack, I'll let you kill-kill if you wash David's oh you know what rubs against my man's skin that's against our religion." Isn't that just like her?

NARRATOR, JESUS, JOSEPH, HOLY GHOST

Just like her.

JESUS

Mother, Mother,
Jewish wife,
shield our mirrors
from the light.

MARY

So I agreed. She gives me the duck. I have the duck. I have the duck in my hands and I'm walking down the road. The sun is directly overhead. I cast no shadows. I pass a stone house. I pass a wagon full of soldiers. They are sleeping. I pass a rich man's rose bush. I pass a brown mouse and a white rabbit.

NARRATOR, JESUS, JOSEPH, HOLY GHOST

White rabbit.

NARRATOR

Mary, Mary,
Queen of light,
shield our mirrors
from the night.

MARY

I have the duck. Where does the duck end; where do my hands begin? Is such softness possible? It's quiet. The duck quacks.
(*The rest of the cast make a brief but loud quacking sound.*)

JESUS

Mother, Mother,
Mother of me,
open their eyes
and let them see.

MARY

A dog answers the duck; a frog answers the dog; a bird answers
the frog. The sun moves slightly. I cast a light shadow.

NARRATOR, JESUS, JOSEPH, HOLY GHOST

Light shadow.

NARRATOR

Mary, Mary,
walking slow,
show us all
the golden road.
(*Build tempo and volume.*)

MARY

I was bent over washing clothes and I was thinking about the duck
and the golden road.

NARRATOR, JESUS, JOSEPH, HOLY GHOST

The golden road.

MARY

It must have been the heat.

NARRATOR, JESUS, JOSEPH, HOLY GHOST

Heat.

MARY

There were drops of sweat on my forehead and I was wet beneath
my breasts.

NARRATOR, JESUS, JOSEPH, HOLY GHOST

Breasts.

MARY

The palms of my hands were slippery and I——

NARRATOR, JESUS, JOSEPH, HOLY GHOST

DROPPED THE DUCK!

MARY

I dropped the duck. It waddled down the road and turned into a bigger duck and then a bigger one——

NARRATOR

The Miracle of the Duck!

MARY

Soon there was a duck the size of a camel running away down and up the road—eeee-ooooo (*The highest sound the actress can make sliding down to the lowest. Everyone is doing duck imitations. The stage is full of ducks.*) straddling the road. The duck was running away from me and (MARY *becomes a young girl running*) I was running after it as fast as a girl can run. I ran a mile after my duck, which kept on growing until it was the size of a ooooo-eeeeee (MARY's *lowest sound to her highest. Loud!*). Everyone was inside sleeping, except a naked little boy. He came out of his yard and ran after me. (HOLY GHOST *pursues* MARY.)

NARRATOR, JESUS, JOSEPH, HOLY GHOST

Ran after me.

NARRATOR

And then she said——

MARY

Ran after me.

NARRATOR

And then she said——

MARY

Ran after me.
("And then she said" *and* "Ran after me" *are repeated over and over again to establish a beat for clapping and tambourines. The words are then dropped.* MARY *and the* HOLY GHOST *dance to that steady beat in* MARY's *area of the stage. From his place,* JOSEPH, *the jealous husband, watches* MARY *and the* HOLY GHOST *do their erotic dance until he can stand it no longer. He tries to interrupt them.*

They mock him with their dancing. Joseph is Puerto Rican or Mexi-can. In Canada, the speech should be translated into French Cana-dian. In this version the speech is in Puerto Rican Spanish. JESUS *and the* NARRATOR *keep the beat for* MARY *and the* HOLY GHOST *until it is time for the* NARRATOR *to speak. His cue is* JOSEPH's *line "La puta."* JESUS *alone then keeps the beat.* MARY *and the* HOLY GHOST *reach their high point at "La puta," but continue a slow hypnotic dance until* MARY's *line at the end of the scene, under the* NAR-RATOR's *speech.*

The placement of the actors after JOSEPH's *speech is:)*

X

XX	(JOSEPH)	X (JESUS)
(MARY and HOLY GHOST		X (NARRATOR)
dancing)		

JOSEPH

Mi mujer Maria estaba lavando rope a mano. ¡Mielda! No le peudo comprar un washer-dryer. Quizas el año que viene. Quizas en el año que viene no trabajo. Este negro viene con una pinga como un salami. Este negro pendejo viene y mira a mi mujer. Yo no soy el mismo hom-bre de antes. Yo cantaba, yo bailaba con las muchachas. No me deja-ban quieto. Yo era el typo sabroso. Ave Maria, mira lo que has hecho. Este come mielda con pelo de Brillo. Yo trabajo, yo trabajo fuelte, pa la union pensión y pal social security. Quiero morir contento. Y Maria, que se muera. ¡La puta! Le tengo tanto odio en mi corazon que si se estuviera muriendo de sed ni le doy meao. ¡Ay me muero de asma! ¡Arranca mi corazon y cómetelo! Ese negro tuerto y apestoso. Lo cogió en sus brazos, le besó la cara fea y le dió la chocha. ¡Mira que cosa! ¡Mira que cosa! Dios mio, mira que cosa.

NARRATOR

(*The* NARRATOR's *speech should come from a newspaper and cover some item of local political interest. It can change nightly if de-sired. The speech, which overlaps* JOSEPH's, *should run about five minutes. The one here is from the* Berkeley Barb, *May, 1969.*)
If one can forget the horrible wounds sustained by our brothers, there are many reasons for being hopeful. First, we have all known —since Chicago or earlier—that in fact we do live in a police state and Reagan's measures here have forced that fact into the resistant

heads of much larger numbers of people. From now on, the regime cannot afford to be as coy. Second, the occupation of Berkeley is extremely expensive for the regime. Police forces throughout the Bay Area are strung thin. (At Palo Alto Friday, police had to wait three hours for sufficient reinforcements to move against a small group of Stanford protesters.) If young people can stimulate similar repressions simultaneously in a couple of dozen cities around the country, they might soon bring down the American dollar. After that, the old-timers probably would make important concessions to us. Third, the National Guard here is half to two-thirds sympathetic to us, and in an all-out civil war, large numbers of them would defect to our side. One young lady here asked a group of fifteen National Guardsmen whether they'd fire on us. Eight of them remained silent—but not hostilely so—and the other seven said under no circumstances would they shoot. Fourth, the quality of the nine-to-twelve age group is downright inspiring. They understand. The revolution is in their heads at the deepest psychic level and the regime never will be able to eradicate it. But what has to be understood—and somehow accepted—is that hundreds, perhaps thousands of us are going to be murdered before the old-timers concede anything real. We must try to accept this and try not to blame old-timers as individuals. Their conditioning has been so lengthy and so complex that it is almost impossible for them to understand. It is now noon. In an hour we gather at Herrick Hospital to hold a vigil for our wounded. I hear sirens in the distance but I don't know what they mean. (*Perhaps* JESUS *clashes cymbals lightly.*)

MARY

(*Simply*)

I was washing clothes and thinking.

8: PROGRESSION

Complete the progression; that is, the HOLY GHOST *walks back to his place. Then, immediately:*

9: PROGRESSION (GIANT STEPS)

An abstract, compressed version of the earlier Giant Steps. Everyone moves and talks all at once. MARY *repeats,* "No, you may not. No, you may not. Go back. Go back. Go back." *The game ends at*

the point that MARY *and the* HOLY GHOST *are together again. This
time (as she speaks)* MARY *comes center, to deliver:*

10: THE ANNUNCIATION

(*Mary's monologue should have a low musical accompaniment,
preferably live. The kind of song is Buffy Saint-Marie's "Until It's
Time for You to Go." The same song, full volume, should be used
to cover the progression that follows and the Conception, which
follows that.*)

MARY

(*Word by word at first*)
I had the impression that, well, oh, it's strange to say. Yes, what was
I saying? It was so beautiful to be there talking and my words came
out with no lumps and I felt no duty to make my words skiddle to
my feelings. My feelings were going every which way! And my
words were flying out of my sweet mouth like birds. I loved my
words and I loved my feelings and there were colors and smells and
the Lord touched me. It was pleasant?—good?—bad?—to be
touched all over at once. It felt more as if I were touching—no, I
was being touched—by air? Well, it eeeee-ooooo (*highest to lowest note, casually, reasonably*) very quickly and you can scarcely
expect a poor woman like myself to remember what exactly ooooo-
eeeeee (*lowest to highest*) so you can write it down to remind
yourselves what happened to a person—as if it could happen to you
if you remember in detail what happened to me. (*Catches her
breath. She's amused by herself.*)
   Now, I would say—I would say anything if my toes would stop
wiggling (*her toes wiggle*)—you know how it is. Toes, I said stop.
Stop. Please? (*wriggling*) What can you do? Oh, dear, now my
legs. My thighs. Well, it seems to be happening again. (*Her whole
body is trembling.*) Look at the body move, trying to touch as much
air or whatever as possible, all at once, out of con-trol, as they say.
Well, I must be crazy but I'm happy just standing here twitching,
trembling, touching air, saying things. (*The trembling might be
accompanied by a tremulous flute or noisemakers. The other music
has momentarily stopped.*) I'm probably crazy. Next she'll say the
Lord's doing it to her. I say that I'm doing it *with* the Lord; he's the

air and all of this is me, including the words which are really swallowed air made into *ssounnds!* (*Sings a few unrelated notes.*)

(*À la Mae West*) Well, this is what it was like if you really want to know.

NARRATOR

(*Catching* MARY, *who was going to her place*)
What about the colors, Mary?

MARY

(*Music resumes.*)
Colors. Oh, I forgot to mention colors. Thank you. (*Winks at the* NARRATOR.) It wasn't as if someone brought on colors. No, no one drugged out those colors. I just blinked (*lights blink*), and when I opened my eyes, why, there they were! (*The stage is bathed in gorgeous light.*) You should have seen the apple tree. And the garden. And my dress. And there were sounds, ordinary garden sounds and I was washing clothes—and smells—no perfumes, but grass and cowshit and water. I was twitching and trembling. (*Ecstatic*) The Lord entered me and I entered the Lord! (*Cut music.*) But not like these words.
(*Song up and immediately:*)

11: PROGRESSION

Complete the progression; that is, the HOLY GHOST *walks back to his place, exactly as on page 135–6. If there are facilities for a light show, this is the place for it. Nothing is happening onstage for a few minutes, just the song. Toward the end of the song:*

12: THE CONCEPTION

The cast is in their places, sitting. GOD *and the* HOLY GHOST *bring out a rolled-up length of foam rubber. It should be about three feet wide and as long as the playing area. Untied and aimed properly, the foam rubber will open itself across the stage. A magic carpet. The rubber might be covered with silver glitter. As it unrolls,* JESUS *walks across it to* MARY, *who stands. The song ends.*

13: THE BIRTH

Under the entire scene, the slow movement (recorded over and over again) from the Bach-Vivaldi Concerto for Four Harpsichords should be played at low volume. A physicalization of MARY *giving birth should be developed by director and cast. In any case,* JESUS *should end up back near* GOD *and the* HOLY GHOST, *facing them. In turn, as insistently as the music, but never harshly—sometimes even whispering—the men ask Mary:*

"Oh, Mary, whatta ya gonna name that pretty little baby?"

To which she replies, consecutively:

Contentment.
Waiting.
Clumsy.
Heavy.
Swollen feet.
Burden.
Pain.
Pain.
Pain!
Pain!!
Pain!!!
PAIN!!!
Bloody.
Wet.
Warm.
Wonder.
Milk.
Love.
Peace.
Sunshine.
(*The men's questions, which have become rather indistinct and overlapping, are now clear.*)
Emmanuel.
Emmanuel.
Emmanuel.
Jesus! Blackout.
(*Music out.*)

14: SOME QUESTIONS

GOD

Jesus pushed past the words that hold us down.

HOLY GHOST

Jig-a-jig-a-jig-jig
Jig-a-jig-a-jig-jig
Jig jig

GOD

Jesus pushed past the words that hold us down.

HOLY GHOST

Jig-a (etc.)

JESUS

(*Does a somersault before each question.*)
Daddy, Joseph tells me it is holy not to eat pork, but you tell me
that my skin is full of holes and lets in rain and that I'm the pig
I'm not supposed to eat. Eili, Eili, if I can eat a lettuce-me or a
cow-me, why can't I eat a pig-me?
(GOD *will answer each question with a knowledgeable gesture, perhaps from corny paintings of* GOD *or* JESUS. *The* HOLY GHOST *will
then affirm* GOD's *gesture with his "jigs."*)

JESUS

Daddy, Joseph tells me it is holy not to touch my doodly-hoop and
not to play with boohmahs, but you tell me that you *are* a doodly-
hoop squirting gafney into a floating boohmah.
(*Gesture. Jig*)

JESUS

Daddy, Joseph tells me that all men have kikis, but you tell me that
kikis are booloo. Eili, Eili, should I go out into the shima and get a
kiki?
(*Gesture. Jig*)

JESUS

(*With growing frustration*)
Daddy, Joseph tells me that the old men in the temple are gana,

but you tell me they are goonoo like me. Eili, Eili, should I go to them and tell them they are goonoo?
(*Gesture. Jig*)

JESUS

Daddy, Joseph tells me that Judas ba-swani, but you tell me niba-niba Judas ba-swani lacrima dei. Eili, Eili, Judas ba-swani, Judas ba-linda?
(*Gesture. Jig*)

JESUS

(*Furious, agonized*)
Daddy, Joseph di-lalla, lalla di-poinas. Poinas-li at poinas nunc? Nunc poinas! Eili, Eili, lama sabachtani?!
The grandest gesture. The HOLY GHOST *drives* JESUS *into the ground with his "jigs." The scene ends with* JESUS *on the floor near* MARY *and* JOSEPH. *The* HOLY GHOST *and* GOD [*who will play the* JUDGE *in the following scene*] *are in their usual places.*)

15: THE COURTROOM

HOLY GHOST

(*As court bailiff*)
(*Chanted*)
Hear ye, hear ye, the fourteenth district state nation graph structure federal official important flag tribe book law God shape number velocity axis American chief judge power-power kill fist justice thank you fear get out of his way here he comes he comes he comes he comes he comes the judge will tell us what to do here comes the judge de judge de judge de judge! (*Hands the* JUDGE *a bullwhip.*)

JUDGE

(*Turns to audience. Chants.*)
I am one thing you are many things I know what to exclude one side is good the other side is bad I am what I am what I am what I am. (MARY *and* JOSEPH *have picked* JESUS *up off the floor. They rock him, singing Brahms' "Lullaby."*) I have taken a stand which must should has to compelled jail what can you do black white lines right right right right side yes right side (*flung to the heavens:*) kiss my ass I'm better than you my children go to college my wife wears

underwear my daughter got married in the *Times* cigars monograms manicures I won't die I won't die my wife shaves her legs nuns nuns nuns nuns nuns nuns I use Burma Shave lead soldiers I never danced why should I dance heavy heavy heavy (*his voice has become deep and heavy*) I won't die respect me! (*Whip*) respect me! (*Whip*) respect me! (*Whip is cracked at the audience. The* JUDGE *turns to the court.*)

LAWYER

(*The* HOLY GHOST. *Sung:*)
OBJECTION!

JUDGE

(*Sung as the resolution of a chord*)
OVERRULED! (*Silence*) Will the defendant please step forward. (HOLY GHOST *as the* LAWYER *drags* JESUS *away from* MARY *and* JOSEPH *and brings him to the* JUDGE.)

MARY and JOSEPH

He's innocent!

JUDGE

(*Sung:*)
Order in the court. (*To* JESUS) You didn't say may I. Go back. (LAWYER *pushes* JESUS back.) Well?

JESUS

(*Trying to please but not understanding what is being asked of him. Dumb sounds, smiling with each of his attempts to come across*)
Uh. Uh? Uh.

LAWYER

(*Whisper*)
Say, "May I?"

JESUS

(*Mimicking him*)
Ay ay I. Ay ay I? Uh?

JUDGE

What's wrong with your client-client?

LAWYER
He was all right this morning when they were torturing him.

JESUS
Ay I. Ay I.

MARY and JOSEPH
May I. May I.

JESUS
(*Recognizing them*)
Ma-ma. Da-da.

JUDGE
You sure he's not some kind of *nigger?*

LAWYER, MARY, JOSEPH
(*Cringe away from* JESUS, *as one person*)
NIGGER??

JESUS
(*Has picked up on "nigger"*)
Ih-er. Ih-er?

LAWYER
Say may I, dammit!

JESUS
(*Like a parrot*)
Same eye, dmt!

LAWYER, MARY, JOSEPH
(*Patiently*)
May——

JESUS
Mmm-eheh—ii

LAWYER, MARY, JOSEPH
(*Pointing to their eyes*)
I.

JESUS
(*Pointing to his eye*)
Ah-ii.

LAWYER, MARY, JOSEPH
May—I.

JESUS
Mehii yai. (*Whenever he says this phrase, he points to his eye on* "*I.*") Meyai, meyai?

LAWYER
Good boy.

MARY
Good boy.

JOSEPH
Good boy.

JUDGE
(*Topping them*)
Good boy. It sure does my heart glad. I was worried for a moment that we had a nigger on our hands.

LAWYER
(*Sung*)
Objection!

JUDGE
What is your objection?

LAWYER
(*Approaches* JUDGE)
If it please the court, I would like it stricken-chicken from the record that I might in any way be, might be, or has been associated in body, mind, or soul with danger. I have a wife and a color-television set to worry about. Repairs are expensive. There are your real criminals—TV repairmen.

JUDGE
(*Sung*)
Sustained. (*Not sung*) You are in no danger. Only your client is in

danger. Proceed with the case; I like your face. (*Runs his whip across the* LAWYER's *face, gently.*)

LAWYER
Under protest.

JESUS
(*Has been frantically looking for a place to take a leak. He is holding his crotch in pain.* MARY *and* JOSEPH *try to hide him.* JESUS *raises his hand as if in school.*)
Oo-oo-oo.
(MARY *and* JOSEPH *cover their faces in shame.*)

LAWYER
My client wishes to speak.

JUDGE
State your name age make and serial number.

JESUS
Mmm-muh-mh-muh-muh pee? Pee-pee?

JUDGE
I think he's trying to tell us something.

LAWYER
Something about his front central sexio-excretory region.

JUDGE
Watch your language. I'll have none of that filth in my court.

JESUS
Pee-pee. Pee-pee?
(*He's jumping up and down in pain.*)

LAWYER and JUDGE
Bad, bad.

JESUS
Pee.

MARY and JOSEPH
Shame.

JESUS
Pee.

LAWYER and JUDGE
Bad, bad.

JESUS
Pee.

MARY and JOSEPH
Shame.

JESUS
(*Takes out a water pistol and "pees" on the* JUDGE, LAWYER, MARY, *and* JOSEPH. *The* LAWYER *tries to hide behind the* JUDGE *and* JOSEPH *tries to hide behind* MARY.)
Pee-pee, pee-pee, pee-pee . . . ? (etc.)

JUDGE
This is a court of law. (JESUS *shoots him.*) Now cut that out! Something's happening!

LAWYER
Something's happening. That's never happened before.

JUDGE
I'm holding you responsible!

MARY and JOSEPH
Innocent, innocent . . . (*etc. to the end of the scene*)

JESUS
May I? May I? May I pee-pee? Pee-pee? (*To the end of the scene*)

LAWYER
(*Sung*)
Objection!

JUDGE
Overruled. Where's my book?

LAWYER
I'm innocent.

JUDGE

I'm not guilty! This court is adjourned!
(*The* JUDGE *is savagely whipping on all sides. Cries of "Innocent,"*
"Guilty," "Pee-Pee." Tremendous noise. Blackout.)

16: THE LAST WORDS OF JESUS

The tone should be light, sometimes sarcastic, when it is not sav-
age. JESUS *starts his first line in the blackout and on the floor. He*
repeats that line until the stage is light and he is standing. The
position of the actors:

	JESUS	
JOSEPH X		X HOLY GHOST
	X	
MARY X		X GOD

JESUS

It won't stay the same. There's nothing to it. Help, I'm whating,
slumbling in it. A costume party with guests hiding guns in their
jewels. A drag queen does his best, and poor creatures, rich young
debutantes hide their tears and grins and go to make-believe make-
believes. What other subject is there, Buster?

Why it just keeps on happening over and over, each time in a new
way. God, that seems so bad that I would like to kill someone about
it. Who's to complain to? Is it a joke? Whose idea of a joke is this?
So I half close my eyes and as politely as I can I go on with what
I'm doing. I expect that's how I shall die. They can't take death
away from you; they try to make you forget that you were born.

They tell you a story, an obvious lie, or at best a fearfully demented interpretation based on second-hand information. A man is
born; he moves his body; he ingests vegetable matter or transformed
vegetable matter; he egests the same, somewhat altered. He smiles;
he suffers; he gives pleasure; he feels pleasure. Someone interprets
these actions and tries to endow them with motivation: animal
needs, social pressures, gods, an unconscious, the stars, the way
things are. You call their bluff and if you're lucky they lock you up.
You say, Mister, I don't mean to be impolite but you're speaking
blah-blah; besides you're also stepping on my toes, Mister (*angry*),
get off my back. I don't care if they're Cong or pigs or hippie-
faggot-nigger-Jews—that don't mean shit to me. Shove your concept-

gun up your ass, I'm busy replanting the field you ruined yesterday during the Unity Parade!

Then they give you an easy rule of thumb about what's real. If it hurts it's real; if it's moderately painful it's true; if it's just so-so you have your choice. Well, it's now real. It's real. And it's real. It's real. It's real. It's real. (*Continues saying this until it's "real" to the actor.*) Are you happy? It's real.

So I half-close my eyes and politely as I can I go on with what I'm doing. I'm dying. They can't take that away from me. (*Sung like a Broadway tune:*) "No, they can't take death away from you." They tried to make me forget I was born. Don't try to take away my death. Don't ask me for an attitude about my death. Don't even ask me for a grimace. May I please just die, with no attitude, no explanation, silent, except for those noises that come from me like an orgasm, those unexpected sounds that *are* me? May I cast away —GHUN°—the rotten shit of words GHUN and take my GHUNful place among the GHUN?

Our Father, which art in GHUN, hallowed be Thy GHUN. Thy GHUNdom come, Thy GHUN be done, on GHUN as it is in GHUN-GHUN. Give us this GHUN our daily GHUN, and GHUN us our GHUN, as we GHUNgive our GHUNGHUNers. And GHUN us not into GHUNation but GHUN us from GHUN. For GHUN is the GHUNdom and the GHUNer and GHUNy forGHUN. Amen. A-GHUN.

(*Bach chorale from beginning, "O Haupt Voll Blut und Wunden," fades in.*)

And now the world will stop and the silver wire binding me to the golden plug, the bright orange insulation unravels, the tiny platinum screws unscrew, and the blue juice ceases to flow. I am weak

---

° *The sounds indicated by "GHUN" are nonverbal, incoherent noises produced deep down in the actor and released by him when he relaxes his defenses. They are sounds of the moment and cannot be "acted." During the Lord's Prayer, which follows, the sounds, if produced properly, will take over the prayer and take the actor way out. In the last paragraph of the speech, the tension of the actor way out, trying to pull himself back in, should be dramatic and suspenseful.*

Some of the sounds will be loud, some will be soft. They can't be faked (they come from stomach breathing). If the sounds are genuine, the effect should be hair-raising.

and growing weaker. GHUN, ghun. (*Fainter and fainter*) I am some kind of man, some kind of child. Ghun, ghun. If you subtract a man from infinity you get zero. Ghun, ghun. One man plus one GHUN equals infinity. Any child knows that. Open their eyes and let them see. GHUN. The paint is peeling, the wood splinters, the machine whines. Bring me my cat, the tiger-striped one, and my rubber duck that can't quack. No, I don't want anything, thank you. No, no thanks. (*Lights are fading.*) It's all right. I'm tired. (*Gentle*) Oh, yes, please close the door when you leave.
(*The stage is black.*)

END

THE POOR LITTLE MATCH GIRL

A Christmas Comedy

by Arthur Williams

Dedicated to Lula P.,
and memories of CHRISTMAS, 1936

THE POOR LITTLE MATCH GIRL was first presented by the Judson Poets'
Theater in association with the New Gaiety American Operetta Theater Company at Judson Memorial Church on December 22, 1968. The music and songs
were by Alvin Carmines, the direction and choreography by James Waring, the
set by Teresa King and Ivan Taub, the lighting design by Earl Eidman, the
costumes by Norvel Bullock, and the cast was as follows:

LULU	Arlene Rothlein
GRANDMA, LAME WOMAN	Teresa King
POOR WOMAN	Aileen Passloff
HAWKSLEY	George McGrath
RICH MAN, SYLVAN	Bill Maloney
COACHMAN, BLIND MAN, WATCHMAN	Bryan Hayes
KITTY	Joanna Vischer
STREETWALKERS	Teri Loren
	Aileen Passloff
	Lynn Warhoftig
POLICEMEN	Craig Kuehl
	Lyon Phelps
JOHN ROYALL	David Vaughan
TOMMY GOODY, ANGEL	Edward Barton
SAILOR	Roy London
BOB	Delmer Petersen
BILL	Mark Russel
TERPSICHORE	Gretchen MacLane
NYMPHS	Teri Loren
	Lynn Warhoftig

161

CUPID	Marian Sarach
DOWN-AND-OUTER	Craig Kuehl
RICH WOMAN	Gretchen MacLane
CAROLERS	Teri Loren
	Delmer Petersen
	Mark Russel
	David Tice
	Lynn Warhoftig
SOUL OF THE MATCH GIRL	Eloise Harris
	(or) Mary Lou Harris
CHORUS OF BLESSED SOULS	Jeffery Apter
	Gayl Fowler
	Lee Guilliatt
	Teresa King
	Philippa Koopman
	Roy London
PIANIST	Al Carmines

ARTHUR WILLIAMS was born at Cape Girardeau, Missouri, in 1930. He attended Anderson College in Anderson, Indiana, Hartford Theological Seminary, and the School of Library Services of Columbia University. He is the author of *The Sideshow,* a one-act play produced in 1965 by the American Theatre for Poets; of "America's Speech and Song" from *The Pageant of the Four Continents,* a monologue performed at Caffe Cino in 1966; and of *Dreams for Sale* and *The Winner,* one-act plays done at the Open Space in 1970. In addition to acting in several Off-Off Broadway productions, he has appeared with the Judson Poets' Theater and Off Broadway in *In Circles and Peace.* He, together with John Herbert McDowell and James Waring, is a founder and a director of the New Gaiety American Operetta Theater Company.

SCENE 1: *Grandma's room.*
SCENE 2: *The North River docks.*
BALLET-PANTOMIME: *Arcadia.*
SCENE 3: *In front of Royall's dry-goods store,*
        East Fourteenth Street.
SCENE 4: *The torch of the Statue of Liberty.*

TIME: *The late 1880's.*
PLACE: *New York City.*

SCENE 1

(New York in the eighteen-eighties. A poor, mean ground-floor room near the North River docks. A window and door give onto the sidewalk; there is a bed, and a trap door in the floor. The room is littered with great piles of rubbish. LULU is sitting on the bed dressing her doll. When she is satisfied with it, she breaks the doll's head on the bedstead, and begins picking it to pieces. The POOR WOMAN appears outside and taps on the window. GRANDMA enters from the cellar through the trap door, goes to the window, and opens it.)

GRANDMA

What do you want?

POOR WOMAN

You know what I want, you wicked old fiend. Hurry, I'm so cold out here.

GRANDMA

It ain't getting any warmer in my house, when I have to open the window every second minute. Have you got money?

POOR WOMAN

I've got forty-five cents. You can let me have a little bit for that.

GRANDMA

I've told you not to come around here with less than half a dollar. *(GRANDMA starts to close the windows, but the POOR WOMAN puts her hands inside. GRANDMA slams the window down and the POOR WOMAN cries out, but raises the window again.)*

POOR WOMAN

For God's sake, it's Christmas Eve. My children are at home, hungry, but I swear to you, if I had another nickel I'd give it to you. You know I would. Please, oh, please.

GRANDMA

If you're so worried about your children, take your forty-five cents home to them.

POOR WOMAN

You're right. It doesn't matter what happens to me, and surely God will help me if I do without for their sakes.

(*The* POOR WOMAN *starts to leave, but* GRANDMA *reaches through the window and catches hold of her shawl.*)

GRANDMA

Well, all right, if you have to have it so bad, I'll give it to you for forty-five cents and your shawl. You can get the shawl back for ten cents.

POOR WOMAN

But I'll freeze if you take my shawl.

GRANDMA

(*Slowly closing the window*) I've told you my terms for doing business. If you don't want it——

POOR WOMAN

No, wait. Give it to me. It doesn't matter. The filthy brats hate me, anyhow.
(*The* POOR WOMAN *gives money to* GRANDMA, *who rummages around on the floor, finally coming up with a small bundle that she hands out through the window. The* POOR WOMAN *snatches it and starts to run away, but* GRANDMA *pulls the shawl off her shoulders. The* POOR WOMAN *runs out with a shriek, clutching the bundle.*)

GRANDMA

(*Closing window*) That is a pitiful wreck of a woman. I hope I never come to such a state as that.
(LULU, *rising from the bed, reaches out to touch the shawl.* GRANDMA *strikes her on the side of the head, knocking her all the way across the room.* LULU *picks up the poker and throws it violently, missing* GRANDMA. GRANDMA *goes to her and pounds her head against the wall until she is quiet and dazed.*
Enter RICH MAN *outside; he taps on the window.* GRANDMA *goes to the window and opens it.*)

GRANDMA

Ah, good evening, sir! I've been wondering when we'd see you again.

RICH MAN

You need never fear losing me as a customer, Grannie. You've got what the doctor ordered.

GRANDMA

It's good of you to say so, sir. How much will you have today?

RICH MAN

Five dollars' worth should get me through the holidays, I think.
(GRANDMA *gathers up three quite large bundles.* LULU *gets up and goes to the window, staring out at the* RICH MAN.)

RICH MAN

And who may you be, little girl?

LULU

(*She has a cleft palate.*) Lulu.

RICH MAN

(*To* GRANDMA, *who has come to the window with the bundles*) What did she say?

GRANDMA

She said her name is Lulu. She don't talk good.

RICH MAN

I'll say she doesn't. Shouldn't you wipe her nose?

GRANDMA

Wipe your nose, Lulu.
(*The* RICH MAN'S COACHMAN *has come up to the window, and* GRANDMA *hands the bundles through to him. The* RICH MAN *then gives* GRANDMA *a five-dollar bill.*)

GRANDMA

She's my granddaughter, sir, and she's not right in the head. Thank you so much for your business, sir, and Merry Christmas. I hope I'll be seeing you again soon.

RICH MAN

That you will, Grannie. Merry Christmas, and Merry Christmas to you, Lulu. A most peculiar-looking child. Treat those carefully, Charles. They've got to last till next week.
(*Exeunt* RICH MAN *and* COACHMAN. GRANDMA *closes window.*)

GRANDMA

I've told you I don't want you hanging around that window when I've got customers. You're sickening.

LULU

Grannie.

GRANDMA

What?

LULU

It's Christmas.

GRANDMA

It's Christmas Eve. Christmas is tomorrow.

LULU

Will I get a present?

GRANDMA

Will you get a what?

LULU

A present.

GRANDMA

Well, I should say not. Who do you think would get you a present, pray tell? How much money did you bring home last night? How much?

LULU

Three cents.

GRANDMA

A present! You're not even worth feeding.

LULU

Santa Claus will bring me a muff.

GRANDMA

Are you still whining about that muff? It costs two dollars. At the rate you work, it will be cold weather again before you've brought home that much.

LULU

Santa Claus will bring me one.

GRANDMA

He'd just as well not bother, because if he does I'll sell it to pay me a little for the expense I'm put to keeping you. You need your hands to tend to your business, not to keep in a muff.

(LULU *begins to weep bitterly and throws herself onto the bed. Enter* FRANK HAWKSLEY *outside. He taps on the window, and* GRANDMA *opens it.*)

GRANDMA

What can I do for you, young sir?

HAWKSLEY

I need a small bundle, quick, Grannie, and I heard that you've got it.

GRANDMA

I've got it if you have. My smallest price is fifty cents.

HAWKSLEY

All right, give me that much.

(GRANDMA *begins to search for a small bundle. Meanwhile* HAWKSLEY *unpins his badge from the inside of his coat. When* GRANDMA *returns and hands him the bundle, he drops the badge into her outstretched hand.*)

GRANDMA

Wait a minute! That's no half dollar!

(*She holds the badge up to the light and gives a shriek of terror.*)

A badge! You're a copper! (HAWKSLEY *vaults the window sill and twists* GRANDMA's *arm. She groans in pain and drops the badge into his hand. He releases her and she stands nursing her twisted arm while he pins the badge on the outside of his coat, then looks down at it, admiring the effect.*)

HAWKSLEY

That's right, Grannie, you're fairly caught. But you may boast, when you're behind bars, that you were put there by Frank Hawksley, the sharpest man on the detective force.

GRANDMA

Well, Frank Hawksley, if that's what you're called, you're a fine one, going around doing old women out of their only means of livelihood. And what about my poor little grandchild, my darling? What will happen to her?

HAWKSLEY

Stuff a sock in it, Grannie. Do you think I'm not busy making my own living? I'll get a promotion for this. I've already been promised.

GRANDMA

You have, huh? Then that means the heat is on someplace. Let me think—I get it! It's John Royall, the mayor's brother-in-law. He's trying to start an operation in his dry-goods store uptown. Ain't that right? I thought so. Now, you listen to me, young man. You carry me off to the Tombs, and the only way you'll get a promotion is to move to Chicago.

HAWKSLEY

Come on, Grannie, you haven't got a bigger contact than the mayor's brother-in-law.

GRANDMA

Four city councilmen are customers of mine. Can you match that?

HAWKSLEY

But what can I do? I've *got* to make an arrest.

GRANDMA

I don't see what concern that is of mine. You just keep your fat hands off me. Wait a minute! Maybe we can do a little something for each other. Lulu, dear, come to your old Grannie. Go close the window, will you, dear? It's getting cold in here.
(LULU *hesitates, and* GRANDMA *shoves her violently to the window, which she closes. She turns and stares at* GRANDMA *and* HAWKSLEY.)

GRANDMA

And now, dear, I know you won't mind going down in the cellar for a bit, while this gentleman and I talk over some business.

LULU

It's dark down there.

GRANDMA

I know it's dark down there, you fool. Now go on, or I'll knock the side of your head in.

HAWKSLEY

There's certainly something bad wrong with that one. How can you stand to have her around? Why doesn't she wipe her nose? (LULU *quickly bites his leg.* HAWKSLEY *kicks her off with a shout of anger and pain.* GRANDMA *catches up a stick, but* LULU *rolls to the trap door and pushes it shut, although she herself is crouching behind the bed.*)

GRANDMA

That's my granddaughter, and you can have her.

HAWKSLEY

What would I do with a thing like that?

GRANDMA

Arrest her instead of me. I'll lie low, you'll get promoted, and I'll go burn down John Royall's dry-goods store—I'd been intending to do that anyway—then after a while I'll open up again at the old stand, and you get a nice bonus from old Grannie. How does that strike you?

HAWKSLEY

Now, wait a minute. What if you're lying to me? But if you're right, it would put me way ahead.

DUTY DUET

HAWKSLEY

> Where does the path of duty lie?
> Should I keep going straight ahead
> And do as I'd already planned,
> Or should I take a chance for more?

GRANDMA

> The dangerousest thing that you could do
> Would be to take a chance on crossing me.
>
> Duty bids you step aside
> And take advantage of the job
> I offer you to help you out
> And make some money on the side.

HAWKSLEY

> I think you're right about what duty bids:
> I'll make a little money on the side.

GRANDMA

Perhaps I can help you make up your mind. You walk around by the mayor's brother-in-law's dry-goods store sometime tomorrow, and if it's still standing, come and arrest me. But if I go up there and burn it out tonight, you'll have to do business with me, and you can still have Lulu and your promotion.

HAWKSLEY

Done, Grannie. You're square: a fellow couldn't ask for a fairer proposition than that. All right, I'll come back and get her tomorrow night.
(KITTY, *heavily veiled, enters outside and taps on the window.*)

GRANDMA

Can this be a customer? Christmas Eve is usually a slow time.
(*She opens the window, recognizes* KITTY, *motions to her to come in by the door, and closes the window.*)
This is a very special customer, so you go on, now, and come back tomorrow evening. I'll have her ready for you then.
(KITTY *enters by the door, and starts back at the sight of* HAWKSLEY.)

GRANDMA

It's all right, Miss. This gentleman was just leaving. Goodbye, sir, I think our association will work to the profit of both of us.
(HAWKSLEY *leaves through the door.*)

KITTY

(*Lifting her veils*) Ma, I've brought you some money. I can't per-
suade John not to try and take over your business, but I'll pay you,
Ma, honest I will. Promise me you won't burn his store down.

GRANDMA

You just set your mind at rest on that score, my dear. I've decided
not to bother your John's precious store. You just rest easy tonight.
Everything's going to be all right. How much money did you bring
me?

KITTY

Here it is. I've got to go; it wouldn't do if anybody down here
recognized me.

GRANDMA

If John Royall ever found out who you were before he met you
there would be no more fine dinners at the mayor's house, would
there? You'd be back on the docks hustling sailors in about fifteen
minutes.

KITTY

I can't bear to think of it. He's had himself made a special deputy
so he can go out with the police rounding up streetwalkers. I think
he would kill me if he knew.

GRANDMA

Kitty, dear, I've some bad news for you. Poor little Lulu was caught
stealing apples this morning and they've carried her off to jail.
Don't take it too hard.

KITTY

I'll take it easy. I just hope they throw away the key. Sometimes
I dream I'm walking in the street with John and we come upon the
little monster and she calls me Mama.

GRANDMA

Don't be silly. She doesn't know you. I told her her Mama was dead
—and her Papa, too.

KITTY

Oh! Don't mention that molly-boy to me. What's he doing now?

GRANDMA

Sailors. Kitty, I can't understand how you let Tommy Goody give you a baby. From the time he was in the third grade, he was making lunch money off the high-school boys. How could you get a kid from him?

KITTY

I've told you a thousand times, Ma, we were just talking, and I bet him he couldn't do it, and he did, and I wasn't prepared. That's all.

GRANDMA

He still lives on the third floor. Every time he sees Lulu, he jumps and turns pale, as well he might.

KITTY

Well, if she's in jail for a while, that will be a rest for you. Besides, when she's here you don't feed her much, and you knock her around a lot, so she gives you a little fun. I've got to go. Thanks for not burning down the dry-goods store, Ma. I'll still work on John to drop the new business.

GRANDMA

Goodbye, Kitty, dear.
(KITTY *leaves.*)
And I promise I'll not burn the store more than once. Such a grand lady, and she brings her poor old mother only sixty dollars for Christmas. I ought to burn her house, too.
(*Goes to trap door, opens it, and calls down.*)
Lulu! Come on up. It's time to get out to work.

LULU

(*Stands up behind the bed*)
Grannie, was that pretty lady my Mama?

GRANDMA

Did you hear what we said? Were you here all the time?

LULU

Is Tommy Goody my papa?

GRANDMA

I'll kill you, you little sneak.

LULU

I'll go to my papa. He won't let them take me to jail.

GRANDMA

(*Searches around the floor until she finds a considerable length of rope. She stalks* LULU.)
Now listen to Grannie, dear. If you were ever to tell anybody that that pretty lady is your Mama, it would cause some people to be very angry with her. And if you don't go to jail, it will cause Grandma a lot of inconvenience. You don't want those awful things to happen, do you? And as for that Papa of yours, if he thought you knew about him, I think he'd help me send you to jail. So you see, dear, I'm just thinking of your own good. Wipe your nose, dear. (*As* LULU *wipes her nose,* GRANDMA *springs with the rope, but* LULU *is too quick for her. After a struggle,* LULU *grabs a brick and begins to beat* GRANDMA *on the head. When* GRANDMA *is quite bloody and still,* LULU *rolls her into the cellar and puts down the door. Then, singing* "Merry Christmas, Grannie," *she puts on the* POOR WOMAN'S *shawl, takes up her matches, and leaves.*)

SCENE 2

(*The North River waterfront. It is snowing heavily. Three* STREET-
WALKERS *enter.*)

WHORES' SONG

STREETWALKERS

We hate the wintertime and snow,
We'd like to see the sun.
But that can't be because, you know,
The night's the time for fun.

We'll give to any man or boy
Who'll spend six bits or so
An hour within our loving arms,
Instead of in the snow.

(JOHN ROYALL *enters with two* POLICEMEN. *The* POLICEMEN *appre-
hend the* STREETWALKERS *and take them off. Re-enter* POLICEMEN.)

POLICEMEN

Well, that lot is safely off to night court. It's a great work you do
among the wicked of this city, Mr. Royall.

ROYALL

I do my modest best, officer. You two go down that way, and
search for more evil-doers. I'll stay here and see that this area remains clear.
(*Exeunt* POLICEMEN. *Enter* LULU.)

LULU

Will you buy my matches, kind sir?

ROYALL

Certainly not, filthy little girl. Why don't you wipe your nose?
(LULU *raises her hand to strike him, reconsiders, wipes her nose.*)
What are you doing out on the streets this kind of night? It's not
respectable.

LULU

I have to sell my matches, or Grannie will beat me. (*Giggles.*) She
won't beat me tonight.

ROYALL

Well, on second thought, I guess you're not likely to go bad with men, anyway. Probably steals, though.

LULU

Won't you buy my matches, please?

ROYALL

No. Now stop bothering me.
(*Enter* TOMMY GOODY.)

TOMMY

Excuse me, sir, have you got a match?
(LULU *comes forward and proffers her matches, but both ignore her.*)

ROYALL

No, I haven't. I don't smoke.

TOMMY

(*Searches his pockets.*)
Would you believe it? I had some all the time. This is an awfully cold, snowy night for a gentleman to be standing out.

ROYALL

Ah, young man, you are not old enough to realize what late, unseasonable hours wickedness keeps in this city. I'm down here trying to rid the streets of the immoral women who tempt the sailors just come off the boats. I hope you never have anything to do with evil girls.

TOMMY

Oh, no, sir. I wish you would drive them all off the street.

ROYALL

An excellent sentiment, and I hope I will be able to gratify your wish. What is your name, young man?

TOMMY

Tommy Goody.

ROYALL

Goody—that's an odd name.

TOMMY

You won't think so when you get to know me better.

ROYALL

I'd like to know you better, but it will have to be some other evening, because I am down here working with the police tonight.

TOMMY

The police! Well, I must be going, but any time you want to be better friends, just come down here. I'm always around. Merry Christmas. (*Exit.*)

ROYALL

Merry Christmas.

LULU

(*Fondly*)
That's my Papa.

ROYALL

A very manly, handsome young fellow. I always like to help that kind.

RIGHTEOUS SONG
Recitative and Hymn

O Lord, I thank thee that thou hast seen fit
To grant thy servant success in the holy war against sin.
And I thank thee, Lord, for the material success
That has crowned my efforts in thy behalf.
Truly the Prophet saith, I have not seen the righteous
    forsaken,
Nor his seed begging bread.

> All good and perfect gifts, 'tis said
>   Come from God above,
> And rest upon the righteous head
>   As tokens of His love.

The wicked loses all he has,
    The righteous takes it up,
And God will bless his happy life
    With overflowing cup.

(*Enter* SAILOR.)

ROYALL

Ah, there, fellow, stop a moment. May I ask, are you just off a boat?

SAILOR

Yes, I am, if it's any of your business.

ROYALL

I just feel I should say a word of warning to you against the un-savory sort of thing that sailors so often do when they get to port. There are so much better ways to spend your time and money.

SAILOR

I see. Thanks for the offer, Pop, but I'd really prefer a girl. Nothing personal, you understand.
(*Exit* SAILOR.)

ROYALL

Abandoned wretch! Go your way to perdition!
(*Enter* POLICEMEN.)

POLICEMAN ONE

What's the matter, Mr. Royall?

ROYALL

That bestial sailor, shamelessly seeking a woman. Did you find anything down that way?

POLICEMAN TWO

Just Rosie and Sal, Mr. Royall, and they both slipped us some-thing, so we let them be.

ROYALL

A little extra Christmas treat for the kiddies, eh? That's nice. But speaking of Christmas, I really should be back up at the dry-goods store. We always do a big business on Christmas Eve. Come along, men, I'll give you a bit of something to warm you after this cold work.

POLICEMAN ONE

We're right with you, sir.
(*Exeunt* ROYALL *and* POLICEMEN, LULU *alone.*)

LULU

It's so cold, and nobody is going to buy me a present. Not even Grannie.
(*Enter* BOB *and* BILL, *two sailors.*)

BOB

Do you reckon we'll find one here?

BILL

I don't know. How would I know?

BOB

Well, I don't know.

BILL

Here comes somebody.
(*Enter* TOMMY.)

TOMMY

Well, hello, boys. Out looking for a good time?

BILL

Why, yes, we are, thank you for inquiring.

BOB

But we don't know where to find one, you might say.

TOMMY

What! This is your first time in the big city?

BOB

Yes, we just got a job working on the Albany boat.

TOMMY

Fresh off the farm, I'll bet.

BILL

Well, we ain't been away from it long.

TOMMY

Now listen, men, it's Christmas Eve, and I'm willing to help you find a little entertainment.

TOMMY'S SONG

Every night just after sundown,
    When the stars begin to shine,
Tommy, too, comes out and twinkles—
    All the sailors form a line.

All along the docks they're saying,
    Isn't he just fine?
All you sailors, count your money,
    Tommy's coming down the line.

All the sailors follow Tommy,
    He's the sailors' joy.
Tommy's cute and Tommy's clever,
    He's the trickiest kind of boy.

BILL

That's mighty kind of you. We've got money—we'll pay.

BOB

Would the entertainment be—kind of—like girls?

TOMMY

I'd say that was a fair way to describe it—kind of like girls.

BOB

Hoo, boy, that's for us, huh, Bill?

BILL

You just lead on, Mister. We're right behind you.

TOMMY

That's the way.
(*Exeunt* BOB *and* BILL *and* TOMMY.)

LULU

Why would they pay a girl?
(*Enter* HAWKSLEY.)

HAWKSLEY

Ah, there, Lulu, isn't it awfully cold for you to be out this evening?

LULU

It's better than being in jail.

HAWKSLEY

What do you mean?

LULU

You're going to put me in jail after Grannie burns a store. I know.

HAWKSLEY

Has that old fool been babbling to this child? Why, if I do arrest her now, she'll tell everything. At least I can go warn the old woman not to burn the store.
(*Exit* HAWKSLEY. *Enter* POOR WOMAN, *shivering in the cold. She sees her shawl around* LULU's *shoulders.*)

POOR WOMAN

It's an awful night to be out, isn't it, dear?

LULU

Yes, I'm cold.

POOR WOMAN

But you have such a nice warm shawl. Where did you get it?
(*Puts her hand on the shawl.*)

LULU

It's my Grannie's.
(*Pulls the shawl tight and holds onto it.*)

POOR WOMAN

It *is* my shawl. I must have it.

LULU

Lady.

POOR WOMAN

Yes, dear.

LULU

Why do the sailors give money to girls?

POOR WOMAN

So they will take them home with them and let them—do things.

LULU

Do the sailors pay you?

POOR WOMAN

(*Weeps*)
No, I can't make anything any more. Give me my shawl, you ugly
idiot. I'm dying of the cold.

LULU

(*Kicking and beating the* POOR WOMAN)
No, no.
(POOR WOMAN *runs off. If the ballet interlude is not done, skip to*
BOB *and* BILL's *entrance and* BOB's *line:* Well! That was a surprise . . .
If the ballet interlude is done, LULU *runs off in pursuit of the* POOR
WOMAN.)

TERPSICHORE IN LOVE
Ballet-Pantomime

(*Enter* TERPSICHORE *with attendant* NYMPHS.)

TERPSICHORE

> I've hurried down from Mount Parnassus fair,
> Terpsichore, the goddess of the dance,
> In disguise, on purpose here to meet
> The lovely shepherd lad whom I adore.
>
> But O, my heart misgives me cruelly:
>
> For I'm a minor deity
>   And he's a shepherd boy.
> How can a happy union be
>   Betwixt such two as we.

(*Enter* SYLVAN.)

SYLVAN

> I've never seen that lovely maid before,
> But ere she flees I'll claim her for my own.
> O maiden fair, I pray you be my wife,
> And side by side we'll live a happy life.

> She spurns my love! What recourse have I now?

TERPSICHORE & SYLVAN

> For I'm (she's) a minor (very) deity, etc.

(*Enter* CUPID *with bow and arrows. He shoots* SYLVAN *and* TERPSICHORE.)

CUPID

> Their plight demands that Cupid give some aid,
> But what to do is not within my scope.
> I'll hie me to Olympus for advice,
> And there I'll get some help from mighty Zeus.

> So please don't worry, I will be right back.

TERPSICHORE

> Go ask almighty Jupiter for help.

CUPID

> I'll ask great Zeus what he can do to help.

SYLVAN

> Go beg Jove the Thunderer his help.

TERPSICHORE, SYLVAN, & CUPID

> For I'm (she's) a minor (very) deity, etc.

(*Exit* CUPID.)

TERPSICHORE

> My heart expands with joy and hope sublime.

SYLVAN

> If all goes well I think she'll soon be mine.

TERPSICHORE
>   We'll tend the sheep and while away the day,

SYLVAN
>   And tender little games of love we'll play.

TERPSICHORE & SYLVAN
>   If only Cupid brings us help divine.
>   For I'm (she's) a minor (very) deity, etc.
>   See! Cupid comes, and help is on the way!

(CUPID *enters, pursued by* LULU, *who now has his bow and arrows.*)

CUPID

Help....

(LULU *chases* TERPSICHORE, SYLVAN, CUPID, *and the* NYMPHS *offstage and runs off after them. There should be an intermission at this point, and the second half would resume with* LULU *onstage when* BOB *and* BILL *enter. If the ballet interlude is not done, there need not be an intermission.*

Enter BOB *and* BILL.)

BOB

Well! That was a surprise. Didn't it surprise you?

BILL

Yes, I thought it was a surprise.

BOB

I sure didn't expect anything like that. Did you?

BILL

No, I didn't expect nothing like that.

BOB

No, sir, I sure figured he was going to show us something else. But I thought it was worth the money. Didn't you, Bill?

BILL

Yes, I think it was worth the money. (*Puts his arm around* BOB.) And it kind of gives me an idea, you might say.

BOB

(*Puzzles over this for a moment—he's slow—then brightens, puts his arm around* BILL.)

Say, you know, I think you're right. That fellow might just have given us an idea.

(*Exeunt* BOB *and* BILL.)

LULU

Did they pay him?

(*Enter* SAILOR.)

Will you buy my matches, please, sir?

SAILOR

No, I don't want any matches. Say, kid, where can I find a girl around here?

LULU

I'm a girl.

(*The* SAILOR *laughs.*)

I am! Look.

(*She reaches down to pick up her skirt. The* SAILOR *covers his eyes in horror.*)

SAILOR

All right, all right, I believe you.

LULU

I'll take you home with me if you give me two dollars.

SAILOR

Two dollars! I wouldn't give Lillian Russell two dollars.

LULU

I want two dollars awful bad. I'll take fifty cents.

SAILOR

You don't even know what it's all about.

LULU

Thirty-five cents?

SAILOR

God, you turn my stomach, little girl. I'm going uptown.
(*Exit.* LULU *weeps. Suddenly she is swept by a fit of terrible rage.*)

LULU

(*Calling after the* SAILOR)
Don't you laugh at me, you son of a bitch!
(*Enter* TOMMY.)

LULU

Here comes my Papa. Papa!

TOMMY

Wipe your nose, Lulu. What did you say?

LULU

I said, Papa. You're my Papa.

TOMMY

(*Knocks* LULU *down and kicks her two or three times.*)
Don't you ever say that word to me again, you filthy little turd.
What ever gave you such an idea, anyway?

LULU

I heard my Mama and Grannie talking. They said so.

TOMMY

Your mother! That cheap bitch! Listen, Lulu, you mustn't believe
everything she tells you.

LULU

Then you're not my Papa?

TOMMY

How am I to know? Honest, Lulu, it's the only time I ever did such
a thing, and I don't see why I should have to suffer for it for the rest
of my life.

LULU

When the policeman arrests me, I'm going to tell them you're my
Papa, and you can tell them I didn't do nothing.

TOMMY

You wouldn't tell them, would you, Lulu? You wouldn't tell anybody that.

LULU

Yes. I don't want to go to jail. And it's true: you're my Papa. (*Shouts*) You're my Papa!

TOMMY

(*Covering her mouth with his hand*)
I'd be ruined if this got out. I'd be laughed off the docks.
(LULU *bites his hand, and drops to the ground when he lets go of her. He makes a dive for her, but she picks up a piece of ice and stuns him with it. She removes his belt and ties his hands. Then she searches his pockets. She pulls out a dollar.*)

LULU

My goodness, they gave him a dollar.
(*She searches further, finds another dollar. Outraged*)
They gave him a dollar apiece.

TOMMY

(*Still groggy*)
Of course. I always get a dollar! Hey! Give me that money! Untie me, you monster!

LULU

No. I'm going to keep you tied until they come to arrest me. And I'm going to buy me a muff.

TOMMY

I'm warning you, Lulu, the minute I get my hands loose I'll kill you.

LULU

You will?

TOMMY

I'll tear you apart. Help! Help!
(LULU *looks around desperately, then rolls* TOMMY *over the edge of the dock into the water. Enter* HAWKSLEY.)

HAWKSLEY

I thought I heard someone shouting for help. Was it you, Lulu?

LULU

I didn't hear nothing.

HAWKSLEY

Lulu, something terrible has happened to your Grandma.

LULU

I know. I hit her with a brick.

HAWKSLEY

Well, you've killed her, you little beast, and now she won't give me the money she promised me. At least she won't burn down John Royall's dry-goods store. Listen, Lulu, I've decided not to take you to jail, but I'm going to take you somewhere nice, where you'll be out of trouble, and nobody will bother you.

LULU

No.

HAWKSLEY

Why not?

LULU

I'm going to buy me a muff.
(*Runs off.*)

HAWKSLEY

I've got to think: How can I still get money out of John Royall? And I've got to get that idiot kid.
(*Exit.*)

SCENE 3

(*East 14th Street, in front of John "Royall's Dry-Goods Emporium." It is snowing heavily. Enter three* BEGGARS: *a blind man, a lame woman, and a down-and-outer.*)

BEGGARS' SONG

Our lives are hard, your lives are soft—
You've only got to ask for bread.
Therefore we make bold to beg:
    Won't you spare a little change
    To help a poor man on?

You know the money's in your purse,
You'd rather keep it there.
Your guilty conscience is our friend:
    You'd better spare some change
    To help a poor man on.

(*Exeunt* BEGGARS. *Enter* LULU.)

LULU

I've got two dollars now, and I'm going to get me a muff. I'm going to get the white one in the window.
(LULU *starts to enter the store as the* RICH WOMAN *comes out.* RICH WOMAN *holds a coin to her.*)

RICH WOMAN

This is for some good little girl for Christmas. Have you been a good little girl?

LULU

Yes, ma'am.

RICH WOMAN

Have you gone to Sunday School every Sunday this year?

LULU

Yes, ma'am.

RICH WOMAN

And what did you learn in Sunday School?

LULU

I don't know.

RICH WOMAN

Surely you remember something, or there wouldn't be any use
in your going, would there? Now I'm certain that if I were to give
you this five-cent piece you would be able to remember a little song
you learned in Sunday School.

LULU

Yes, ma'am.

RICH WOMAN

That's a good girl. Now, wipe your nose, and sing me a song.
(*She gives* LULU *the nickel.* LULU *sings.*)

I'M READY WHEN YOU ARE

Beneath the trees a maiden and a soldier walked,
    Their arms entwined, their hearts beat high with joy.
The soldier whispered in the maiden's pretty ear;
    Then blushing she addressed the gallant boy:

    I'm ready when you are;
I hope you'll not make me wait all day.
    Stop hanging around, now,
Your soldierly task is set for you.
    Stand up to attention;
I promise you'll be well satisfied:
    I'm ready when you are.

(*The* RICH WOMAN *beats* LULU *vigorously with her heavy handbag,
snatches the five cents from her pocket, and marches off in a rage.*
LULU *lies swooning on the sidewalk.* CAROLERS *enter, singing* "O
Little Town of Bethlehem." JOHN ROYALL *comes to the door of the
store to greet them.*)

ROYALL

Thank you for your music, my friends. I'll be glad to contribute to
your cause. But may I first know to what use you will be putting
this money?

CAROLER

It's to pay for Christmas dinners for the children of deserving poor families.

ROYALL

Isn't that sweet! Since it's for that, I will give you double the amount I had intended.
(*He gives the* CAROLER *a handful of money.*)

CAROLERS

Thank you, Sir. God bless you, Mr. Royall. Merry Christmas. Good night.

ROYALL

Good night, and may God bless you, dear young people.
(CAROLERS *exeunt, stepping over* LULU, *who still lies on the sidewalk. Enter* KITTY.)
Ah, good evening, Catherine, my dear! Isn't it rather cold for you to be stirring?

KITTY

Yes, John, it is, but I'm very nervous. What if that terrible person down by the waterfront were to try to harm you or your store?

ROYALL

Catherine, Catherine, you're so inexperienced in these matters. I suppose you never so much as heard of dealings like these out in the country. Here in town we know how to take care of ourselves. I already have the commissioner of police working with me on this. In fact, I hope to hear that the woman who runs the business has been arrested this evening.

LULU

(*Coming to*)
Mama!
(KITTY *gives a little scream.*)

KITTY

Lulu!

ROYALL

Catherine! Do you know this wretched child?

KITTY

No! Yes! I mean— She came to the back door begging once, when I was in the kitchen, that's all.

LULU

(*Displays the two dollars*)
Look, Mama, I'm going to buy me a muff.

ROYALL

Why does she keep calling you Mama?

KITTY

Because I gave her some money, John. She's feeble-minded. She doesn't know what she's saying.

ROYALL

Well, I wish you wouldn't encourage people like that, Catherine. There are already too many of them in the world. Tell me, little girl, where were you intending to buy your muff? I have some very pretty ones inside. And for just two dollars, too. Why don't you come inside with me?

LULU

I want that one.

ROYALL

Oh, that's a lovely one. You wait here and I'll go in and get it for you. So you won't have a chance to slip anything into your pocket.
(ROYALL *goes inside and takes muff from window.*)

KITTY

(*Taking nail scissors from handbag*)
If you call me Mama one more time, you hideous little animal, I promise you, I'll slit your throat.
(*Returns scissors to handbag.*)

LULU

Why don't you like me?

ROYALL

(*Re-entering*)
Don't, I beg you, Catherine, give the child any more. If she had

more money she would just spend it foolishly, as she has two dollars on this muff. Come on inside, dear. It's so cold out here.
(ROYALL *and* KITTY *go into the store.*)

LULU

(*Puts on the muff and admires it, strutting up and down, posing with it.*)
I'm not cold any more. Beautiful, beautiful. Soft, soft. It's like a kitten.
(*The muff begins to separate at the seams and fall apart, and at last it lies at her feet in many pieces.* LULU *contemplates it, immobilized by overwhelming grief. Enter* RICH WOMAN *and* RICH MAN.)

RICH WOMAN

There she is, Henry. She sang an extremely improper song to me. Extremely.

RICH MAN

Ah, Emily, I know this child to be one of the dregs of the city. You were fortunate indeed that you escaped her presence merely having heard of wickedness. You, there, match girl, what do you mean by insulting my wife with your filthy bar-room songs?
(LULU *slowly turns and lifts her skirt, offering him her behind to kiss. The* RICH MAN *strikes her with his cane, but* LULU *grabs it away from him and begins beating him and his wife unmercifully. They run off with* LULU *after them. Enter* ROYALL *and* KITTY *from the store.*)

ROYALL

So you see, my dear, there's nothing to worry about. Everything will be taken care of. Go on home and sit down by the fire; I'll be there very soon.
(KITTY *sings.*)

KITTY'S SONG

> I used to call the cows at break of day,
> I used to pick potatoes off the vine,
> I used to hoe the rows of oats and rye;
> A happy life, for ev'ryone I knew was good.

Now, New York City is a wicked place:
    It's full of lust and violence.
To think about the wicked people here
    Makes me desire that peaceful farm.

O Husband, on a night like this
How much I long to see again
My long ago Long Island home.

(*Enter* FRANK HAWKSLEY.)

ROYALL

Ah, Hawksley, there you are. Have you effected the arrest of the person you went after? My wife has been very anxious about this affair.

HAWKSLEY

Well, no, sir. Things have taken an odd turn. I discovered that the operation was run by a young girl who lived with her grandmother. When I went to arrest the girl, the grandmother found out what had been going on, and in the ensuing argument the girl killed her by beating her head in with a brick.

KITTY

Ma! Dead!

HAWKSLEY

She escaped, but I know who she is, and I hope to earn that bonus yet, by her capture.

ROYALL

Catherine, whatever is the meaning of this? Do you know this old woman, too? (*To* HAWKSLEY) You have indeed brought disturbing news. Go inside and get warm while I say goodbye to Mrs. Royall. She is just leaving.
(HAWKSLEY *goes inside.*)

ROYALL

Now, Catherine, can you explain your acquaintance with these people who are so obviously not respectable?
(*Enter* SAILOR.)

SAILOR

Kitty! By God, Kitty, you don't know how glad I am to see you. (*Embraces her.*) It's certainly been a long-enough time.

ROYALL

I beg your pardon, fellow.

SAILOR

Oh, hi, Pop. Are you a friend of Kitty's? Come on, Kitty, let's ditch Auntie here and go somewhere and have a good time.

ROYALL

Catherine, do you know this man?

KITTY

No, John, no. It's a lie; it's all a lie.

SAILOR

Does she know me? I'll say she knows me, and the best way, too, don't you, Kitty Cat? But I haven't seen you in so long, Kitty. Whatever happened to your old lady and that simple kid of yours?

ROYALL

Simple kid? Your mother? Catherine, you've lied to me. You're not from Long Island at all. You're a—— You've been a common—— I can't say the word. (*Shouts.*) Bad woman!
(*Lifts his arm to strike her. The* SAILOR *intervenes.*)

SAILOR

Okay, Pop. That's enough of that. Nobody but me gets to bat Kitty around.

ROYALL

Very well. I leave her to you. But mark this, Catherine, you are never to darken my doors again. Indeed, I forbid you to come within my sight any more. I intend to lodge an information against you with the police in the morning.
(*Goes into store.*)

KITTY

Goddamn you, you fool, you've spoiled everything. He's my husband. Now he's kicked me out.

SAILOR

Ah, what do you want him for. He's an old fairy. Now me, I'm a man, and I've got three days in town. Come on, I'll show you a good time.

KITTY

Will you get away from me? You've ruined my life, and now I'll have to go back on the streets. Go away! Go away before I kill you. I've got to get him to take me back.
(*Runs into the store.*)

SAILOR

I thought she'd be glad to see me.
(*Goes out.* LULU *enters, swaggering, with broken-off half of* RICH MAN's *stick in her hand. She sees the pieces of the muff, becomes sorrowful again. Takes matches out of pocket to offer them for sale, gets an idea, goes into store. Enter* RICH MAN *and* RICH WOMAN, *much battered, with two* POLICEMEN.)

RICH MAN

She was right here, officer. She attacked us physically.

RICH WOMAN

She is literally a scandal in the streets. You must do something.
(*There is a scream from within the store.* LULU *comes running out, laughing wildly, and runs off.* KITTY *and* HAWKSLEY *come to the door at the same time and try to squeeze through together.* HAWKSLEY *pushes* KITTY *aside, knocking her into the display in the show window.*)

HAWKSLEY

(*To* POLICEMEN)
You men follow me. I've got to catch her.
(HAWKSLEY *and the* POLICEMEN *run off. The store is burning brightly by now, and a crowd gathers to watch* KITTY, *who was injured when she fell, vainly try to break the window and escape the flames.*)

SCENE 4

(*The platform around the torch of the Statue of Liberty. The door giving access to the ladder down the arm of the statue. It is snowing heavily. Enter* LULU *through the door. She runs all the way around the torch.*)

LULU

There's no way out.

(*She runs around in back of the torch out of sight. Enter* HAWKSLEY *and two* POLICEMEN.)

HAWKSLEY

She's trapped, now, men; you go this way, and you go that. I'll stay here and guard the door.

(POLICEMEN *go around torch in opposite ways. One of them is heard to cry out in terror, the cry dying away as he falls from the torch. The other* POLICEMAN *returns.*)

HAWKSLEY

What happened?

POLICEMAN

It was terrible, sir. She just sprang out of the shadows and pushed him over before he had a chance to see what was happening. What a terrible way to die.

HAWKSLEY

Well, never mind. They say that when a person falls from a great height like that he's already dead before he hits the ground.

(LULU *creeps stealthily around the torch toward the two men, who have their backs to her. Suddenly she puts her head down and runs at* HAWKSLEY, *butting him in the back. He, thrown off balance, falls against the* POLICEMAN, *who is pushed over the railing. The* POLICEMAN *grabs* HAWKSLEY'S *coat.*)

POLICEMAN

Help me, sir!

HAWKSLEY

Stop it, you fool, you're tearing my coat. Catch hold of the rail, and I'll help you up.

POLICEMAN

I can't sir, my hands are too cold. Help me!
(HAWKSLEY *pries the* POLICEMAN's *hands loose, but is unable to hold onto him. The* POLICEMAN *drops with a scream.*)

HAWKSLEY

Now you see what you've done. When I do get you, I'll kill you.

LULU

I'll kill you. It's easy. I could have killed them all whenever they hit me. And I will, now.
(LULU *advances on* HAWKSLEY; *she is beginning to enjoy a new and delightful sense of power.* HAWKSLEY *suddenly panics.*)

HAWKSLEY

Don't touch me! I'm going to go down and signal for help. You can't get away. There's only one way out, and that will be watched.
(LULU *rushes him, he runs for the door, hits his head on the top of it. Dazed, he staggers back to the rail.* LULU *picks up his feet and tips him over. She watches him fall with considerable satisfaction. Then she goes and closes the door.*)

LULU

I'm tired. I'm cold. I'm so cold. I'll build a fire. Nothing to burn.
(*Lights match.*)
Grannie won't beat me any more.
(*Blows out match, lights another.*)
I got two dollars from Papa.
(*Blows out match, lights another.*)
Mama didn't like me.
(*Blows out match, lights another.*)
The cops can't take me to jail.
(*Blows out match, lights another.*)
How can I get away from here?
(*Watches match burn out.*)
It's Christmas and I'm so cold. Once at Christmas I made a big fire. Grannie beat me, though.
(*Weeps.*)
I won't get a present and nobody likes me. I don't care. I'll bash them. I'll hit them. I'll kill them. Santa Claus likes me. He'll bring

me a good muff. He'll see me good up here. Oh! Oh! There he is! Santa Claus! Santa Claus! Here! Here! My hands are so cold. Can't I have my muff? Santa Claus! Come back, come back.

(*She is too stricken for tears at this, and although her eyes are beginning to dim, still she searches the sky. Suddenly, she is joyous.*)

He's coming back. Oh, Santa Claus, you heard me. You're coming back.

(*She collapses in tears and dies. The flame of the torch dissolves into a vision of the mystic rose in the tenth heaven. A beautiful* ANGEL *stands forth and speaks to the dead match girl.*)

ANGEL

No, Lulu, not Santa Claus, but one who brings you more than even Santa can. I bring warmth, but I bring coolness; I bring you safety among loving companions; I bring you rest, but I bring you joy; I alone can give you life, for I am Death. Poor little match girl, come with me, and these bright souls will teach you the song they sing.

(*The* SOUL OF THE MATCH GIRL *in the form of a beautiful child clad in white takes his hand.*)

Bow to them, for they are your brothers and sisters, and they bid you welcome.

(*The* CHORUS OF THE BLESSED SOULS *sings* "Welcome, Lulu, welcome," *and the angel leads* LULU's SOUL *to its place in the circle. The vision fades. Enter* WATCHMAN.)

WATCHMAN

What is happening up here? Three bodies have fallen with terrible cries from this torch, disturbing my sleep. Can murder be done on Christmas Eve?

(*The body of the little match girl rises. The face has become that of the Wolf Man in the Lon Chaney movies. The body lumbers awkwardly over to the* WATCHMAN, *who starts back in horror. With a swipe of its claw the body kills him, and exits through the door.*)

WILLIE THE GERM

by Murray Mednick

WILLIE THE GERM was first presented by Theater Genesis at St. Mark's Church in-the-Bouwerie on April 1st, 1968. It was directed by Ralph Cook, with lighting by Johnny Dodd, sound and visuals by Domenick Capobianco and Elfi Schuselka, and the following cast:

FLAMINIA	Michele Collison
PANTS	Gene Elman
CYNTHIA	Delia Duke
MARTIN	Tom Lillard
WILLIE	Victor Eschbach
BUTTON PUSHER	Pat Cook
DR. SAM	Jerry Lipani

MURRAY MEDNICK, who was born in Brooklyn on August 24, 1939, grew up in the Catskills, but returned to New York at age seventeen. All his plays have been presented at Theater Genesis, beginning with *The Box, Mark of Zorro,* and *Sand.* With Sam Shepard and Eddie Hicks, he formed a musical group called The Heavy Metal Kid. *The Hawk,* a collaboration with Tony Barsha and the Keystone group, was also produced Off Broadway. *The Hawk, The Hunter,* and *The Deer Kill* (which won an Obie award) have been published in separate volumes by Bobbs-Merrill. As playwright-in-residence at Theatre Five in San Diego, Mednick wrote and directed *The Shadow Ripens,* which is based on Eskimo ritual. He has received two Rockefeller Foundation grants and a poetry award from the National Council on the Arts, and a book of his poems will soon be published by Bobbs-Merrill.

(THE SCENE: *A narrow stage with a black curtain as background. A sizable area in front of the stage is roped off. To the side, near the theater entrance, is a large platform on wheels. Above the playing area are hung several mirrors. One, large, stage rear, faces the audience; the others, smaller, face the stage; all are slanted so as to reflect the action proper and each other. Portraits of George C. Tilyou and other carny heroes adorn the walls.*

Ideally, the audience should be forced to stand, as they would at a freak show.

This play should be done FAST, up tempo all the way, by SPEED FREAKS—it is, in fact, a freak show in a spook house at a carnival, and everything possible should be done to create a carny atmosphere in and around it.

CYNTHIA, FLAMINIA, *and* PANTS *sit on stools onstage. There is another stool, unoccupied. They all wear whiteface.* CYNTHIA, *a girl about fifteen years old, wears a mini skirt.* PANTS *and* FLAMINIA *are dressed in a style reminiscent of the commedia dell'arte.* FLAMINIA *has a great mane of red hair.* PANTS' *fly is open. They are the parents of* CYNTHIA *and* MARTIN. MARTIN, *also in whiteface, is a young man in a sharp black suit. He stands at the theater door, taking charge of the rope, ushering in the audience, while the others make faces and obscene noises.*

As this is going on, the PROLOGUE, *in* WILLIE'S *voice, is heard over and over again, outside the theater as well as in, against a background of carny sounds—cackling, barkers, crazy laughter, calliope, etc.*)

PROLOGUE

I have had many weird dreams about waterfronts. Circus-type waterfronts, with sideshows and freaks. Slanting warehouses, tipsy piers, rolling promenades. Waterfronts that are carnivals, blaring on the edge of the sea. There I have a variety of nightmares, but I am always looking for the right THE END, somewhere near a bandstand in the sun, where the technicolor is real, and the black and white shadows disappear like witches into the moon. Without fail it will be beyond the next mirror, or the next, threatening, obliquely, like the Mona Lisa, to become three-dimensional. Having found my way there during the hunt, to have happened on this circus water-front, cringing in alleys, has never been a surprise. It is a repetitive chase played out in my brain, in which only the characters change, to protect the guilty; a recurring journey taken at night, by the sub-conscious.

In the beginning I walk before recognizable strangers, the puz-zled faces of the waking life, those to whom one smiles through one's detachment; they who flicker in the imagination, as in shadow plays, staccato marionettes. The world rises ahead and slips away behind, without smell, without touch; I am waiting for my own soundless footsteps in what appears to be the entrance of a circus. . . .

Mirrors are signs, leading into or becoming doorways; and door-ways becoming corridors, endlessly opening corridors in a gray light. Out there is the wide water without sound, the whiteness be-loved of poets, upon which are dark boats floating, funereal caskets carrying the deaths of the day's enemies. What may have been is no longer the question. Time resolves it within the urgent sense of the hunted in a hunting game, like a schizophrenic clock, the melting tick of the heart. Drifting, mirrors sliding through mirrors . . . a crime has been committed! What crime?

Ah! I am the sole spectator of my distortions—the sideshows are under my direction, the freaks are in my image! The scene changes, recurs—the interlocking, perpetually embracing rings of the circus. There my ancient Self, my Ringmaster, cracks His whip and howls.

(*When all of the audience is inside, the* BUTTON PUSHER, *an ordinary-looking, middle-aged woman wearing a white lab coat, enters and joins the audience somewhere in front. She carries a but-ton mechanism that is attached by wire to an unseen oscillator or operates by remote control. . . .*

MARTIN *secures the rope and wheels the platform to the stage so that it makes an extension jutting out toward the audience. He then takes his seat onstage with the others.*

WILLIE THE GERM *is rolled tightly in a ball, exactly in the right front corner of the platform.*

He remains in this position for some time.)

FLAMINIA

Come on, Willie. Get up.

PANTS

Get up, Willie.

MARTIN

Rise and shine, Willie. It's not that bad.

CYNTHIA

Poor Willie.
(*Finally* WILLIE *moves. He uncurls slowly, in bits and pieces. We hear heavy breathing on tape, the body breathes in unison. He opens his eyes. He attempts to rise, fails, tries again, gets up on his knees. He waves to himself in the mirror several times, each time with more despair. He laughs at the audience. The freaks laugh at him. His final gesture is hopeless. He is dressed in a white busboy's jacket and baggy black waiter's pants, no shoes, no whiteface. He contemplates his image.*)

WILLIE

What crap . . . the corpse . . .
(*He slowly lifts his right arm, in such a way as to avoid the edge of the platform.*)
. . . moves . . .
(*Staring straight ahead, he approaches, carefully, the edge, with his right hand. He hesitates an inch away. He takes the plunge. Instantly there is tremendous static and a flashing strobe light.* WILLIE *pulls back his hand, as if burned, and howls with pain. The others laugh.*)

FLAMINIA

I told you not to fuck with the energy around here, Willie.

MARTIN

No liberties, Willie, no fringe benefits.

PANTS

You ought to know better by now, Willie.

WILLIE

(*A harsh whisper*)
. . . through a strange dream . . .

CYNTHIA

(*Giggling*)

See if you can get it up, Willie.

WILLIE

... composed of a series of temptations ...

MARTIN

What?

WILLIE

... in which he tries to be good. ...

MARTIN

Oh?

WILLIE

That's correct, Martin.

FLAMINIA

Well, how do you feel, Willie?

WILLIE

I feel all right. How do you feel?

FLAMINIA

I feel fine ... a bit tired, maybe.

WILLIE

It's a bit sticky. ...

PANTS

It's a bit damp. My feet hurt.

CYNTHIA

It's dark. I'm scared of the dark.

MARTIN

Get on with it, Willie.

WILLIE

Get on ... with it ... (*He tries a little dance, sings.*) It was Willie what got drownded ... (*Fails, gives up*).

CYNTHIA

That's not it, Willie. (*Sings*) It was Willie what got drownded in the deep, blue sea. . . .

FLAMINIA

Very good. That's very good. Not bad at all, dear.

WILLIE

I can't sing.

MARTIN

Try harder, Willie.

PANTS

You got to make an effort, kid.

WILLIE

My voice is changing. (*Horrified*) It's getting higher!

MARTIN

Then sing higher!
(*They laugh.* FLAMINIA *comes forward.*)

FLAMINIA

Try this one, Willie.
(*She sings, in falsetto:*)
Gonna build me a log cabin
on a mountain so high
so I can see Willie
as he goes riding on by . . .
(*She stops, flustered.*)

WILLIE

(*Cracking up*)
I can't do that one either, Flaminia!

MARTIN

(*Embarrassed*)
Mother!
(*He hands her a broom.*)

FLAMINIA

Uh . . . yes . . . (*Harshly*) Here, then sweep!

WILLIE

Here, sweep . . . (*He sweeps.*) Here, sweep . . . (*he smells something, stops to sniff*) sweep. . . . (*Drops the broom, begins sniffing himself*) Uh, oh . . . I'm disturbed . . . spiritually fucked up . . . and stone-broke on top of that . . . and I have a cold . . . and my overcoat was stolen in the employment agency—I can't believe it! Black cashmere! Warm as hell! No coat! No boots, either! I lost my boots in the Port of Authority . . . in the dead of winter . . . twenty below! That's life . . . but I'm a working man again . . . I've got a job! . . . I'll be nice and people will like me . . . I'll give up drugs . . . I'll get ahead in the world. . . .

(*He has sniffed himself up and down until he ends up with his head between his legs, looking to the rear. A pause.*)

Wow . . . there is an evil biped in the premises. There are several evil bipeds in the premises. I'd better watch my ass.

(FLAMINIA *picks up the broom and whacks him across the buttocks with it. The others laugh.*)

OW!

(*He recoils to the edge. Static. He gets a shock.*)

OW!

FLAMINIA

Sweep.

WILLIE

(*Sweeping*)

Okay, I'll sweep. You don't have to come on that way about it . . . (*Looks seriously at the audience*) You don't have to come on so strong . . . I'll sweep . . . (*Whispers, sweeping*) Which of you is the Button Pusher? . . . I piss on you . . . (*He finishes sweeping, stops, turns to the others*) I think of Willie what got drownded, walking on a cloud in the sky, wearing a bowler hat and a loincloth.

(*Applause*)

PANTS

Excellent.

FLAMINIA

You did a good job.

CYNTHIA

Bravo, Willie.
(*Other appropriate ejaculations*)

MARTIN

Oh, for God's sake! What did he do? He didn't do a damn thing!

WILLIE

Well, I tried.

MARTIN

(*Stalking him with the broom*)
Try harder.

WILLIE

(*Sinking to his knees*)
Okay, Mart.

MARTIN

(*Eyeball to eyeball*)
Do something!

WILLIE

Yuk a luck, fuck a duck. I feel stuck in the muck with a shmuck.
When you don't have a buck, you suck.

MARTIN

(*Thrusting the broom handle into* WILLIE's *mouth*)
You suck!
(*Applause. He returns to his stool.* CYNTHIA *comes forward.*)

CYNTHIA

Poor boy, poor boy. Hang around, be a clown. Poor boy, poor boy,
hang around, be a clown.
(*Returns.* FLAMINIA *comes forward.*)

FLAMINIA

Ladies and gentlemen, this unregenerate person has been rescued
from the street, by us, for your amusement. He's something of a
wise guy, but he's getting hip.
(*Returns.* PANTS *comes forward.*)

PANTS

I agree wholeheartedly and one-hundred cents' worth with my very
high and very esteemed wife.
(*He returns, cuffing* WILLIE *on the way.*)

WILLIE

Your fly is open, Dad.
(PANTS *turns, glares.*)

FLAMINIA

That's enough for now. It's almost lunchtime.

WILLIE

Lunchtime? Lunchtime?

FLAMINIA

Yes, yes, of course. Get moving!
(WILLIE *tries to escape. Static, a shock, etc. The others move their
stools to the platform and make a circle. What follows is an exaggerated pantomime of a meal, a grotesque one, with sounds—grunts,
moans, grabbing, gurgles, etc., with* WILLIE *acting as servant. He is
kept busy and humiliated, setting the table, serving the food, pleasing*
FLAMINIA, *and so on.* WILLIE *has a running monologue throughout,
sometimes to himself, sometimes to the audience, sometimes as if in
answer to something someone has "said."*)

WILLIE

Oh, certainly . . . yes, you may . . . with pleasure, my dear . . . but,
of course . . . very good! . . . thank God it's dead . . . yes, aren't you
glad you didn't have to go out and kill it yourself? . . . no? . . . yes?
. . . more blood, perhaps? . . . your belly hurts? . . . already? . . .
don't eat so fast . . . pig! . . . what now? . . . she wants cream cheese
for her celery . . . right away, my sweet . . . here you are . . . a
banana for your mouth . . . and a mushroom for your hot little
pussy . . . remember me in bed . . . itch! . . . You'll never be satisfied . . . oh, that's nice . . . eat! eat! . . . tomorrow you die . . . up
against the wall! . . . aw, Martin, you're depressed . . . too bad . . .
he needs a new convertible and an M-16 rifle—he's a big man on
campus . . . tch, tch . . . Mr. Pants, here, is a pinball operator . . .

that's right . . . he's got three machines—Big Blonde, Little Blue
Baby, and Heavy Hippie Momma . . . he used to have quite a few
more, but they're disappearing . . . it's very strange . . . meanwhile,
he's giving Doctor Sam a screwing . . . five-hundred-dollars' worth
. . . success! . . . he's terrified . . . Flaminia is quite pleased . . . but
suspicious . . . he's holding out . . . she expects me to spy on his
wheelings and dealings . . . it's not my line, exactly . . . eat! eat!
. . . shit! shit! . . . never fear while Willie's here! . . . I flush their
toilets and perfume their corpses . . . I oil the machine . . . I'm axle
grease, that's what! . . . ha! . . . not rare enough for you? . . . you
like it rare? . . . hmmmm . . . horny little animal, aren't you . . .
there, there . . . don't get excited . . . it's only food, after all . . .
you say you're paying for the service? . . . no denying that, is there?
. . . I'll do my best, sir . . . half prune juice, half hot water? . . . a
compote for the missus? . . . Pepsi for Martin? . . . hot chocolate
for little Cynthia? . . . coming right up! . . . eat! eat! . . . oh? . . .
you don't say? . . . tell me all about it . . . yes, indeed . . . go fuck
yourself . . . die in bed, why don't you? . . . and you, you little cunt,
shove a chocolate bon-bon up your . . .

CYNTHIA

(*Leaping into language*)
Recite a poem!

WILLIE

(*Breathless*)
Recite a poem?

PANTS

Yeah, a short one.

MARTIN

Make it topical.

FLAMINIA

Make it rhyme.

WILLIE

It's not my job.

PANTS

Make it fast.

FLAMINIA
We'll have it with our tea.

WILLIE
I think of Willie what got . . .

CYNTHIA
Not that one, a new one!

FLAMINIA
Will you pour?

MARTIN
Certainly, Mother.

FLAMINIA
All right, begin.

WILLIE
Yes . . . uh . . .

CYNTHIA
Go on!

WILLIE
Well . . . uh . . . I was sitting between two windows. Two windows.
Yes. I was sitting between two windows, in an ordinary room.
But the windows were mirrors. Okay.
(*Playing with his reflection in the mirrors*)
I was sitting between two windows,
in an ordinary room,
but the windows were mirrors.

PANTS
That's no poem.

CYNTHIA
Come on, Willie, I want more.

FLAMINIA
Terrible, Willie. Let's go. (*Leading the others back*) You get worse
and worse, I must say.

CYNTHIA

Shit, Willie, why don't you write about love?

WILLIE

Love?

MARTIN

Get on with it.

WILLIE

(*Turning to audience*)

See, the windows faced each other perfectly. That is to say, they were directly opposite. One another. Naturally, a person likes to look out the window from time to time. Or climb out on the fire escape. Or open the window for a little air. It's a natural thing, to want to do that. But the fucking windows were mirrors.

FLAMINIA

So you cracked up.

WILLIE

Yes, I did.

PANTS

It's certainly not art.

MARTIN

Certainly not. Come along, Cynthia, it's time! (*Exits*)

CYNTHIA

It's all right, Willie. I really do like it. (*Exits*)

WILLIE

If only I could get my head through . . . (*Stares at the audience.*)

FLAMINIA

Clear the table!

WILLIE

(*Contorting*)

OW!

FLAMINIA

Clear the table, clear the table, shut your mouth and clear the table! (WILLIE *stops and approaches the edge. He hesitates, pulls back, regards the audience.*)

WILLIE

I would sometimes see faces in the window . . . (*Sits in the yoga position, meditates a moment, rises.*) But it would turn out to be an illusion . . . every time. . . .
(*Again he approaches the edge. He touches and gets a shock, as before, whispers:*)
Which of you is the Button Pusher?
(*He addresses the audience with an apologetic bow.*)
And so, you see, I had nowhere to turn, for a change of scene, but inward. It is a deliciously abysmal direction. Into a bottomless pit. Yes, that's what the doctor said: "a bottomless pit." Exactly . . . You see, the hum in your head is the sound of your nervous system. Oh, something else: I have always considered the phrase "nervous system" to be kind of perverted . . . as if the system was being nervous . . . a question of describing the energy of the process, rather than its form . . . or something . . . its structure. . . . And that is because . . . I am a very nervous person . . . it seemed to me a highly accurate analysis of the situation. . . .
(*He is violently interrupted by* PANTS, *who seems to have had a sudden anxiety attack.*)

PANTS

Hey! Cut it out, will ya? Cut it out! What are you trying to do? Huh? Huh? You wanna get me in trouble or something? Huh? Huh? (*Implying* FLAMINIA, *behind them*) With the old lady? Just keep it cool, you understand? Keep it cool, you understand? You understand?

WILLIE

What are you talking about, Pants?

PANTS

Huh? You know what I'm talking about! You know what I'm talking about! Doctor SAM! Okay? Doctor SAM! Okay? Okay? I gotta go! Okay? I gotta go!

(*He exits hurriedly, waving and smiling at* FLAMINIA, *who waves and smiles back.*)

WILLIE

I mean . . . as I was saying . . . I present myself to you all. . . . (*He feels his body.*) I present my . . . SELF . . . SELF . . . to YOU . . . to YOU . . . all . . . in various guises . . . of which I am not sure . . . SELF . . . of which I could never be sure . . . SELF . . . and I have the feeling that I have overstayed my presence. . . . (*Disgust at his body. He howls.*)

FLAMINIA

What's the matter with you?

WILLIE

I can't make it. (*Diddling his lower lip*) I can't make it, Flaminia!

FLAMINIA

(*Coming forward*)
Well, stop it. Here, have some of this. (*She produces a small tin-foil packet.*)

WILLIE

I don't want any.

FLAMINIA

Go on, it'll make you feel better. (*She sniffs a pinch of white powder from the packet.*) I'll have some with you.

WILLIE

I don't want any.

FLAMINIA

Go ahead, Willie. I'm trying to help you.

WILLIE

Yeah? (*He takes the packet and sniffs greedily.*) Help is on its way.

FLAMINIA

Besides, I need you to do something for me.

WILLIE

(*Snorting*)
I thought so.

(CYNTHIA *re-enters, a finger in her mouth, and stands by* FLAMINIA. *We hear a tape recording of* MARTIN *giving* CYNTHIA *a beating. Horrendous wailing and shouting.*)

WILLIE

What's that?

CYNTHIA

It's me. I'm being beaten up.
(FLAMINIA *strikes an innocent pose.* WILLIE *and* CYNTHIA *stare at one another until the beating is over.*)

WILLIE

That's a shame.

FLAMINIA

It's a family affair.

PANTS

(*Rushing in as* CYNTHIA *runs off*)
Flaminia! Flaminia! Where's Martin? Huh? They're after me! The heat's on! I can feel it! They're after me! (*Rushes off.*)

FLAMINIA

What? Who's after you? Come back here! Pants?

WILLIE

Maybe he's right, heh, heh.

FLAMINIA

Yeah? (*Grabbing the packet*) Look, Willie, Pants isn't what he used to be. I don't think he can handle it. He's a little off his beam.

WILLIE

So?

FLAMINIA

I want you to contact Doctor Sam, and change the code.

WILLIE

Why don't you send Martin?

FLAMINIA

Martin goes to college.

WILLIE

Oh, I forgot. Heaven forbid.

FLAMINIA

I wouldn't want him to blow his thing, after all.

PANTS

(*Offstage*)
Flaminia! They're after me! The heat's on! I can feel it! They're after me! Flaminia! (FLAMINIA *exits left.*)

WILLIE

(*Shouting after her*)
I'll think about it!

PANTS

(*Entering right*)
Where's my wife? Huh?

WILLIE

How should I know?

PANTS

She was just here. I can smell her remains.

WILLIE

She left.

PANTS

That woman is up to something. Where'd she go? Huh? Huh?

WILLIE

She didn't say.

PANTS

(*Cuffing him*)
What's going on? Huh? Who is in on it? Come on, come on, what are you trying to do to me? Huh? Huh?

WILLIE

We were talking about an old face we used to know. A bad face, come to think of it. From the old days. Don't do that.

PANTS

(*Hitting him*)

Who? Who? Tell me! Tell me, or I'll drown you in a pinball machine! So help me. I'm gonna take you, and I'm gonna wire you to one of my machines, and I'm gonna dump you in the ocean!

WILLIE

Stop that. My left eye twitches for hours when you do that. Don't do that.

PANTS

Okay, let's have it. Out with it!

WILLIE

Doctor Sam.

PANTS

(*Terrified*)

Doctor Sam? Yeah? Doctor Sam? Yeah? So? So?

WILLIE

So, nothing.

PANTS

What do you mean, nothing? Nothing?

WILLIE

Just talk, Pants, I swear it. A reminiscence. Your fly is open.

PANTS

(*Running off right*)

I'll kill her!

WILLIE

(*Pointing left*)

She went that way!

(PANTS *reverses direction, runs off left.*)

PANTS

I'll kill her!

WILLIE

Shmuck!
(FLAMINIA *comes back in right.*)

FLAMINIA

Listen, now do what I tell you, or else. I want you to take the following message to Doctor Sam.

WILLIE

No. Doctor Sam? No.

FLAMINIA

Yes. Tell him: The Cowboy is dead. Period.

WILLIE

No, I don't want to. I'm scared.

FLAMINIA

Here, have another snort. There's nothing to be afraid of. You got that? The Cowboy is dead. Repeat after me: The Cowboy is dead.

WILLIE

The Cowboy is dead.

FLAMINIA

Right. That's all. I'll be back. (*Exits*)

WILLIE

The Cowboy is dead. Terrific.
(*He sinks to his knees, rolls his eyes, clasps his hands, and prays.*)
Doctor Sam? Doctor Sam? Doctor Sam?

VOICE OFF

(*Deep business-head drawl*)
Yes?

WILLIE

Doctor Sam?

VOICE

Yes?

WILLIE

(*Astonished*)

Doctor Sam?

VOICE

(*Annoyed*)

I hear you, boy!

WILLIE

(*In tears*)

Doctor Sam?

VOICE

What!

WILLIE

Why . . . it's a terrible thing that's happened, sir . . . a terrible, terrible thing, sir. . . .

VOICE

Yes? Go on.

WILLIE

Yes, sir . . . it's about the Cowboy, sir, the Cowboy . . . he was going down the road, just going down the road, sir, minding his own business. And he was riding his favorite horse, Spot, sir . . . and he was enjoying the peace, sir, of the early evening, and feeling nice and relaxed . . . smoking a cigarette, as a matter of fact, sir . . . riding off into the night . . . and . . .

VOICE

Yes?

WILLIE

Yes, sir . . . and he was riding quietly into the night . . . and . . . and he was attacked by Indians, sir. . . .

VOICE

Go on, son.

WILLIE

And the Indians attacked him, sir . . . and . . .

VOICE

Yeah?

WILLIE

And . . . and . . . and they ate him, sir.
(*A silence*)

VOICE

(*Slow and even*)
Listen, boy.

WILLIE

Yes, sir. Yes, Doctor Sam. I'm listening, sir.

VOICE

Don't bother to call here no more, boy. Tear up my number. You read me, boy?

WILLIE

Yes, sir. I read you, sir.

VOICE

You are no longer useful to the industry, boy.
(*Click*)

WILLIE

Yes, Doctor Sam. . . .
(*A pause. He whispers:*)
Which of you is the Button Pusher?
(PANTS *enters, distraught.*)

PANTS

Something is fishy around here. I can feel it in my bowels.

WILLIE

You need an enema.

PANTS

(*Hitting him*)
I told you not to make smart remarks! Didn't I? I told you that, didn't I? Huh? Didn't I?

WILLIE

Yes, you did. You did. You told me, Pants.

PANTS

Now, be quiet—I've got to concentrate. I'm getting shafted. You hear me? They've been stealing my machines. That's for sure. You hear me? I just don't know who! Who! Who! Who! I've got to think!

WILLIE

Oh, I have a telegram for you.

PANTS

A telegram? A telegram?

WILLIE

Yes, it's from Doctor Sam.

PANTS

(*Hitting him*)
Doctor Sam? Doctor Sam? Why didn't you tell me before? Huh? What's the matter with you? Huh?

WILLIE

I just got it, Pants! Leave me alone! I just got it!

PANTS

Okay, read it to me. Fast.

WILLIE

(*Produces telegram, on a matchbook cover, reads fast.*)
To: Mr. Pants. Spook house. Coney Island. Brooklyn. Big Blonde down. Gives good head. Dead Little Blue Baby. Watch your Heavy Hippie Momma. Perpetually yours. Stop. Doctor Sam. Hollywood, California.

PANTS

What? What? That's too fast! Read it again! Fast!

WILLIE

To: Mr. Pants. Spook house. Coney Island. Brooklyn. Stuff bad. Death rate up. Fifteen-per-cent margin. Watch your ass. Blow your beak. Perpetually yours. Stop. Doctor Sam. Hollywood, California.

PANTS

(*Backing off*)
What? What? What? Oh, my God!
(*Rushes off left.* FLAMINIA *enters right. They have a very rapid face to face rap.*)

FLAMINIA

What was that all about?

WILLIE

Nothing. He smells a rat——

FLAMINIA

He smells his own crap in the wind——

WILLIE

You shouldn't talk like that in front of people——

FLAMINIA

You're highly sensitive, aren't you?

WILLIE

Highly. See? My right eye twitches. It's my nerves——

FLAMINIA

Too much speed——

WILLIE

Yeah. You're probably right——

FLAMINIA

You ought to get off it for a while——

WILLIE

I know. It's not easy——

FLAMINIA

Too bad. You're ruining your health——

WILLIE

I know——

FLAMINIA

Maybe you could switch to No-Doz——

WILLIE

I did try Benzidrex one time——

FLAMINIA

No good, eh?

WILLIE

No good——

FLAMINIA

How'd you get started, Will?

WILLIE

Oh, I was working as a hairdresser, up in the mountains——

FLAMINIA

In the mountains. No kidding. What town?

WILLIE

South Fallsburgh——

FLAMINIA

Shit, I know that town. There's a traffic light at the bottom of a hill next to a movie house. The Rivoli. Then one short, frantic street ending with another traffic light——

WILLIE

That's the town, Flames! I started with them one-a-day green-and-white spansules. Just to make it, you dig——

FLAMINIA

Sure, I can see how you'd need them, working as a hairdresser up there——

WILLIE

And the soda jerk in the drugstore next door was feeding me bennies. Irving, his name was——

FLAMINIA

Irving Murgatroy?

WILLIE

You know Irving?

FLAMINIA

Sure, sure I know Irving. He was the best busboy in the mountains at one time. Before he retired. Very strung out on pills, though.

WILLIE

That's right!

FLAMINIA

Good friend of mine. We used to sit on his station, for goodness sake, every season, season after season, at the old River View Hotel——

WILLIE

That's right!

FLAMINIA

Yes, indeed. Those were the good old days. Legit. He had a younger brother named Eddie, as I recall. Irving did——

WILLIE

That's right!

FLAMINIA

It's a small world——

WILLIE

Sure is——
(*A pause.* MARTIN *appears on the floor area.* FLAMINIA, *seeing him, slaps* WILLIE *across the face, hard.*)

FLAMINIA

Later, Willie. (*Exits*)
(WILLIE, *on his knees, holds his face and regards the audience. Whispers.*)

WILLIE

Where are you? The one with the button? Don't worry, I'll get you. I'll get you, motherfucker!
(*He feels around the floor of the platform, putting his fingertips*

to his nose and snorting. He gives up, crawls to the edge, almost touches, changes his mind, withdraws. MARTIN, *watching him, goes over to the* BUTTON PUSHER, *with whom he has a casual conversation. The lights dim out.*)

WILLIE

Aha! Hey, Martin! Is that you out there, Martin? This is for you, Martin. . . .
(*He takes a prayer candle from his jacket pocket, lights it, contemplates it in the dark.*)
This is how it all began, Martin, see? With a light in the dark, that's all . . . it's lovely . . . it's a lovely fountain, see . . . nothing else is necessary . . . nothing . . . you never get bored, looking at a prayer candle. When your head is right. (*A long pause. Voices*) And then I heard voices, Martin . . . which disturbed my peace. But I said to myself: "Go on, man, go out and join the others . . . express your joy with them. . . ." (*He rises. Music—"The End," by The Doors— begins here and builds until* CYNTHIA's *line.*) Oh, it was marvelous, Martin! Dancers! Musicians! Drums! Flutes! Tambourines! Vibrations! Lights! Moving pictures! Magical blue guitars!
(*He dances, growing more ecstatic, the candle in his hand.* CYNTHIA *enters, draws him into dancing with her, tempting him severely. The music builds to a crescendo and then fades down.*)

CYNTHIA

Can you get it up, Willie? (*No reply*) See if you can get it up, Willie, come on. . . . (*Giggles*) Come on, Willie. . . .

WILLIE

Can I get it up? Can I get it up? No, I can't.

CYNTHIA

Oh, Willie . . . poor Willie . . . too bad. . . . (*A pause*)

WILLIE

I don't mind. (*Another pause*)

CYNTHIA

I'll tell you a secret, Willie.

WILLIE

What's that?

CYNTHIA

Promise not to tell.

WILLIE

Okay, I promise.

CYNTHIA

I hate my parents, because they don't like Negroes. And I love Negroes. (*A pause*)

WILLIE

Negroes?
(PANTS *rushes in, with* MARTIN.)

PANTS

Silence!
(*The music stops.* WILLIE *blows out the candle.*)

WILLIE

Darkness!

MARTIN

Cynthia!

CYNTHIA

(*Annoyed*)
What?
(*A spot comes on to reveal* WILLIE *crawling to the edge of the platform. Static, a shock, etc. He freezes.*)

MARTIN

Willie is a bad man. He never sees the good side of things. He's maladjusted. When he looks at a flower, he sees death. When he looks at people, he sees creeps. He is mentally deranged and morally demented. You shouldn't play with him.

CYNTHIA

I can play with him if I want to!

MARTIN

No, you can't!
(*He leads* CYNTHIA *off.*)

FLAMINIA

(*Offstage*)
CYNTHIA!
(*A pause.* WILLIE *and* PANTS *are alone.*)

PANTS

(*Hitting him as the stage lights come back up.*)
Listen, you! I don't like little men in general. (*Hits him.*) They're
sly and they have sneaky ways. I like you even less. There's something wrong with you.

WILLIE

I have eyes. That's what's wrong with me. If I didn't have eyes, that
would be wrong with me. And people would say: Look at Willie,
he ain't got no eyes. But I do. I have eyes.

PANTS

I think I'm going to have to get rid of you.

WILLIE

Get rid of me?

PANTS

You heard me. My son says you're not functioning properly.
(MARTIN *enters.*)

WILLIE

Get rid of me? YAAAAAAA! That's a joke.

MARTIN

You're not functioning properly.

WILLIE

(*Pointing at his eyes*)
These aren't eyes, they're marbles. Really. One's a puree and one's a
jumbo.

MARTIN

That's what I mean. We allow you to stay here, but you rave. . . .

WILLIE

You allow me to stay here?

MARTIN

And you have to behave yourself.

WILLIE

(*Incredulous*)
Here?

PANTS

You got it, kid.

MARTIN

Correct.

WILLIE

Thanks. That's nice of you. Why don't you just turn me loose? You know, I don't want to be a hassle to you folks. I'm crazy, anyway. Why don't you just get that woman with the button out of here and fire me, let me go? But first you got to get rid of that goddamn Button Pusher.

MARTIN

You know that's not up to us, Willie. It's up to Doctor Sam.

WILLIE

Where is she? (*He looks.*) He'll do it for you, Pants. Won't he? You're a big man. Why don't you ask him?

PANTS

(*Hitting him*)
That's fast, smart talk, Willie. I told you about smart talk, didn't I, Willie? Ain't gonna do you a bit of good. Might even get you iced, Willie. Iced! Ha, ha!

WILLIE

(*Hysterical*)
Ha, ha, ha!

MARTIN

This is a new scene, Willie, a new era. We are undergoing tremendous change. Technological change, teleological change, metaphysical change. These, of course, will cause sociological chaos. Momentarily. Political, economical, societal, and sexual evolution. Not revolution, mind you, evolution.

WILLIE

I can't wait, kids. Sounds like a riot. Lots of fun for the boys in East New York. Me? Just let me go my own way. I'll go back to the mountains. I was a damn good busboy once. Maybe I'll even make waiter this time.

PANTS

Oh, yeah? Where'd you ever work?

WILLIE

All over. Zalkin's Birchwood Lodge. The Avon Lodge. The Nevele Country Club. Chester's Zunbarg. The River View. . . .

PANTS

The River View? The River View?

WILLIE

Damn right.

PANTS

The River View? No kidding?

WILLIE

Yeah. I was the head children's busboy. Captain of the busboys in the children's dining room.

PANTS

Now, that's something. Used to go there myself. As a guest, of course. Let's see, the waiter's name was Tosh. Harry Tosh. That's something. Comes back to me now. Sure, he had the best busboy in the mountains, as I remember . . . best busboy in the entire mountains . . . name was——

WILLIE

Irving.

PANTS

Irving! That's it, Irving! They called him . . . They called him——

MARTIN and PANTS

Murgatroy Box!

PANTS

Murgatroy Box! Because his feet stunk, heh, heh. You get it? Damn good busboy!

MARTIN

I was a waiter at the Concord!

PANTS

That's right!

WILLIE

Big deal. It's the worst joint in the mountains. I know that place. It's a gigantic nuthouse. Twenty-five a weekend for group therapy with two thousand strangers just like you. Meanwhile, all the help is at each other's throats, hustling the inmates. You have to fight for your goddamn silverware to set the tables with! And the coffee cups! Forget about the coffee cups! And take shit from a whole race of degenerate dining-room employees, mountain rats! Not to mention the guests—those whining women with metal hair! And their fucked-up slobbering kids! And their fat husbands trying to act like *machers!*

PANTS

Machers?

WILLIE

You could puke from it! And in the kitchen it's worse! Everybody takes it seriously! It's life or death! Waitresses push you around . . . cooks scream at you . . . dishwashers spit at you . . . and . . .

MARTIN

You're just bitter, Willie. I did all right.

WILLIE

I bet you did.

MARTIN

I worked my way through college.

WILLIE

(*Spitting into a hand*)
Here's a medal for you.
(*Wipes his hand on* MARTIN's *jacket*)
Now, take it home and show it to your mommy now, before it dries.

MARTIN

You'll be sorry you did that, Willie.

WILLIE

I'm sorry already.

MARTIN

I will finish what I began to say.

WILLIE

Straight ahead, Marty.

MARTIN

I have studied carefully, and thought hard. I have many friends who think as I do. We are armed and in contact with the best in the country. The cream. It will take a bitter effort and struggle to get rid of the scum, but once we get control the transition will be easier. Hard times, discipline, love of country, better business practices, new markets, and states' rights! (*Makes the Nazi salute.*)

PANTS

Stick around, kid.

WILLIE

Oh, fuck that, man—what if I don't want to?

PANTS

We'll have to cut your balls off.

MARTIN

We just might have to do that.
(*A pause*)

WILLIE
(*Searching the audience*)
Changes . . . I go through changes all the time . . . what's that? . . .
First they ask for hot prune juice, then they give you shock treat-
ments, then they cut your nuts off. What's that? (*To* MARTIN)
Where'd you learn all that stuff?

MARTIN
In school.

WILLIE
It figured. I'm getting out of here! (*He leaps for the edge—static,
a shock, flashing lights.*) Shit. (*To the audience*) Whoever you are, I'll
get you. Remember me, I'll get you. I'll get your children and your
children's children and your nice little grandma in your home town. A
plague on you, and all your house. A plague on you.

PANTS
(*To* MARTIN)
Listen to that! (*To* WILLIE) We don't like your attitude. It's unco-
operative and resentful. No wonder you had so many different jobs.

MARTIN
Right. Resentful and uncooperative.

WILLIE
Hey, man, I was just getting the hang of things around here.

MARTIN
I'm out of school now, Willie. Don't forget that. It's time to get
serious. It's time to move.

PANTS
(*Hitting him*)
We're not fuckin' around!

WILLIE
I can tell! I can tell!

PANTS
You've got to be more humble, kid.

MARTIN

There's money to be made in intellectual circles these days, Willie, and important political work to be done. We've got to get this country moving forward again. You're not stupid.

WILLIE

Yes, I am. I'm just an uneducated meth freak, Martin.

MARTIN

We want nothing less than a new breed of man, a new breed altogether!

PANTS

And new markets.

WILLIE

Martin?

MARTIN

What!

WILLIE

Please don't yell. It makes my eyes twitch. By the way, who is the Button Pusher?

MARTIN

We will tolerate no insubordination, no questions, no diversions, no unclean thoughts, and no kinks!

PANTS

That's a fact.

WILLIE

I believe you, I believe you.

MARTIN

And our women must be protected. It's a question of good up-bringing, bad influences, and strange temptations. Purity is the only desirable state, in the long run.

PANTS

For a woman, for a woman . . . uh . . . and for everybody else, too— right?

MARTIN
Right.

WILLIE
Look, boys, purity is the last thing I need right now; if you don't mind, I'd just as soon split.

PANTS
We took you in, kid. We gave you a home.

WILLIE
I was abducted.

MARTIN
It is a proper domicile.

WILLIE
A what?

PANTS
Take a look around. You see any dirt? Not a particle of dust or a blemish—anywhere.

MARTIN
Mother is a good woman.

PANTS
It's spotless.

WILLIE
What about Doctor Sam? What about the Cowboy?

PANTS
(*Frightened*)
Doctor Sam? The Cowboy?

MARTIN
(*Uptight*)
I believe only in the epistemologically clear!

WILLIE
What?

MARTIN

The cut of the real, goddamn it!

PANTS

Exactly right. I'm behind you one hundred percent, son.
(FLAMINIA *enters.* WILLIE *rushes up to her.*)

WILLIE

Flaminia! You've got to do something. Call Doctor Sam!

FLAMINIA

It's time you kicked, Will. Calm down, Martin.

WILLIE

What? I don't want anything. Nothing! I'm out of my skull! I'm no good to anyone in this ... condition. .... Turn me loose!

FLAMINIA

Oh, Willie—it's beyond our control. We just work here. You know that.

PANTS

We do the best we can, making ends meet, pleasing the public. Brooklyn ain't what it used to be, you know.

WILLIE

I'm tired. I want to go to the country. I need a rest. What's happening?

PANTS

Hang in there, kid.

FLAMINIA

Leave it alone, Will ... it's better that way.

PANTS

Yeah, don't worry so much. We're going to get everything straight. Aren't we, son?

MARTIN

We sure are, Dad.

FLAMINIA

(*To* PANTS, *as they return to their stools, arm in arm*)
Button your fly, dear. Where's Cynthia? Oh, here she comes.
(CYNTHIA *enters, carrying a whip.* WILLIE *sinks to his knees.*)

CYNTHIA

Oh, Willie. It's too bad, you know . . . Poor Willie . . . (*She joins her parents.*)

MARTIN

Take it easy, Willie. (*He jumps off platform and leaves area.*)

WILLIE

(*To audience*)
I piss on you . . . .
(PANTS, FLAMINIA, *and* CYNTHIA *wave and make faces at the audience.*)

WILLIE

(*Toward the stage*) Listen to me! So I finally put my head through the window, and it bled! It bled for hours . . . (*To the audience*) He didn't feel a thing . . . he saw a head smash through the window streaked with blood, like war paint. It made an exquisite sound, the sound of broken glass cutting the flesh. . . .
(*The "telephone" rings.* WILLIE *answers despondently.*)
Hello.

VOICE OF DOCTOR SAM

Listen, boy.

WILLIE

I'm listening, Doc.

VOICE

Somebody is trying to confuse my mind.

WILLIE

It ain't me.

VOICE

I don't take kindly to it.

WILLIE

What happens next, Doc?

VOICE

Oh, nothing out of the ordinary, Will. It's business as usual. Like to know who's been playing with my head, though.

WILLIE

It ain't me, Doc. I swear!

VOICE

Never did like that sort of thing.

WILLIE

Well, how do you think I feel?

VOICE

How do I think you feel? . . . That's vague, boy. That's irrelevant. Nothing to do with the problem.

WILLIE

They want to clean up the mess down here, Doc. Everything's gonna be nice and white. No garbage, no losers.

VOICE

That's all right with me. I like clean streets.

WILLIE

Sure, Doc.

VOICE

We'll change the uniforms.

WILLIE

Groovy.

VOICE

So long, son. Be good, now. (*Click*)
(WILLIE *bows his head. A silence. He looks up, raises his arms to the audience. His eyes are twitching.*)

WILLIE

THE FREAKS ARE . . . PER-PETUALLY . . . HUNTED . . . (*He is having difficulty getting the words out. He tries harder as the others begin to razz him.*) I WALK . . . ALWAYS . . . I WALK . . . STRANGERS . . . MIRRORS . . . DRIFTING . . . MY IMAGE. . . (*The others get louder, taunting him:* Get on with it, Willie. More, Willie. Say it, Willie, *etc.*) I . . . I . . . MY . . . SELF . . . SELF . . . HOWLS . . . ON . . . MARION-ETTES . . . MAR . . . I . . . OH . . . NETTEEES. . . .
(*Finally he can no longer speak at all. He rasps and growls, attempting to speak. He cannot. The others come forward. They become as animal trainers, with* WILLIE *as the terrified animal. He screams and froths at the mouth. He attacks and is driven back.* MARTIN *helps the others from the floor, shouting and beating on the platform, until* WILLIE *is cornered. Then he sets up a soapbox and microphone on the floor in front of the audience.*
WILLIE *makes a last desperate attempt to break the invisible barrier around the platform. A loud, long blast of static, etc.* WILLIE *screams and crumples into a heap.*
A silence.
The BUTTON PUSHER *suddenly rushes under the rope and out of the theater.*
PANTS, FLAMINIA *and* CYNTHIA *wheel the platform back to its original position. The stage lights go out and a spot comes on the soapbox and microphone.* MARTIN *climbs the box officiously, clears his throat, tests the microphone, and speaks.*)

MARTIN

I have never asked the impossible. Nor have I promised it. Not to myself, nor anyone else. Consequently, I have no illusions. I deal only with reality, with the issues before us. A fantasy is a cold in the mind, after all. Dreamers are not to be trusted, are usually failures, and carry little weight in the community. We need strong, firm men of high character—men who will not flinch at responsibility—men who will shoulder the burden of a new society, a righteous, purified one, one organized according to the highest principles of order and light; in a word, of Christian virtue. The time to begin is NOW. Thank you very much.

(The spot goes out. We hear the snapping of fingers at one-second intervals three times. On the third snap the stage area is brightly illumined with silvery light. There, as if clipped onto the black wall, is a perfect effigy of WILLIE THE GERM. *He is naked from the waist down, arms stiffly at his sides, eyes staring straight ahead. His balls are bleeding. High static.*

Three seconds. The light goes out, the curtain closes on the effigy, the stage lights come back up. The FREAKS *wheel the platform up to the stage, as before, and take their places.)*

FLAMINIA

Come on, Willie. Get up.

PANTS

Get up, Willie.

MARTIN

Rise and shine, Willie, it's not that bad.

CYNTHIA

Poor Willie.
    (They all freeze.)

FLITE CAGE

by Walter Hadler

FLITE CAGE was first produced by Theatre Genesis at St. Mark's Church in-the-Bouwerie in May, 1969. It was directed by Ralph Cook, with the following cast:

MOSSBACK CASH	Ron Gold
WILMA	Nern Barab
BAYLOR	Sully Boyar
SHERIFF	Tom Lillard
MRS. WILLIAMS	Pat Cook
MRS. FREED	Sally Sommer
MR. WILLIAMS	Richard Bright
MR. FREED	Gene Elman

WALTER HADLER. Grew up in Houston and Pennsylvania. Attended Air Force and the University of Maryland. Acted and directed Off-Off and Off Broadway productions. Current play MUTILATION first produced at Theatre Genesis.

MOSS *and* WILMA *lying spread-eagled, head to head, on blanket at opening. Middle of a flat desert. Opens in early morning, to gray, to midday. Lights should be desert; gray for Baylos-Moss scene. At opening, light comes from dusk to morning.*

MOSS
Listen to that.

WILMA
No sound.

MOSS
Wow.

WILMA
Wow.

MOSS *and* WILMA
Wow.

WILMA
Look at that.

MOSS
Wow. Can you hear it?

WILMA
What?

MOSS
Crows. The crows are awake. Hear them?

WILMA
Yes.

MOSS
They're down the canyon looking for jack rabbits and mice.

WILMA
And lizards. They like lizards.

MOSS *and* WILMA
Wow. Wow. Wow.

WILMA

This is the most fantastic thing I've ever seen.

MOSS

Me too.

WILMA

I'd like to stay here forever. I'm so sick of that rain.

MOSS

I like it here.

WILMA

Wouldn't you like to stay here? We could build a shack and farm this land.

MOSS

I like it here.

WILMA

You used to live on a farm, didn't you?

MOSS

Wow.

WILMA

We could live here, stay here, never go back to that rotten place.

MOSS

Listen, one of the crows spotted a rabbit.
(*Sounds of crows from four speakers*)

WILMA

I don't think those are crows.

MOSS

Sure they are. I know crows. There's four of em. (*Sound four up*)

WILMA

(*Sits up.*)
No. Look over there. That's a sparrow hawk.

MOSS

Where?

WILMA

Up there. See it?

MOSS

My God, that's an eagle or something.

WILMA

It's a sparrow hawk.

MOSS

No, he's too big. Look at his neck. God, he's huge.

WILMA

He's probably been up there since the sun got there. They come over with the sun. Sometimes they'll start fifty miles away or more when the sun's rising up back there. And they'll glide in on the first rays. Almost like surfers only they're on the crest of the light. They ride on the edge of the morning till they see something.

MOSS

He's circling.

WILMA

He sees the crows.

MOSS

There is four crows.

WILMA

He don't care how many crows.

MOSS

He's watching us. He's directly over us. (Crow) How'd you know that?

WILMA

He sees something.

MOSS

(*Crows louder.*)

So do the crows. (*Eagle screech*) It must be near us. Maybe it's that rabbit we saw back there on the road.

WILMA

They like fresh meat.

MOSS

(*Crows loud*)

Listen to em, they're like scouts. They're calling in the roost.

WILMA

Calling in the roost?

MOSS

Yeah. They're scouts for the flock.

WILMA

They're afraid of that hawk.

MOSS

Naw. Not crows.

WILMA

He'd tear those crows to ribbons.

MOSS

You don't know crows.

WILMA

He'd tear their wings off with one slash.

MOSS

(*Crows*)

There's more an four of em now. (*Sits up.*)

WILMA

He's diving. Look. Look at that bastard.
(*Two loud sonic booms.* MOSS *and* WILMA *both fall down. Silence.*)
Bastards! Bastards! Those bastards!

MOSS

It's getting really lit up now. My God, those mountains look fantastic.

WILMA

They start up there beyond Collins Valley and they roar over the *miestra*. They think it doesn't matter out here.

MOSS

They don't do that back home.

WILMA

Hell no, they don't. They're afraid to. They think this whole place is a testing lab.

MOSS

(*Stands*)
You motherfuckers.

WILMA

Just because there's no shopping-center windows to bust or god-damn hospitals, they think they can rip the place to pieces.
(*Two more booms, louder.* MOSS *turns with them.*)

MOSS

Motherfuckers! Motherfuckers! Look, look way up there. See those two tiny silver dots? See? See? They're barrel-rolling on top of each other.

WILMA

Where?

MOSS

See? See the sun on their wings? Silver and black. First one, then the other. They're like a ferris wheel.

WILMA

Oh, yes. Yes, I see them. They look like a mirror. They're playing in the sun.

MOSS

I know. I know. Unbelievable. My God. I always wanted to do that.

WILMA

They're trying to catch each other. See. They're getting closer. They're trying to eat each other up. Look at the one in the light. Look at its mouth. It's open.

MOSS

Wow!

WILMA

Look at the mouth. It's getting wider and wider. It's silver. A silver mouth. Look, a silver hole in the sky. It's a blue eye now. I can't look any more. (*Falls to knees.*)

MOSS

They're making a figure eight. Must be over fifty thousand feet. Wow. It's like someone ice-skating. It's like we're under water. All you can see is the blades on the ice. They're going higher. Getting smaller, smaller. (*Crow sounds, one speaker*) Those crows must have found something. Boy, they're really going to town. I wonder where they drink. There's no water around here. Is there? (*She's on hands and knees.*) What do they do for water? Hey, are you all right? What's wrong?

WILMA

Nothing. Nothing. I feel a little sick. I'll just lie down. I'll be all right.

MOSS

Maybe you should finger.

WILMA

No. No. I'm all right. I just need to lie down. I feel dizzy. My head's spinning. It's just my head.

MOSS

You don't feel sick?

WILMA

No. No. My head. Inside there's a thing spinning inside. Everything else is all right. Don't you feel sick?

MOSS

No.

WILMA

Don't you feel dizzy?

MOSS

No. I . . . yeah, I do a little.

WILMA

You should lie down and be still.

MOSS

It feels like I've got a hairball in my stomach.

WILMA

Here, lie down and close your eyes. (*He does.*) Is that better? The best thing to do is to lay still and it'll go away.

MOSS

It feels like it's moving.

WILMA

Sh-h-h-h. Don't think.

MOSS

It's moving around. (*Sits up.*) I mean it's crawling toward my lungs.

WILMA

Shhhh. Be still.

MOSS

(*Stands.*)
I can't lay down. It's no good for me. I have to keep moving. I mean, as long as I'm up it's O.K. When I lay down, it starts to close in. When it moves around, I've got to move around.

WILMA

You should be still. I'm feeling better already. Aren't you ever still?

MOSS

(*Jumping*)
I don't know what it is. It's getting warmer. I'm getting hot. Aren't you? It really gets hot fast here. (*Begins undressing to shorts.*) It's a lot warmer than I thought it was. (*Crows*) They're still eating. That's all they do—sleep and fly and scream at each other. They're really incredible animals. They know how to deal with anything. Remember those crows we saw with the falcons? They kept the eagles from tearing themselves to pieces. Aren't you hot?

WILMA

I feel better.

MOSS

Why don't you take off your clothes?

WILMA

Slow down. Slow down, will you? I will. Give me a breather.

MOSS

Oh, yeah. O.K., O.K. Man, I can feel my legs and arms. (*Crows*) Listen to those bastards. They're really having a blast out there. It really heats up fast. You could be dead before you know it. I mean the lizards or anyone. You think it's just warmin their blood and pretty soon it's bakin their blood an they can't move. That's why they try to stay around the flat rocks. In case they forget they can just flop off the side and land in the shade. That's important, the shade. They try to do everything in the morning before it gets too hot. (*He's stripped here.*) You don't realize it at first. I really need this. I can feel it pourin into me. I can't even stop it. I'm tryin to and it won't stop. Wow. (*Crows*) Listen to that. Listen to that. Caw! Caw! Caw! Caw! Caw! Caw! (*Crows. He starts slowly walking toward sound.*) Wow, it won't stop. See them going down and up. Black. Black. You can almost see rainbows on their black wings. Son of a bitch. There's a white one. Do you see that—a white crow? No wonder we couldn't see him. They're dive-bombing. They must have him out of his hole. Bang-bang. (*He stands on his toes or a high stop.*) They're banging into his head. Goddamn. (*Crouches.*) Goddamn. The white one's diving at his eyes. (*He leaps to another stop, like an Indian.*) The rest go for his neck. (*Cautiously*) Caw! Caw! Caw! (*Crows*) Caw! Caw! Caw! (*He caws offstage.*)

(WILMA *rests a bit. Rises, looks around. Begins to undress. Boots. Blouse. We hear* MOSS *whoop twice. She stops a second, squints up at sky. Takes off trousers. Lies back enjoying the sun. A car door slams. She doesn't notice. A man in a California sheriff's khaki outfit appears. He is shorter than* MOSS—*about as tall as* WILMA—*stocky, wearing Stetson, badge, boots, gun, and sunglasses. He approaches, above* WILMA. *Watches, adjusts sunglasses, seems a little drunk, begins to fondle pistol. Stops. Loosens the gun. Stops. Rubs hands. Stops. Looks up. Fondles gun. Takes it out. Stops. Looks up. Looks at her—crows on speaker one—takes out gun. Aims it at her. Sights up and down her body. Stops at her pussy. Cocks the trigger. She coughs twice, sits up. He lowers gun. Uncocks trigger. She looks up. Coughs. Crows on speaker one. She gets on all fours, crawls to edge of blanket. Tries to puke. Dry heaves. He puts gun away.* MOSS *whoops offstage. She turns to sound. Smiles. Lies back down. He whoops. She whoops. Cop steps offstage covertly.* WILMA *digs an ant hill, sits up.*)

WILMA

Crazy hillbilly. Who the hell's he think he is? (*Crows on four speakers. She looks up.* MOSS *enters, smiling, bleeding in several spots on the chest, one spot on face. Out of breath.*) What happened to you, man? Jesus Christ. Did you fall or what? Hey, those are deep. What happened?

MOSS

I found a spring. That's where they were diving.

WILMA

How'd you get all cut up?

MOSS

They were trying to get this fawn. I thought it was a jack rabbit till I got up close.

WILMA

Where was the mother?

MOSS

She was trying to keep em off her fawn but they were too fast and the fawn's leg was twisted around an old tree. So I went in and got it out.

WILMA

What happened? How? Did the deer cut you?

MOSS

No. No, the deer split. And those bastards came after me.

WILMA

Jesus Christ.

MOSS

They got in but I ran up a gulley into some trees and they backed off and waited. I threw some rocks at the bastards and took off across the flat.

WILMA

We better clean those up, man. They look awful.

MOSS

No, they're O.K. I feel fantastic. It's unbelievable, babe. I mean everything's pouring out from between my legs. All this unbelievable power. I really feel like I belong on this land. I mean my toes, each one of em talks to the sand every time I move. When I was running, it was fantastic. Everything was silent. The mesquite, the sand, no wind. Just my feet tappin on the ground. A little behind me and very light. I was barely touchin the ground. I looked back and all I was leaving were toe prints.

WILMA

You're really nuts, man. Are you sure those things don't hurt you? Maybe we ought to go in and get you a tetanus shot.

MOSS

Yeah. Yeah. This is the best I've ever felt on the land. I mean I can feel the earth. My hands and feet. Goddamn. China. It's good.

WILMA

It is good. I know it's good. (*Crows on one speaker. They both check sky.*) They're still down there. Maybe we should leave before they remember we're here.

MOSS

No. I know crows. They like to play. They're not gonna leave that spring to come up here to fuck with us. There's too many other things goin on down there. They like to rap on everybody who needs a drink.

WILMA

Yeah. I see how they like to rap.

MOSS

No. No, babe. It was that albino bastard that did this. The other ones just watched and waited and squawked while he tried to do his number. It's really weird. He had a hooked beak.

WILMA

Next time we come out, we'll bring a gun.

MOSS

Babe, we don't need no guns out here. We just run with the wind. Don't you feel it? Isn't it too fucking much? I mean, baby, I thought we lost it. I thought it was bred out or never was, but it is. It's there. Right here (*holds groin and thinks*) in all of us. It's untapped nuclear energy. I was talking to the cactus and the rocks. I don't mean babbling my guts—my skin was singin to the cactus. Even the needles feel good.

WILMA

Wow. Let me look at your feet. Do they hurt?

MOSS

No, they're all the way inside. They itch. I got most of em out rubbin my feet in the sand. How do you feel?

WILMA

Much better. Much better now.

MOSS

Did you get sick?

WILMA

No. I tried to throw up but nothing came. I feel much better. I needed to rest for a while. I was diggin this ant hill. Look at this.

MOSS

Wow. Look at those bastards. They go all day long like that.

WILMA

(*Stares*)
They seem to be all movin to the same rhythm. Squint your eyes and watch.
(*He does, lets out several whoops, looks up, arms extended, makes sound to it. She is looking at him. He is silent with arms extended. She kisses his leg. Hugs his leg. He kneels and kisses her. Lies on top of her. It doesn't get to fucking. They begin to really dig each other's body. He kisses her stomach, legs, fingers. Vice versa. Cop reappears as soon as they lie down. He approaches very cautiously, hand on gun. At some point they hear him and freeze. Everybody freezes. Crows on four speakers.* MOSS *slowly looks up. Gets up.*)

MOSS

What's your problem?

COP

Let's see some identification.

WILMA

Where'd the fuck he come from?

COP

How old are you?

WILMA

I'm twenty-one.

COP

Have any identification?

WILMA
Jesus Christ.

COP
Don't put your pants on.

MOSS
If you don't mind, I want to put my pants on.

COP
Leave em off. You don't need your pants on to show me your identification. You either, Miss. You don't have to get dressed to show me your identification. (*She slips on blouse. Cop pulls gun.*) I said, don't get dressed.

WILMA
Afraid I'll disappear?

MOSS
What's the charge?

COP
Never mind the charge. Let's see your identification.

MOSS
(*Gets wallet.*)
Christ, this is a drag.

COP
Take it out of your wallet. (*He does.*) Ever been arrested before?

MOSS
Yes.

COP
Ever had any traffic violations?

MOSS
Yes.

COP
Sit down, please. Where's yours? (*She hands him paper.*) Twenty-one? (*He goes back to Moss's.*) This doesn't look like you. Looks

like you bin in a fight. Did you do that to him? I'll bet he tried to get fresh with you, didn't he? This is private property out here. This ain't no city park. I bin watchin you two for quite a while. These don't match. (*Four speakers crows*) You know you're not supposed to touch the deer in here. It's against the law. Do you have a license to hunt?

WILMA

There are no deer in here.

COP

You've got false identification and an illegal driver's license, plus you were hunting deer out of season without a license. Got anything to say about that?

MOSS

I'd like to put my trousers on.

COP

You just take it easy. (*He does. She reaches. They move as the* COP *indicates, or just stare.*) Hold it. I didn't say you could. What are you doing out here? Why'd you come out here on other people's property and take your clothes off? I didn't say you could put on your shoes. I didn't see a car. How'd you people get out here? You think because there's a lotta open space out here you can come out here and run wild. What were you hiding in that gulch? I watched you running away from something. What were you doing down there? I suppose you think you can carry on any way you see fit out here. How come your eyes are all red? (*They both look at sky.*) I think she's probly a minor. You know it's a felony in this county for a man to be runnin around with minors. It's even worse when they're both naked like you two. You bes answer my questions or you'll be booked for resisting arrest. I saw you down on your hands and knees, pukin. I figure you're pregnant or on dope— which is it? You hear what I said?
(*Two sonic booms.* COP *flinches,* MOSS *gets gun, pushes* COP *to ground.*) Please. Please don't shoot me. I'm only doin my job. I've got these kids. Listen, I was only trying to scare you a little bit. It gets kinda lonely out here. I was gonna let you go. I always do. I was just kiddin. Don't point that gun at me.

(MOSS *goes through self-course in how to fire a gun till he learns it fully and does.*)
I was only kiddin. I'll drive you to your car. O.K.? Please. Please don't do something you'll regret the rest of your life. I'm not kiddin. I'm willing to forget all of this. Please, Mr. Cash. Don't do something like this. You'll never get away with it. They'll hunt you forever. C'mon, sir, don't be crazy. Tell him, Miss Jackson. Please tell him I've got three kids back there. For God's sake, tell him he'll never get away with it. I was only kiddin about I.D.s, honest. And that deer thing was just a joke. Everybody shoots em on sight at night. It's a joke out here. I shot one last week when he stopped in my headlights. Mother of God, Miss Jackson, tell him, for God's sake. Tell him. Listen, you were in the service. You know what these jobs are like—they drive you crazy. You go nuts waitin for something to do. Hell, all I wanted to do was stop and shoot the breeze. I didn't mean for all this to happen. For God's sake. I've got three kids. Nobody's perfect. I could've just put you both in irons and gone on if I was serious. Couldn't you tell I was kiddin? You could tell, couldn't you, Miss Jackson? I beg you, Mr. Cash, don't go do something like this. You'll never in a million billion years get . . .
(*Six shots into* COP. *Crows on one speaker.* WILMA *gets dressed.*)

WILMA

How do you feel?

MOSS

I don't know.

WILMA

Are you sick?

MOSS

I don't know. He was right. I can't feel the space any more. There's something in it now. A great silence. The silence of ice. It'll never be open here now. There's something here. He felt it, too. It had to be filled with something or we had to get out.

WILMA

You shouldn't start feeling bad.

MOSS

I'm not feeling bad or glad. This spot is full now.

WILMA

What do you mean?

MOSS

The whole thing. Colonies or cities or whatever we call them attempt to get through this emptiness. Fill it with anything. Plastic, bombs, bodies, houses, lights, factories, or cows. Occupy and control it.

WILMA

Christ, don't start talking like an idiot because you killed a pig. He had it coming.

MOSS

He knew it.

WILMA

All right then. Stop worrying.

MOSS

He knew about it. He was doing it. I wasn't. I was doing something else. I was trying to bring, to bring, to bring, us, or me to the land. No, I mean trying to let its energy and my energy find themselves.

WILMA

Oh God, Moss. You sound like some nut. Stop playin with yourself. We've got to remember where we are, not where we were or wish we were. You know that. You've taught it to me.

MOSS

Yes. I know. I've just killed a man. He's laying there. He was shot six times. The first thing I do is put on my pants.

WILMA

Look at those two. They're up there ice-skating and playing ferris wheel through the whole thing.

MOSS

I don't hear the crows.

WILMA

The vultures probably got them.

MOSS

Maybe the shots scared them out of the valley.
(*He puts on shirt.*)

WILMA

Maybe the vultures ate the sound man. The second thing they eat
are your fingers.

MOSS

If we leave him, the buzzards will attract attention.

WILMA

That'll take up plenty of space. All those birds overhead, then all
the tourists gathered around for the hunt. How about if we put him
in a cave with . . .

MOSS

I'll take him with us.

WILMA

Don't be silly! Take him with us. Are you completely cracked? What
about the space you were talking about?

MOSS

Help me pull him out of the way. (*They take him upstage.*) It's
almost dark.

WILMA

Are you gonna continue with this unbelievable number?

MOSS

It's probly gonna rain. It's rained ten inches here in two weeks.
Did you know that?

WILMA

No, I did not. I hate rain. If you like rain, why don't you go live
in Oregon?

MOSS

The rain affects the energy I was talking about. It keeps trying to clean the land. Open it up. It's starting to rain. It's coming over the mountains. See it up there?

WILMA

Yes, I see it.

MOSS

Looks like gray plastic sheets.

WILMA

Listen, Moss, I'm pullin out of this. Let me know what you finally decide to do. I'm going back where we were.
(*She exits. Lights go to gray.*)

MOSS

O.K. O.K. You go back. I'll stay. It's time I stayed. Damn, it's cold. It's worse than Canada. It doesn't seem cold but it is. Where the hell's everybody? Maybe the rain's keepin em away. Baylos should be around. (*Kneels, wraps blanket.*) This is better. Ummm. It's warmer . . . what the hell's that? Damn building's moving. Naw, not up here. Wow! It's floating. Goddamn! Naw. Naw. Ol Baylos built this place outta real wood and concrete.
(*Enter* BAYLOS. *Cigar butt, thick glasses, carrying wide broom. He sweeps entire stage throughout, toward body, as though it were the final pile in a circle. He's also carrying an Easter basket with three eggs in it.*)

BAYLOS

Howdy, boy. How long you bin home?

MOSS

About two hours.

BAYLOS

Pretty rough over there, ain't it?

MOSS

Yeah, it was.

BAYLOS

You done us all proud. Real proud.

MOSS

I'm thinking about gettin married, Dad. Might keep me from getting drafted.

BAYLOS

I don't give a fuck if you get married or run off and live with a herd of hogs. You can knock up a log for all I care.

MOSS

I brought you a souvenir. (*Produces lighter.*)

BAYLOS

Does it work?

MOSS

Yeah, I've used it.

BAYLOS

It might work over there but will it work here? What are you gonna do with yourself now that yur back? Are you gonna work or are you gonna lay around on that damn floor like a drunken squaw?

MOSS

I think I'll take a breather, before I look.

BAYLOS

It's too late to be taking breathers. This whole place is sinkin. The buildings are fallin down, boy.

MOSS

Christ, I felt it earlier. It's not our place, is it?

BAYLOS

Every goddamn place is on the move. The whole damn coast's turned into shit. Yuh didn't know that, did yuh? Naw, how could yuh out there? Everywhere yuh look yuh see tons a garbage. People are even sellin it, boy. Luinpoc County's buying it offa ten different cities. The mayor wants to cover the whole desert with the crap. People are shittin on everything, boy. Damn shit's messed up my matches. Yuh got a match on yuh?

MOSS

No. I don't. I'm sorry.

BAYLOS

Nothin tuh be sorry for. Yuh either do or yuh don't. What the hell yuh doin on the floor? Oh, that's right, yur takin a breather. I wouldn't count on no breathers, boy. Not in these times. Yuh don't know what yur liable to be breathin.

MOSS

I'm trying to get warm. I feel like I've got the bends.

BAYLOS

Any moron'll tell yuh that's no place tuh git warm. Not any more. Ground around here's freezin up. Used to be you could lay on the ground an it would be like layin on yur mother. Not any more, though. Cold as hell now. Whole country's freezin up. All the fires are goin or gone. No way a stokin em neither. Too much shit coverin everything. Couldn't get it goin again even if yuh had a mind to.

MOSS

I've gotten warmer since I laid down here.

BAYLOS

Yuh have, have yuh? Yur one in a million, Mossback, one in a million.

MOSS

I'm not all that warm. I still feel cold inside.

BAYLOS

Tuh tell yuh the truth, I didn't think yuh were. Yuh see, son, yuh can't fool me. Ain't nothin warms out here no more. Used to see tomatoes plastered all over these hills. Wild flowers growin everywhere. Yuh could smell the perfume fifty miles at sea. Now yuh hate tuh come in. The shit's ten feet thick an risin all the time. No way fur it tuh warm up neither. They keep pourin in here and shittin on top of each other. Yuh can't even get a streetcar through, trains ain't runnin, only thing movin are the birds.

MOSS

I'd think the shit would be good. It's warm and wet, and it makes things grow.

BAYLOS

Amigo, shit's as warm as the man who makes it. These ol boys runnin in here is shittin icicles, that's what. I mean they's shittin snowballs. Yuh think that's mud out there fillin up the streets? Hell, no, that's cold shit.

MOSS

Is it still rainin out there?

BAYLOS

Naw, it's just dribblin. I don't understand why yur so damn cold, son.

MOSS

I'm not all that cold. My head's cold.

BAYLOS

Look up at that light. (*Examines.*) Hmm, that's funny.

MOSS

What's funny?

BAYLOS

Yur eyeballs. They look like blue ice. Turn your head. Damn funny. The whites are like snot. Yur head's kinda clammy and yur chest's as warm as my hand. I tell yuh what yuh do—go down tuh the beach, bury yourself in the sand, but keep yur head up. That ol sun'll cut right through that.

MOSS

It didn't work.

BAYLOS

What didn't work?

MOSS

I tried it. It didn't work. That's why I came back here. You think I came back to hear you shoot the shit about shit? I got a million things on my mind.

BAYLOS

That's what I'm tellin yuh. Why'd yuh think them turtles lay around with their heads floppin on rocks? They gotta have that sunlight tuh git their damn brain cells cookin. Yuh do what I say, Wilkie, an nobody'll notice the difference.

MOSS

Listen, you old bastard, I'm not Wilkie.

BAYLOS

And I'm not Napoleon, am I?

MOSS

Who the hell said you're Napoleon?

BAYLOS

Same dates, boy, August fifteen. Same age. Same height. Same times, boy, two hundred years apiece, son. Four hundred years between us. That's right here in this room. I'm tellin yuh what I know. Yuh can listen an learn or not. It's up tuh you, Wilkie.

MOSS

I'm not Wilkie. And I'm not gonna lay on no beach an get my damn head kicked off.

BAYLOS

That's up to yuh, Wilkie. Just don't tell me who I am or am not. Or else I might up an kill yuh.

MOSS

(*Stands at once, drops blanket.*)
Where in hell'd that come from?

BAYLOS

Stop askin all these dumb-ass questions, Wilkie. Yuh finally got yur butt outta that damn blanket, didn't yuh?

MOSS

Look, pop, my name's Mossback, not Wilkie, goddamn it, and what the hell's this about the blanket?

BAYLOS

I don't know how you're supposed to get your ass up layin aroun wrapped in some blanket. Yuh can lay aroun havin a breather. Yuh can lay aroun tryin to get warm. Yuh can lay aroun askin all these dumb questions. Yuh got a job to do an yuh bes do it.

MOSS

What job? What the hell job are you talkin about?

BAYLOS

Now you know damn well what I mean. Yuh bes stop actin like one a those lazy-ass Yaquis. I saved yuh those eggs. Yuh want tuh take care of em cuz it's all yur gettin. (*Crows*)

MOSS

Listen, Baylos, crows. What's crows doin here?

BAYLOS

I don't wanna see yuh lose yur hair, Wilkie, or I told yuh I might have tuh kill yuh. (*Slowly*) I might have tuh chop yur head off. I might have tuh chop everybody's head off if they don't stop the shit.

MOSS

I thought you killed all them crows. Hey, come back here. Hey! Baylos, I thought you killed all them crows! Come back in here for a minute, you old fuck. Aw, shit. "Do yur job. Or I'll kill yuh." Who the hell you bullshittin, Baylos? What the hell you gonna do— sweep our heads off? All that shit about the shit. Man, all I wanted to do is ask you a few things about us. Can't you hear, you stupid bastard? You goddamn galley slave.
(*He exits. Sound of a car door slamming. Desert lights up. Enter* MR. *and* MRS. WILLIAMS *and* MR. *and* MRS. FREED, *in their fifties. Both women have high hairdos. They're eating popcorn and throwing it on the ground for the birds.*)

MRS. FREED

Well, this is our little homestead, Mildred.

MRS. WILLIAMS

Why, it's absolutely fantastic, Ina. It's really adorable.

MRS. FREED

Yes. We bought it for Morris's asthma.

MRS. WILLIAMS

How lovely. Have you thought about building on it?

MRS. FREED

Heavens no. We're waiting for the highway to be finished, then we'll sell the land at a nice price.

MRS. WILLIAMS

That's smart. I wish my Arthur had one-fifth the brain your Morris has about these things. (MORRIS *coughs.*)

MRS. FREED

Isn't that awful? You'd think the fresh air would make him stop that. Morris, if you must cough like that, please use your handkerchief. Honestly.

MRS. WILLIAMS

Mine's no better. He wouldn't leave the backyard if it hadn't rained so hard he couldn't tend to his crab grass.

MRS. FREED

Crab grass. Oh, come on, Vi, you don't mean you have crab grass?

MRS. WILLIAMS

Oh, yes. Papa calls it "devil grass"! It gives him a thrill, I think. I don't think it would live if he didn't water it every day.

MRS. FREED

I know. Nothing grows out here. Really. Not like it does back home. There's no water.

MRS. WILLIAMS

I know, Flo. Although that rain we're having keeps ruinin our driveway. I didn't think he'd be able to get the car out of the garage. It's so horrible.

MRS. FREED

I know. Everywhere you look. (MORRIS *coughs.*) I tried to get Morris to shovel our walk and I may as well try and find teeth in a rooster. Morris, breathe deeply in this air. It's good for your cough. If we're going to pay for it, we might as well use it.

MRS. WILLIAMS

Arthur, why don't you pay attention to what Florence is saying and not fall asleep? We're not at home. Honestly, sometimes that man is impossible. I swear, he'll sleep through his own funeral.

MRS. FREED

That's the Sierra Muerta over there, Vi.

MRS. WILLIAMS

My, my. Isn't it wonderful to know all that?

MRS. FREED

A Spanish priest named it that because an entire expedition was murdered by the Yaquis.

MRS. WILLIAMS

Yankees?

MRS. FREED

No, dear, Yaquis. That's the name of the local tribe of Indians.

MRS. WILLIAMS

Isn't that fascinating? Did you hear that, Arthur? He's a great one for history.

MRS. FREED

I think there were two hundred people in the party, or it happened two hundred years ago.

MRS. WILLIAMS

My. Lord. I hope there aren't any around here now. I mean I wouldn't like to lose my hair. (MORRIS *coughs.*)

MRS. FREED

Really, Morris. There's no excuse for that out here. He's so mulish sometimes. I think he coughs like that just to irritate me. No. No. They put them up on the tops of mountains so they wouldn't bother people.

MRS. WILLIAMS

Thank God for that little gesture.

MRS. FREED

It amazes me, though. I got Morris to drive up there one Sunday and you just could not believe the filth. It makes you wonder how they could've possibly massacred anybody.

MRS. WILLIAMS

They don't work or anything?

MRS. FREED

Oh, no, they just sit around, just like they did two hundred years ago.

MRS. WILLIAMS

Isn't that revolting?

MRS. FREED

You simply cannot imagine. Morris, must you pick your nose in front of the whole world? Honestly. I thought we might find some nice earthenware or something but it was simply horrible.

MRS. WILLIAMS

I'm glad you told me, Flo. I was going to try and get Arthur to drive up there.

MRS. FREED

Oh no, dear. It's dreadful.

MRS. WILLIAMS

Would you get a load of those two? They act like they're two hundred years old.

MRS. FREED

Take off your coat, Morris, and let a little of this sun on your skin. You'd think he would, after the price we paid for this property.

MRS. WILLIAMS

How much of this is actually yours?

MRS. FREED

I'm not sure, Vi. It's somewhere around two hundred acres. (MOR-
RIS *coughs in handkerchief.*)

MRS. WILLIAMS

I think that's wonderful. To have your own land like that. We
should look into something like that, Arthur, before the highway
is finished.

MRS. FREED

You should. They already started surveying on the other side of the
valley.

MRS. WILLIAMS

What's that, Flo? Over there. See it? It looks like a basket. (MRS.
FREED *goes to it.*)

MRS. FREED

Oh no, dear. This is a nest. We're really very lucky to find this. You
don't know how rare it is to find their breeding grounds.

MRS. WILLIAMS

What kind of eggs are they?

MRS. FREED

They're those disgusting *Corvus Corax* birds. They've been the
bane of hard-working people for centuries. They eat your crops or
newspaper or anything they can get their filthy beaks into.

MRS. WILLIAMS

What should we do with this nest?

MRS. FREED

Lord, Mildred, this is no time to worry about that. We break them.
(*She does.*)

MRS. WILLIAMS

They resemble alligators.
(*Sound of crows from all four speakers. Both men look to sky and
stay looking. Women don't look.*)

MRS. WILLIAMS
What on earth!

MRS. FREED
It's more awful desert birds.

MRS. WILLIAMS
Will they harm you?

MRS. FREED
Lord, no. They're as useless and as lazy as those Yaqui Indians.
I've heard that the Yaquis raise them as pets and eat them. If you
can imagine those filthy black creatures covered with body lice and
God knows what else. Isn't the sun lovely?

MRS. WILLIAMS
The whole vista reminds me of a Japanese silkscreen.

MRS. FREED
I couldn't agree more.

MRS. WILLIAMS
That's really awful.

MRS. FREED
Really, this is too much. Morris, Morris. (*He looks.*) Go back to
the car and get the sprays. (*He does.*)

MRS. WILLIAMS
That is quite strong.

MRS. FREED
Yes, it is.

MRS. WILLIAMS
Do you smell that, Arthur? Arthur. Arthur! What on earth are you
looking at? What is that disgusting odor? (*He looks up.* MORRIS *has
returned with four cans.*)

MRS. FREED
Here we are. We'll each take one.

MRS. WILLIAMS

Arthur. Arthur! (*He looks.*) Will you pay attention to your company and take one of these? (*He does.*) Good. I suggest we each spray a different area.

MRS. FREED

Fine. You go up there, Morris. (*He does.*)

MRS. WILLIAMS

Do what Morris did. (*He does opposite.*) All right, all together. (*They spray, walking backwards till they meet, back to back, at center.*) It is getting worse.

MRS. FREED

I don't know what it could be, Mildred. This place has always been so clean and fresh before. (MORRIS *coughs.*) Oh God, Morris, don't you start.

MRS. WILLIAMS

It's getting worse, Ina. Let's spray our way back to the car.

MRS. FREED

Yes, I think that's the only thing we can do.
(*Crows on one speaker till they leave. Men look up.*)

MRS. WILLIAMS

Do you think it's those birds?

MRS. FREED

It could very well be.

MRS. WILLIAMS

You'd think the game commission would do away with such a nuisance.

MRS. FREED

Oh, God. That is unbearable. Let's go. (*Women begin to walk slowly, spraying.*) C'mon, you two. Morris. Morris, pick up that basket! (*He does.*)

MRS. WILLIAMS

Arthur. Arthur! Would you get your head out of the clouds and come on?

(*They spray off.* WILMA *comes on in bra and panties. Lies down on blanket.* MOSS *appears.*)

WILMA

How do you feel?

MOSS

I don't know. I can't smell anything.

WILMA

Are you getting sick?

MOSS

I don't know. He was right. I can't feel the space any more. There's something in it now. The silence of ice. It'll never be open here. He felt it, too. It had to be filled with something or we had to get out.

WILMA

You shouldn't start feelin bad.

MOSS

I'm not feeling glad or bad. This spot is filled.

WILMA

What do you mean?

MOSS

The whole thing is to try and fill this emptiness. With anything. Bombs, bodies, plastic, popcorn, houses, wire, factories, or cows. We have to relate to it even if we have to empty it.

WILMA

Christ, don't start that moronic routine again just because you killed a pig. That bastard deserves it.

MOSS

He knew it. He was doing it. I wasn't. I was doing something else. I was tryin to let it all happen like it does all at once and still bring us to it. We have to learn to re-find the land, re-fill the emptiness. No. I mean we've—I've got—I've—I want to let it be in me and me in it.

WILMA

We've been here before. Do you realize that? You sound like some nut again. Stop playing with yourself. You know damn well. We've got to remember where we are, not where we were, or where he was, or they were, or where we wish we were. You know that much. You've pounded it into my head.

MOSS

I know. Yes. I've just shot a man to death. He's over there. I shot him six times. I did that. The first thing I did was put on my trousers. (*Two sonic booms*)

WILMA

I don't hear the crows. The vultures probly ate them.

MOSS

They're all dead.

WILMA

Then they ate the sound man's fingers and ears.

MOSS

They're all dead. They were electrocuted.

WILMA

What?

MOSS

The engineers wired every bush, tree, and rock in this valley and electrocuted every bird in here.

WILMA

That's absurd. Why the hell would they do that?

MOSS

They were a nuisance. They shit on everybody and carried syphilis and lice.

WILMA

Listen, Moss, don't let those morons get to you. Look at all the shit they left out here. The place is turned into a garbage heap.

MOSS

(*Touches* COP's *body*)
He's frozen solid.

WILMA

Good. Let him rot.

MOSS

His eyes are open. They look like frozen blue snot.

WILMA

It's time for us to clear out.

MOSS

It's almost dark.

WILMA

Good. Leave him to the crows and buzzards. They'll finish him in a few days. They'll eat his hat and boots, too. So you don't have to worry. (*Two booms*)

MOSS

They're dead. Don't you understand? He'll just lay there.

WILMA

Listen to those bastards. They keep that blasting going all day and all night. Let's get out of here.

MOSS

If we got ten inches of rain, right here in the middle of the valley, this place would become a sea again. That might open it up.

WILMA

Hear those bastards, don't you? They're ripping the mountains down.

MOSS

I hope they do. I hope they level every rock and leaf and feather till there's absolutely nothing left for them to level except the hole they're standing in.

WILMA

I'm going back where we were. (*Starts to leave.*)

MOSS

Once they get to that massive fucking hole, they'll be able to look at each other and know. All they'll have will be their own death and each fucking other to smell.

WILMA

Where the hell will we be during all this?

MOSS

We'll probly be like those crows. Powder. We'll be powder under their feet.

WILMA

I'm not waiting for that. Are you ready or not?

MOSS

I'm staying here.

WILMA

Listen, we've got no water, nothing to eat but this poisoned pop-corn. I'm going back up. (*Exits.* MOSS *squats on blanket with pistol in hand. Two sonic booms*)

MOSS

Good. Good. Keep it up. We're getting closer. We're gonna see each other. I'm gonna watch you watch me. It ain't gonna be like no fuckin buffalo hunt. (*He listens. Crow sounds from the rear speaker.*) Hey, what the fuck? I thought you killed all those crows when I left. You said you did. (*Crows on one speaker*) You said you did! (*Crows on all four speakers*) Shut up! (*Rises.*) Get the hell away from him, you bastards! Git! (*Tries to protect body.*) You all better git yur asses back down there and look for mice. I'm not shittin around now with no goddamn rocks. I'll put a hole in your asses. Scram, you motherfuckers. This ain't for you, you hear me? You hear me! Don't pretend you don't. They don't hear shit. You black bastards. See this fuckin gun, don't you? Too high now. (*Crows out. It gets black.*) That's fine. Just fine. They'll never find us in this light. We're safe now. (*Corpse moans.*) What the fuck's goin on? (*Moan*) Hey! Hey! Get the hell away from him. You hear me! Leave him alone or I'll shoot! (*Moan*) Halt! Halt! (*Bang*) That was a warning, the next one'll go right between your eyes, so come forward! (*Quieter moan*) Halt! Stop that shit, you hear me! Stop it! (*Moan*) Leave him alone. Stay away! Don't move. Don't anybody make a move or I'll shoot your eyes out of your faces! (*Moan*) Don't touch him! (*Fires remaining shots into blackness.* COP *has been moved offstage.* MOSS *exits, light comes up on empty space with blanket and popcorn.*)

GRAND TENEMENT
and
NOVEMBER 22

Two Works in Progress

by Tom Eyen

*To the beautiful cast, 'Ntoni Bastiano, and the
memory of the Playwrights' Workshop.*

NOVEMBER 22ND and GRAND TENEMENT were first presented by and
with the Theatre of the Eye Repertory Company at the Playwrights' Workshop
on November 22, 1967. It was directed by the author, with music by Jonathan
Kramer, sets by Saito, lighting by 'Ntoni Bastiano, and costumes were every
man for himself. Photographs were by James D. Gossage, posters by Paul
Fisher, and the stage manager was Betty Guyes. The casts included:

NOVEMBER 22ND

INTERVIEWER	Bob Mooty
MRS. PRESIDENT	Kaye Michaels

GRAND TENEMENT

APARTMENT 1	(SUPERINTENDENT)	Lucy Silvay
APARTMENT 2	(HIGH-FASHION MODEL)	Karole Kaye Stevenson
APARTMENT 3	(FOLK SINGER)	Jonathan Kramer
APARTMENT 4	(COLUMNIST)	Jane Sanford
APARTMENT 5	(STEWARDESS)	Carolyn Wiswell
APARTMENT 6	(HAIR STYLIST)	William Griffin Duffy

APARTMENT 7		
APARTMENT 8	(SUBWAY-TOKEN SELLER) ————————————	Dan Mason
APARTMENT 9	(KNOCKED-UP SEAMSTRESS) ————————	Carole Silon
APARTMENT 10	(PROFESSOR) —————————————	Wayne Wiener
APARTMENT 11	(BITCHING WIDOW) ————————	Dorothy Farrell
THE ROBBER, RAPIST, DETECTIVE, and JUDGE —————		Monty Montgomery

These are two separate plays written to be performed simultaneously. The time and place for both are the same. NOVEMBER 22 becomes a television program tuned into the apartments of GRAND TENEMENT.

TOM EYEN was born in Cairo, Egypt, a twin Leo, on August 14 during the War. No! Not the Civil!—it was the Second World War, the one Darryl Zanuck overproduced. Tom, due to the fact that his twin brother Jerome beat him by twenty-two seconds, was born the youngest of seven children to Julia and Abraham Eyen, two renowned supporting actors who appeared with Sarah Bernhardt at the Palace during the Divine's fifth final American tour. Mr. Eyen began writing at the age of twelve in Cambridge, Ohio, where his family had fled after being exiled from their home in Egypt. Eight years after the Korean War, he eloped to New York City where his first play, *Frustrata, the Dirty Little Girl with the Red Paper Rose Stuck in Her Head, Is Demented!*, was produced by Ellen Stewart at La Mama E.T.C. on May 7, 1964. He has since written approximately thirty-nine plays, give or take a few dreary Russian translations, all of which have been produced in the holy and hard-to-find sanctuaries of experimental theater. He is the director of his own acting company, the Theatre of the Eye Repertory Company, which has performed his plays from La Mama, the Caffe Cino (alas), the Playwrights' Workshop (also alas), the Festival of Two Worlds in Spoleto (almost alas), and the Extension Theater Club to the Electric Circus. Eyen's second play, *The White Whore and the Bit Player*, has been made into a film by the Cannon Group for release in 1971. His last play (as of May, 1970), entitled *The Dirtiest Show in Town*, received the Screw Award for Best Play of 1970. He is the recipient of a Rockefeller Foundation grant, a Guggenheim Fellowship, and twenty-four eviction notices. Eyen, a social hermit, lives with his French wife, Liza, and their growing French-Arabian sons on a farm four and half miles from J. D. Salinger, whom he has never seen.

TIME

1:32 P.M., November 22.

PLACE

A tenement building and television studio in New York, Paris, London, Rome, or Hong Kong.

SETTING

NOVEMBER 22: A thrust stage, backed by a large multicolored NBC peacock, protrudes over stage right into the GRAND TENEMENT setting. Two chairs used in the interview program wait vulturously in front of the vain peacock.

GRAND TENEMENT: The main stage is divided into eleven sections, numbered from one to eleven, for each of the apartments. Each number, or apartment, is brightly painted in a color from the multicolored tail of the television peacock, and each tenant should be dressed in the color of his/her number or apartment. Apartment seven is completely hidden by a white covering, but we can see red paint coming from this apartment, forming a large red-painted puddle in stage center with a white numeral "1" painted over it. This number-one puddle is the superintendent's apartment. The super, as did Lady Macbeth, tries to wash clean the blood from her floor throughout the play. (Ignore this last statement as it reeks of incrimination of the super who is no more guilty than the others.)

MUSIC

"Grand March," from both *Aida* and *Carmen*. Other than these, the music should come from the interplaying of the performers.

LIGHTS

Lighting should create the illusion of an NBC color spectacular.

FIRST IMAGE

Stage is presented in strange reds and blues or with such an effect to give the stage a surrealistic quality. The "Grand March" from

Aida (selection optional) begins as the model, dressed lavishly in a sexual satin gown with a tear-away front, walks across the GRAND TENEMENT stage to center with several products sold on television commercials. She strikes modelish poses with the products at a rate of sixty poses per minute (throwing products over shoulder when bored with them). She is giving us a very heavy sales pitch but, thankfully, we cannot hear her due to the loud and competitive music. Shortly, the interviewer appears and proceeds to his little "peacock area" and arranges the vulturous chairs nervously, straightens his tie nervously, and zips up his fly nervously. Something seems to be troubling him. Someone is missing. Checking his watch, he begins.

INTERVIEWER

The scheduled program at this time will not be shown——

MODEL

(*Stops posing.*)
What?

INTERVIEWER

In place of "Queen for a Day," the National Broadcasting System brings you with great pride—the first lady of the land in a special interview spectacular, "Mrs. President Speaks!"

MRS. PRESIDENT

(*Running down aisle or from the outside door*)
Oh, Mr. Warren—here I am! I'm so sorry I'm late, but the subways got stuck! (*Climbing onto peacock area*)

INTERVIEWER

I'm sure our guest needs no introduction.

MRS. PRESIDENT

Thank you, Robert.

INTERVIEWER

Bob—please!

MRS. PRESIDENT

Bob—as you please.

INTERVIEWER

Today, Mrs. President will give her views on the world.

MRS. PRESIDENT

Yes, Bob, I thought it was time the American people knew what was really happening.

INTERVIEWER

But first—a word from our sponsor!

MODEL

Headache? Parties make you tense? Classroom has you irritable? Clients impossible? Is your marriage failing because you're too up-tight to put out? Are you knocked up and your lover won't marry you? Do your tenants put their garbage in the halls? Is heterosexuality getting you down? Don't let tension tie you down! Amyl Nitrite (*sniff*) in convenient, all-glamour, jewel-tipped inhaler! (*She exits.*)

INTERVIEWER

(*Handing Mrs. President an inhaler*)
Courtesy of the sponsor!

MRS. PRESIDENT

I thought this was being sponsored by Anacin! (*Rising from chair*)

INTERVIEWER

(*Pulling her back down*)
Now, Mrs. First Lady, you grew up in Texas!

MRS. PRESIDENT

You are informed, Bob!

INTERVIEWER

And I'm sure that the scenery and the people have had a great influence on you. Would you tell us a little bit about what it means to grow up in Texas?

MRS. PRESIDENT

Well, to me, Bob, it meant growing up in what is affectionately called Deep East Texas—which is the economy and the culture and the landscape of the South. My daddy was a merchant and a landowner. He owned Deep East Texas. We lived in a big old red-brick house with white columns, an old noble house built before the Civil War. My greatest delight as a child was to have my mother read to me the great classics—*Gone with the Wind, Uncle Tom's Cabin,* and *Valley of the Dolls.* All red hot American books, Bob.

INTERVIEWER

But, Mrs. President, I wasn't aware that *Valley of the Dolls* was on the market back then.

MRS. PRESIDENT

No, Bob, it wasn't, but since Daddy was wealthier than most, he bought me things long before other people got them. I was also the first girl in Texas to have my very own radio station and personal Honda, which I rode sidesaddle.

INTERVIEWER

Now, Mrs. First Lady, your——

MRS. PRESIDENT

Please, Bob, call me by my childhood nickname, Little Miss Pushy Lady Godiva.

INTERVIEWER

Now, little Miss Pushy Lady Godiva, your father was a very rich and influential person. Tell us, how did he affect your life?

MRS. PRESIDENT

Well, to me, Bob, Daddy did own a lot of land, and was always buying more. He was impressive both financially and physically—six feet three, very broad shoulders, and handsome like all the men in our family, including myself. Of course, he had a great influence on me, Big Daddy Thomas Jefferson Taylor! You can't forget a name like that, Bob, no matter how hard you try—and I have tried!

INTERVIEWER

But, you know, some people say that you are a very good business-woman, too. Has this something to do with watching your father—at work?

MRS. PRESIDENT

Well, to me, Bob, being around Daddy taught me the importance of a solid economic base. In this wonderful country, every man is equal to make of his life what he wants—and why not make the most of it and have a lot of money and television stations? (*Laughing*) But, no, Bob, seriously, I think my business acumen is much exaggerated. Prosperity is just the story of the economic freedom of our wonderful country, no credit to little ole me.

INTERVIEWER

Would you say your childhood was lonely?

MRS. PRESIDENT

Well, to me, Bobby baby, it definitely was not. In spring there were wild cherokee roses and violets in the woods. I spent a lot of time just walking, fishing, and swimming naked with the farm hands in the creeks of Deep East Texas, which accounts for my love of nature and the enjoyment of the beautiful and wonderful country in which I live—and partly own.

INTERVIEWER

Now, as to your education—eight years in a little red brick house one mile from your home, then St. Mary's School for Girls in Dallas, and then the University of Texas.

MRS. PRESIDENT

You're right all the way, Bob. There at the university I felt that the doors of this wonderful country swung open.

INTERVIEWER

Now, how was that?

MRS. PRESIDENT

I got laid, Bob! Hahahaha—I mean—I was floored by education! I realized then that knowledge was the key to world prosperity and peace.

INTERVIEWER

Yes—now, your history shows that you were an outgoing girl, and quite active in school extracurriculars!

MRS. PRESIDENT

Oh, yes, yes, Bob—outgoing! Do you know, I single-handedly formed the C.U.S.T.G.O.I.T.A.A.G.T.E.A.F.T.D.J.A.N.? Could I have a glass of water, Bob?

INTERVIEWER

No! Which committee was that?

MRS. PRESIDENT

The Committee for the United States to Get off Its Tired Ass and Go to Europe and Fight Those Dirty Japs and Nazis! And I was very ahead of my time—that was in 1933 and World War II had not even been planned yet by the American businessman! Other than that, though, I have never messed in politics. A woman's place is in the kitchen—making homemade napalm bombs!

INTERVIEWER

Now—wasn't it unusual for a girl to go to a university in 1933?

MRS. PRESIDENT

Oh, no, no, Bob, not at all! At least one third of the school were females. I would drive to school every day in my pink-and-orange Cadillac convertible and say to myself, "My, isn't it a bitch how many females are at the university!" A homely girl hasn't a chance at U.T.!!

INTERVIEWER

You said you were driving yourself to school in a Cadillac convertible?

MRS. PRESIDENT

I like a man who listens, Bob!

INTERVIEWER

Was it unusual for a girl to have a car back then?

MRS. PRESIDENT

Now, Bob, let's be realistic! I lived fifteen miles out in the country. Abraham Lincoln I'm not. That's my husband; he's the Abraham Lincoln in our family!

INTERVIEWER

So, in a way there was a certain independence already developing in you.

MRS. PRESIDENT

You are getting the total picture now, Bob. I became a woman fast!

INTERVIEWER

When was the first time you met your husband?

MRS. PRESIDENT

I suppose—a girl friend of mine at school introduced me to him—I think—the first of September, 1934, 3:46 A.M. at a college bar. I remember it was time for the last round and everything was very frantic.

INTERVIEWER

Was it a long courtship?

MRS. PRESIDENT

No, no, Bob, from the first of September, 3:46 A.M., until we married on November seventeenth, 12:32 P.M.

INTERVIEWER

So he's really a fast worker!

MRS. PRESIDENT

You are a very alert young man! Are you married?

INTERVIEWER

No. Upon first meeting him, could you tell he was an ambitious person?

MRS. PRESIDENT

Oh, yes, yes, very ambitious! The bartenders in that bar didn't call him "Big Caesar" for nothing! But, to me, he seemed more like a person immersed, enthralled in doing his job to the best of his ability—no matter how tiny that might be. Are you engaged?

INTERVIEWER

No. What was his job then?

MRS. PRESIDENT

He worked for his father, doing odd jobs around the house. He was also secretary to the Texas congressman. Do you have a steady?

INTERVIEWER

No! (*The March from* Carmen *begins softly and the lights on the main stage return.*) Did he ever, as a young man, say to you, "I'd like to become President"?

MRS. PRESIDENT

Oh, no, no! Never, never!! He didn't have to say it—he knew it!!! (*Several of the tenants of Grand Tenement appear going to their apartments and talking to themselves.*)

INTERVIEWER

When did he actually take his first plunge into politics?

MRS. PRESIDENT

The day we married, and I opened a joint account for him in my bank! You do like girls, don't you?

INTERVIEWER

Yes! Now, you didn't actually campaign for your husband, but rather gave him moral support?

MRS. PRESIDENT

Campaign—NO!! Moral support—YES!!
(*More tenants from Grand Tenement appear to the tune of* Carmen. *They are all engaged frantically in their specific occupations; e.g., the super is scrubbing the floor, the folk singer is rehearsing, the token changer is taping nude females on his wall.*)

MRS. PRESIDENT

We couldn't have taken this plunge if it hadn't been for the fact of my inheritance from my recently deceased mother. So I just called Daddy and said, "Can I have a part of it?" and he said, "No, you cannot!!"
(*The rest of the tenants from Grand Tenement appear talking and moving frantically, creating the feeling of a subway station at rush hour.*)

INTERVIEWER

No? He said you couldn't have a part of it?

MRS. PRESIDENT

He said—well, it was on a Sunday when I called, mind you—
"Well, honey, I can't get it for you—not until tomorrow morning
at nine when the banks open!!"

INTERVIEWER

Reports have it that his first political campaign was only short of
lavish!

MRS. PRESIDENT

Not short of nothing, Bob! It was one of the finest campaigns for
Congress you ever saw. We hired a nuns' band from Houston,
dancing elephants from Dallas, and all kinds of nice things like
that! He was elected, of course, and though it took him twenty years,
he paid me back for this. Oh, how he's paid me back for this!!
(*A masked man appears and makes his way to the model and begins attacking her. The tenants of Grand Tenement again begin
taking loudly, and a knocking sound is heard. The super talks over
them.*)

SUPER

Who's knocking out there? Hold on—I'm coming—I'm coming!!
(*Silence—all freeze.*)

FOLK SINGER

> Where is the warm?
> Where is the quiet?
> Why all the hawks out?
> Why all the riot?
> Spring
> sprung
> somewhere else
> this year.

WIDOW

Hey, you potheads! What are you singing for? This isn't Christmas!!

SEAMSTRESS

(*On telephone*)

Louie? Hi!! Guess who? Yeah, it's me—your favorite person in this whole overcrowded emotional jungle!! Oh, you're busy? Yeah, I'll hang on!

HAIRDRESSER

So she came in again, Mrs. Goldberg, and she says to me, "I want something fancy and chic! And with her face she needs something fancy and chic! Now, I consider myself a creative hair designer, but there are limits to even my vast imagination!

PROFESSOR

Parent Report, first term . . . .

COLUMNIST

I recommend without reservations—Princess Pamela's—for the utmost in Southern atmosphere—no, Southern cuisine—no, Southern . . . .

SEAMSTRESS

Yeah, Louie, I'm still hanging on!

COLUMNIST

. . . hospitality!

TOKEN CHANGER

(*To a pinup*)

Gorgeous, gorgeous lady! Are you lonesome?

(*All tenants complain to themselves for five beats.*)

FOLK SINGER

(*Typing*)

November 22. Dear Mom. Weather's fine, mild for winter. Guess it has to do with our cool spring this year. Lots of things happening! Cutting a demo tomorrow, but still waiting for that call— so please send money!

ALL

Please!

MODEL

Can I ask you a serious question? Are they straight—my seams? I'm going up for my first talking commercial today, for Amyl Nitrite!

INTERVIEWER

Now, where Mrs. Kennedy is remembered for being the "Glamour Wife in the Back Seat," you are known as the "Average Wife Driving the Truck."

MRS. PRESIDENT

All a bunch of publicity men, Bob, who don't know their ass from an inkwell. But I suppose that's true, the women of America have come to identify with me. Why, I get letters—I get more letters from housewives than Raquel Welch!! She gets letters from men—I have to get them from housewives—but I love it! And I read every one and personally answer them! I even brought some with me; I thought I could read a few during the commercials.

SUPER

(*To imaginary girl in front of her*)
You looking for an apartment?

ALL

Yeah!

SUPER

So who isn't?

STEWARDESS

We hope you will enjoy your flight with TWA. The time is approximately one twenty-four. We will be flying at an altitude of . . . .

WIDOW

You boys stop playing handball down there! You've broken enough windows already!!

SEAMSTRESS

Yeah, Louie, I'm still here. Where did you think I was? San Juan, Puerto Rico?

PROFESSOR

Pupil one: Lynda S. Byrd. Dear Mr. and Mrs. Harry S. Byrd. Lynda is an intelligent pupil but lacks emotional discipline. Her grades show an up-rise during the first term—but so have her skirts! For the child's sake, please have her wear skirts long enough so as to at least cover her—sacred and holy regions!

COLUMNIST

Regional basketball? Weekends at Madison Square Garden!

SUPER

You don't know what a super is? It's a flunkie—that's what it is! I keep the apartments rented, see that no overt perversion prevails, and wash the halls. In return, I'm given a two and a half free—though I hardly call one room with a kitchenette and a two-foot hallway two and a half, but that's what it says in the lease, so that's what it is! I make extra money for food by baby-sitting, addressing letters at home for a mail-order house, and maybe rolling an occasional drunk in the subways—but not often enough to make it a mortal sin! You are in luck! We have an apartment for rent. Just got an opening—number seven—but you'll have to wait a few minutes until they clear the old body out.

WIDOW

Get out of those garbage cans, you bums!

SUPER

A slight accident. You see, the last tenant got—stuck!

COLUMNIST

Stuck in an old routine? Tired of Howard Johnson's? Goldie's—244 East 53rd Street—small but bouncy!!

SEAMSTRESS

Louie, I'm getting a hernia in my right arm from holding this phone!

TOKEN CHANGER

Gorgeous, gorgeous lady . . .

WIDOW

Brats!!

SUPER

You know why? At the end of each year, they make detailed statistics of how many people are killed by disease, wars, or domestic accidents, so naturally people take the necessary precautions when sick, out driving, or out fighting—and many save themselves. But when it comes to getting stuck—well! most people never heard of it—until it's too late—and, of course, can't save themselves. You know, NYU has a whole research department trying to find the cure for getting stuck! Not that they ever will. You can't find a cure for an invisible death!!

WIDOW

Hey, down there! This is a one-way street! You're driving the wrong way!

TOKEN CHANGER

Now you stay up there—don't move! I want to sit here and absorb you.

SUPER

Getting stuck isn't something that happens in a minute. More like a mental cancer. It absorbs you over a long period of time.

FOLK SINGER

Time, Mom! Believe me, it's only a matter of time and that phone will ring and Brian Epstein will be on the other end, and—I know you don't know who that is—but, well, he's very important. When he calls, Mom, I'll pay you back every cent!

HAIRDRESSER

I ask you, Claire, do you believe her? Listen, I can't talk much longer; I've got to get my lingerie washed.

STEWARDESS

This is a combination parachute and inner tube. Only because of Government regulations must we demonstrate it for you—not that you'll ever need it! Now, step one, take the little string under here . . . .

SUPER

Yes, good references, all right! That'll be one month's rent and one month's security, made payable to the Grand Tenement Ass Period. Garbage collected on Tuesdays and Fridays outside! Sorry about the john in the hall, but the only people that will be using yours are a very sweet hair stylist and a very respectable gent who has decorated it with nude inserts from *Playboy*. But don't let that fool you; he goes to church every Monday—don't ask me why! He says it promotes his individualism!

COLUMNIST

Individualism is the password for Eddie Fisher, now appearing under the palms of the Waldorf-Astoria, and laying lots of coconuts!

STEWARDESS

Now, take the yellow string over the left and . . .

WIDOW

Stop beating up that old lady, you brats!!

STEWARDESS

Please remain calm. There is a reported bomb aboard plane.

ALL

Bomb?

MODEL

Yes!

STEWARDESS

Please bail out according to your seat numbers—first-class passengers will, of course, be allowed to jump first. The Atlantic water temperature is a cool—but not cold—forty-two degrees.

SEAMSTRESS

Listen, Louie, can you call me back?

INTERVIEWER

Now let's jump . . .

MRS. PRESIDENT

Okay!!

INTERVIEWER

. . . twenty years to when your husband ran for President much later.

MRS. PRESIDENT

Much, much later, Bobby baby, Rome wasn't laid in a day!

INTERVIEWER

Then you went on your own whistle-stop campaign tour, which I thought was very courageous and very enterprising. Yet I had certain reservations about it at the time because people were not voting for you, but your husband; therefore, you were using your charm and personality to help him. How do you feel about this?

MRS. PRESIDENT

Good, Bob! It feels good! I mean—I think—to me—I am simply an extension of my husband—unfortunately.

SUPER

Yes, good references. Apartment's just been cleaned up. There's only one thing—do you want it?

ALL

Do you want it
    do you want it
        do you want it?

VISITOR

Do you want it? (*Man falls on top of model, she rolls over and jumps up.*)

MODEL

Now let's talk this whole thing over like two grown, mature, and sensible adults! Your lust for me is only biological, therefore subtracting any true emotions or feelings of real need!

VISITOR

I need you, baby! Believe me, I need you!

COLUMNIST

Are you in need of a new and better Chinese restaurant? Why not try . . . .

MODEL

You have a hard heart? You need me! Can I ask you a personal question? What need are you referring to—the need of one who loves, the need of the lonely man trying to find comfort in companionship, or the need of the modern man looking for a fast fuck?

VISITOR

Look!

SUPER

Yes, yes, the apartment has a lovely view! It faces the back of an NYU boys' dormitory.

VISITOR

It's not as though we didn't know each other! We've seen each other six times.

MODEL

Seeing each other and going together are two separate entities! And, besides, I can't stand it in the mornings!

VISITOR

A friend of mine told me that Bennington girls were a little different, but—Wow! Wow!

ALL

Wow! Wow!

WIDOW

Whose dog is making all that noise down there?

COLUMNIST

Ready for a dog show? Westbury Kennel Association. Sunday, November...

MODEL

Not now! Are my seams straight? I've got to get that commercial!

VISITOR

I know—I know! You're a lesbian!

MODEL

Oh—wouldn't that make it simple if I were? Wouldn't that justify your male ego? Then you could just walk out of here and tell the boys, "She's a dyke, and she only does it with 'bulls'!" Oh, no, darling, you'll just have to admit that there's one decent girl who won't lie back, throw her legs up, and say, "Let's rhumba!"

COLUMNIST

Rhumba—rhumba? When was the last time you went to Roseland? Sunday-afternoon rhumba contests for anyone over twenty-nine and a half!

SEAMSTRESS

No, Louie, I'll hang on—but will you hurry? I'm expecting some-one!

SUPER

What? You're worried about the neighborhood? The Village is the safest area in New York! What? Why are all my windows barred?

PROFESSOR

Pupil number four—Shirley MacLaine. Dear Mrs. Warren Mac-Laine. Shirley is an intelligent student . . . but lacks emotional discipline!

VISITOR

Well, then you're either: one—frigid; two—think I'm sexually un-desirable; or three—never been screwed!

MODEL

Answering your questions in order: One, why must all men classify women who are not instant lays as frigid? Two, I think you're fa-cially attractive and built like a brick shithouse. And three, as to my sexual education, I read the *Kama Sutra* from beginning to end in my fifteenth summer on Cape Cod! Would you like some Fritos?

TOKEN CHANGER

Yes, yes, small-bosom type! You go on the lower wall—next to the Chinese ones!

SUPER

Barred windows are only a psychological protection—I don't really need them!

HAIRDRESSER

So, then, Claire, during the color rinse, she says to me, sexylike, "Would you like to go to the theater with me next week?" Syphilis I got rid of easier than her!

STEWARDESS

And now, the economy class may proceed with bailing out.

VISITOR

Sometimes you escape me!

MODEL

I can only thank my modern-dance classes twice a week for my perpetual agility and maintenance of my modelish cherry.

SUPER

But it's a nice house; no one bothers you. They really don't care . . .

ALL

We really don't care!

SUPER

. . . what you do!

WIDOW

What are you two doing down there? Don't you know public affection is only a sign of insecurity?

HAIRDRESSER

So, I did her hair, anyway—chik and fancylike—but she says to me, "More tease! More tease!" I told her she wasn't going to make it out the front door as it was, but she kept screaming, "More tease! More tease! It's Yom Kippur and I want to be noticed!"

WIDOW

Would you get off my party line? I'm trying to call the weather girl!

HAIRDRESSER

Shut up!!!

SUPER

Not that the tenants aren't friendly; they're all basically small town people. Don't think one of them was born here, except myself. I was born on the edge of Harlem—right on Seventh Avenue and 125th Street.

TOKEN CHANGER

Hmmmm . . . gorgeous, long-legged lady! Top billing—eye level, next to the Italians!

MODEL

I don't want sex! I want an honest answer—are my seams straight?

FOLK SINGER

Hey! Did you hear my phone ring? I just went down to buy a copy of *Billboard,* and—did you hear my phone ring?
(*Tenants resume watching television, while at the same time making non-vocal cries of* "Help!")

INTERVIEWER

Is he ever afraid?

MRS. PRESIDENT

I don't think any really wise, aware person could say that he wasn't ever afraid.

INTERVIEWER

Do you remember when the President discussed with you those alternatives which involved, more or less, fear?

MRS. PRESIDENT

Those several times when there have been those dead-of-the-night calls that violence has erupted in some part of the world, when one doesn't have the luxury of time. You pray you've made the right decision—one which offers the most hope, the least dynamite, and the best-possible press reviews.
(*Tenants now vocalize their cries for help during the stewardess's lines.*)

STEWARDESS

I want to thank you all from the bottom of TWA's heart for keeping calm, and your patience. In only a few days a rescue boat will arrive!

COLUMNIST

Friends arriving from out of town?

ALL

Yes!

COLUMNIST

Want to see a family Christmas show—the Nativity with the Rockettes as thirty-six kicking good shepherds? Radio City Music Hall is still New York's greatest . . .

PROFESSOR

Pupil seven. (*With intense emotion*) Dear parents of pupil seven. Your daughter is a shy girl! She does not join in extra activity! She seems to have no ambitions! She does not leave her desk until dismissal! She cannot make friends! She seems to have no ambitions!

ALL

She seems to have no ambitions?

PROFESSOR

Yes!

COLUMNIST

... is still New York's greatest—greatest ...

SUPER

It's the greatest location—near all subways, three blocks from Eighth Street via the scenic route of Greenwich Avenue, the Park Avenue of the Village—due to the perennial pansies in full bloom!

HAIRDRESSER

Claire ...

WIDOW

You boys down there should be ashamed of yourselves! I'm calling the Humane Society! You dirty up the place and live on the phone! Hey, down there—get off my party line!!

HAIRDRESSER

Honey! Tune in to reality! We haven't got party lines any more! Sorry, Claire, but that bitch upstairs—still thinks she's living in the forties! Still wears rats! (*General demented laughter*) Honestly, this place could drive a more unstable person insane—but I'm getting out of here soon!

ALL

We're all getting out of here soon!

COLUMNIST

Soon spring will be upon us again. Prepare now for your trip to the Bronx Botanical Gardens, flower wonderland of New York!

SUPER

We even have a sunny garden in back which you'll share with the other tenants. It's all yours from 3:00 A.M. to 4:00 A.M. The older tenants have priority, of course. The old apartment eleven has the prime time of noon to one, since she's been here twenty-three years. But, think, someday prime time may be yours at Grand Tenement Ass Period.

MEN

But think!

WOMEN

But think!

MEN

Someday!

WOMEN

Someday!

MEN

Prime time may be yours!

WOMEN

Prime time may be yours!

ALL

At Grand Tenement Ass Period!

SEAMSTRESS

My period, Lou! I haven't had my period for six months and I'm getting a little worried! (*Other tenants assume attitudes of workers in a garment factory.*) I want you to find me a good doctor. I can't miss more work this year! I've already used up my fourteen sick days! No, Louie, not an abortionist—who do you think I am, your first wife? Look, Louie, I know you didn't mean to! We both wanted to wait until you got something better than that switchboard job. I know you wanted to wait until I could open my own clothes shop down here in the Village. I know you wanted to—listen, Louie, forget about what you wanted and take what you've got—a knocked-up seamstress from Union 109 who had a hole in her diaphragm!! Okay, I'll hold on!

SUPER

Heat goes on at 6:00 A.M., shuts off at 10:00 A.M., since most people here work.

TOKEN CHANGER

Work is for the fools, my dear! You and I will vacation on Capri as soon as I shave; and, until our planned voyage on the last sailing of the *Queen Mary* before she becomes a hotel, may I have the honor of glueing you in the choice location, the john's ceiling?

SUPER

Then, of course, back on from 6:00 to 12:00 P.M. It's a quiet apartment, since you're facing back.

SEAMSTRESS

Back, Lou? I know you're not allowed to get outside calls at work, but I couldn't let this thing go on much longer. We can make it, Lou! I can keep my job until I'm eight months and three weeks—it's in my union contract—and your switchboard job at that carpet company has a good hospitalization plan. Okay, I'll hold.

FOLK SINGER

If I can only hold out for a few more weeks, I'm sure that the call will come through. . . .

WIDOW

You threw it! I saw that, you simple, stupid woman! Don't you know there's a twenty-five-dollar fine for throwing paper on the street!

ALL

Yeah!! Yeah!! Yeah!! (*This is followed by five beats of intense shouting by the tenants—preferably in foreign languages.*)

INTERVIEWER

How much help can you give him when a national crisis erupts suddenly?

MRS. PRESIDENT

I can give none, really—except to light the candles in front of St. George, patron saint of war.

INTERVIEWER

Aren't you being too modest?

MRS. PRESIDENT

Modess because. . . .

INTERVIEWER

Because you are a very alert, very intelligent woman?

MRS. PRESIDENT

No, no, I'm terribly average! Of course, in this wonderful country of ours, the terribly average are very alert and intelligent, no credit to me. I just follow the crowd, or they follow me, whichever way it is!

MODEL

I don't care if you did meet me on the street in front of One, Two, Kangaroo—that doesn't make it right! The purpose for sex—the reason God created this divine activity—for man and woman . . .

HAIRDRESSER

Claire, if you could only hear some of the conversations in this place! Are the people in this building misinformed!

MODEL

. . . for marriage, children, decency. What insensitive man took the faith out of faithfulness?

SEAMSTRESS

Faithful, Lou? Who's asking you to be faithful! I'm only asking you to marry me!

HAIRDRESSER

Sometimes, methinks I'm the only normal person in this place! No, Clarence, I don't want to double-date with you and your sick east-side friends! You know I can't stand uptown queens!

MODEL

Do you have time for another question? What immoral idiot put the promise in promiscuity?

SEAMSTRESS

Lou—there, there, don't cry—I'm sure other switchboard operators are fathers. . . .

PROFESSOR

Fathers and mothers cannot always be held responsible for their child, but in this case I feel you have not stimulated the child—pupil seven—to be—to want—it is unnatural not to want. . . .

TOKEN CHANGER

There, there, luscious—I don't want you to try and unglue yourself. Don't think you're up there forever. Just a few more weeks and I'll have enough money to quit my job, and then we'll both sail away on the *Queen Mary*—somewhere warm and quiet. . . .

HAIRDRESSER

No, Clarence—I didn't mean—that. I know you live on East Fifty-seventh Street, but—you're different! Look, Miss Claire, don't give me no more problems! I've got Gladys Goldberg already!!

TOKEN CHANGER

Somewhere serene (*louder*) far away from crazy fairies who talk to themselves!!

HAIRDRESSER

Hold on, Claire, I think the walls are talking again—or could it be apartment eight masturbating in the water closet again?

COLUMNIST

Radio City is still New York's greatest—shit!

FOLK SINGER

Would you two stop fucking so loud in there? I'm trying to rehearse!

SEAMSTRESS

Look, Lou, you'd better marry me, or I'll break your guinea balls!

HAIRDRESSER

Hey, you closet queen! Stop glueing those naked females on my toilet's walls! !

ALL

SOMEONE SHUT THAT SICK FAGGOT'S MOUTH!!

SUPER

It's a respectable house—and we intend keeping it that way!

INTERVIEWER

What do you think, as a mother, of the American youth today?

MRS. PRESIDENT

Merely marvelous! Life is one big happy happening! Well, I suppose you realize that I started this whole flower generation, what with my beautification program! Everyone should grow flowers and love! Are you Italian, Bob?

INTERVIEWER

No—Irish and Hungarian! Now, your special contribution to society—which began right at home in the White House—the beautification program! It has very wide ramifications, hasn't it?

MRS. PRESIDENT

Wide as the Grand Canyon, Bob! Seriously, beautification begins at home. I started doing it in the basement of the White House, but, as the months rode by, it got bigger and bigger, right down to the level of getting people not to throw things out of their cars! Do you realize that it costs the Government thirty-two cents per article to pick up trash on the highway? Someone's getting screwed in that deal!

SUPER

You do want the apartment? Lovely! Grand Tenement doesn't like having its luxury apartments vacant long. Now, what was your name? Oh, never you answer that! Might think I was prying! You're apartment seven. Just mail your check to the Grand Tenement, care of Grand Central. They take care of everything from there. I'm just the super—it's as simple as that. Who you are and what you do is your own business. Besides, nobody here gives much of a damn—whatever you do...

ALL

We've all done it before!
(*Tenants take up positions as customers and hairdressers in a beauty parlor.*)

SUPER

Unfortunately—we've all done it before!

HAIRDRESSER

Before I'm through, Claire, I'm going to shave Gladys Goldberg bald! . . .

TOKEN CHANGER

Bobby pins!

HAIRDRESSER

Then I'm going to stick her under that dryer, and like in the *Story of O* . . .

FOLK SINGER

More tease!

HAIRDRESSER

Shut up, Arnold! . . . I'm going to strap her to that hot chair and have the dryer pre-set on electrocution! And she is going to be squirming like a little Swedish seaman, screaming at the top of her lungs—ahhhhh!! Thinking she's Susan Hayward in *I Want To Live!* But nobody will hear her, because everybody, including you, Claire, will be at the gang-bang in the pink-and-black plastic reception room that I am throwing in honor of her upcoming wake. And then I'm going to push that hair-dryer switch and shhhhhhhhh!! The fanciest, chikest, simplest Yul Brynner hair job she's ever had! And then, when Doris Detective and Lana Law come, I'll be the quintessence of innocence in my deep lavender smock, fluttering my extra-sensitive eyelashes: "But, officer, accidents do happen. Is it my fault she got stuck?" (*Tenants begin talking loudly.*) What, Claire? Turn down that opera! What?

ALL

What?

MODEL

What time is it? I can't be late for that commercial audition! After my sixth robbery last week, I could use the pay.

SUPER

Pay your rent on time, do whatever immoral things you have to do in the dark, and whatever—don't get stuck!

ALL

Yeah!

SUPER

What? Oh, I'm sorry—of course, I forgot the key. Only one like it! And may I now officially . . .

ALL

And may we now officially WELCOME YOU TO GRAND TENE-MENT!!

(*Tenants abruptly return to their own pursuits after welcome. Lights dim to complete blackout. A scream is heard, followed by the sound of police sirens. When the lights come up, the sheet has been removed from apartment seven, revealing the face of a clock with a naked girl spread over the dial and a red numeral 7 in its proper place on the clock face. There is an actual letter opener pinning the girl's body to the center of the clock, and blood issues from the wound down to the bottom of the drawing, where this blood joins that on the floor to form the pool that is apartment one. The tenants of Grand Tenement are frozen in grotesque positions. In the blackness, the* VISITOR *has removed his mask and donned the trench coat of a tough* DETECTIVE.)

DETECTIVE

All right! Nobody move!

ALL

Move?

WOMEN

We wouldn't think of moving, Officer!

MEN

We like it here!

WOMEN

Besides, the rent is so reasonable!

SEAMSTRESS

And you can't get cheap apartments in New York these days!

DETECTIVE

All right! Which one of you did it?

ALL

Did what?

DETECTIVE

A girl has been killed in apartment seven!

WOMEN

(*Straightening up*)
We don't know!

MEN

(*Straightening up*)
We don't know!

ALL

We don't know any girl in apartment seven!

DETECTIVE

Then break down the walls of your limited existence and see!

ALL

Crash! Crash! Crash! Look!

MODEL

Oh, my God! Oh, my God! (*Then very coolly*) You know, that could have been me!

ALL

Rebuild! Rebuild! Rebuild! Slam!

DETECTIVE

(*Sniffs.*)
This smells like an inside job!

ALL

(*Spraying deodorant*)
Sssssssss! He's right!
(MRS. PRESIDENT *and the* INTERVIEWER *have been conversing since the lights came up. Now the volume of their chat rises, and the* DETECTIVE *notices them.*)

DETECTIVE

Who has their TV set on?

ALL

I do, office-sore!

DETECTIVE

Turn it off! This is no time for Peyton Place re-runs!

ALL

Click!
(*Gregorian chants, either sung or played, form the background for the first three statements of the* JUDGE. *The* DETECTIVE *has exchanged his trench coat for black robes, thereby becoming the* JUDGE.)

JUDGE

Hear ye! Hear ye! Harken all ye who have business in this court!

ALL

Hark!

JUDGE

The almighty and powerful country of the United States of America versus the very suspicious people of Grand Tenement!

ALL

OBJECTION!!

FOLK SINGER

What is this?

WIDOW

What's going on here?

SUPER

We demand a postponement, due to the unfair publicity we've received from the press!

STEWARDESS

Have you read the papers?

COLUMNIST

The *Daily News* headlines! "Ten Murderers Living Under One Roof!"

SEAMSTRESS

Things like that can twist the minds of the jury!

JUDGE

Objection overruled!

ALL

Damn!

JUDGE

A jury of twelve decent citizens who voted Democratic in the last election has been picked at random, and will be paid the salary of six dollars per day, plus free lunch!

HAIRDRESSER

I hope they won't be too hostile—getting such a low salary!

COLUMNIST

Or that terrible un-Duncan Hines lunch!

JUDGE

They will be, at all times, quite democratic and fair in their judgment.

ALL

(*Syncopated*)
Quite democratic and fair in their judgment, tshh!

JUDGE

All witnesses will be sworn in the name of God!

ALL

(*Same*)
Witnesses sworn in the name of God, tshh!

JUDGE

To tell the truth, the whole truth, and nothing but the truth!

ALL

(*Same*)
Tell the truth, bop; nothing but the truth, tshh!

JUDGE
Their verdict will be, without question, honest and righteous.

WOMEN
(*A chant*)
A jury, quite democratic,

MEN
Fair in their judgment

WOMEN
All witnesses

MEN
Tell the truth,

WOMEN
Nothing but the truth,

ALL
In the name of God.

WOMEN
Let me out! Let me out! We haven't got a chance!

JUDGE
First witness—where were you at 1:32 P.M.?

ALL
Me?

JUDGE
You!

WOMEN
Me?

MEN
You!

SOME WOMEN
Me?

MEN *and* OTHER WOMEN
You!

COLUMNIST
Me?

OTHERS
YOU!!

COLUMNIST
I—I—don't—know. . . .

OTHERS
Office-sore, office-sore, haven't you forgotten something?

JUDGE
I have forgotten something?

OTHERS
What about our one free call?

JUDGE
Sorry! I forgot!
(*Phone line signals.*)

SEAMSTRESS
I am trying to get that call through!
(*Phone line signals.*)

MODEL
Operator, would you please hurry!

HAIRDRESSER
It's urgent!

FOLK SINGER
Mom!
(*Phone line signals.*)

STEWARDESS
Operator! Quick, give me the Legal Aid Society! (*Others give staccato "Beep!"*)

WIDOW

Operator! Get me the British Embassy! (*"Beep!"*)

FOLK SINGER

Hello, Mom! Now, I don't want to worry you, but I'm being held for murder—so send some money for bail! (*"Beep!"*)

TOKEN CHANGER

Transit Operator 708 reporting in. I'll be late for work today! (*"Beep!"*)

MODEL

Jules, something has come up unexpectedly! No, it's not another excuse! I won't be able to make that audition today—I know you want the commission! (*"Beep!"*)

PROFESSOR

Hello, Lynda! Is your mother out? Good! I can't meet you this afternoon! No, no—don't come up here for your extra lesson until I call you! (*"Beep!"*)

HAIRDRESSER

Clarence—get over here immediately! I'm up for murder! Exciting? You should see the cop! I don't know—wear something black. No, don't you dare wear veils! (*"Beep!"*)

SEAMSTRESS

Hello, Lou? I know I just called, but you've got to get me a doctor up here fast! I can't explain, but there's this cop up here who looks like he beats up Negroes and pregnant women! (*"Beep!"*)

COLUMNIST

Cleaners—please send up my black dress—no back talk—I need it for cocktails at five! (*"Beep!"*)

SUPER

Hello, Smiler's? Send up a roast beef on rye, heavy on the mustard, no pickle—bill it!

JUDGE

Finished?

ALL

(*Relieved*)
Finished!

JUDGE

First witness—where were you at 1:32 P.M.?
(*Through the following, the others back away and abandon the* COLUMNIST *in stage center.*)

ALL

Me?

JUDGE

You!

WOMEN

Me?

MEN

You!

SOME WOMEN

Me?

MEN *and* OTHER WOMEN

You!

COLUMNIST

Me?

OTHERS

YOU!!!!

COLUMNIST

I don't know! I could have been washing my hair, or maybe I was feeding my dogs. I like dogs! I like everything I have, because that's the kind of person I am—one who wouldn't own something he didn't like. Like I like my job. I am a writer for the *New Yorker*. I write columns about where to go, what to do, and whom to do it with. I like that! I like to know what's going on before anyone else. I like to report to the people what to do, so by the time they're doing what I told them to, I'm doing something else, something new! That's the kind of person I am, a frontierswoman!—plowing through mediocrity to find what's really worth doing! So, when you ask me a question like "Where was I at a certain time?"—well, my time is not my own! I'm always moving to find new things to do. That's what I get paid for! I don't know where I was; I only know where I'm going! (*Murderer!*) If . . . (*Murderer!*) if . . . (*Murderer!*) you were kind . . . (*Murderer!*) you would ask me, "Where should I go to impress three business executives on a reasonable budget in the midtown area?" (*Murderer!*) I could answer that easily! (*Murderer!*) That's what I know! (*Murderer!*) I could tell you what to do! (*Murderer!*) I like that—to tell people what to do! (*Murderer!*) That's what I get paid for! (*Murderer!*) I'm telling you what to do! (*MURDERER!!*) DON'T ASK ME QUESTIONS I CAN'T ANSWER!! I don't like that! I won't have anything I don't like! I don't get paid for that! I get paid to tell people what to do— Sign of the Dove, 110 Third Avenue, the elegant eighties and the gay nineties waltz together under swaying candlelight . . .

JUDGE
(*Above "Sign of the . . ."*)
Which of you lived on the murdered girl's floor?
(*Tenants mill about, returning to their apartments and leaving the* HAIRDRESSER *and the* TOKEN CHANGER *in stage center.*)

ALL
Which of us lived on the murdered girl's floor?

TOKEN CHANGER
Me!

HAIRDRESSER
Me!

BOTH
(*Turning and seeing a companion in distress*)
Us!!

JUDGE
Names?

TOKEN CHANGER
Apartment eight.

HAIRDRESSER
Apartment six.

JUDGE
That's your legal name?

TOKEN CHANGER
Only one I've ever had!

HAIRDRESSER
I'm not a criminal!

JUDGE
We'll decide that!

TOKEN CHANGER
He's power crazy, that one!

HAIRDRESSER
Yes, I think he goes to my gym!

INTERVIEWER
And speaking of screwing—I mean, highways!

MRS. PRESIDENT
Highways, Bob! You wicked, wicked weasel, you!

INTERVIEWER
You have begun a country-wide campaign to have litter-bugs on the roads imprisoned for ten years!

MRS. PRESIDENT
After all, the highways of the USA are the biggest public-works program in the history of mankind—bigger than the pyramids of Egypt, the temples of Greece, or the baths of Rome! Those sons of birches don't throw trash on their living-room floors!

JUDGE
Occupation!

TOKEN CHANGER
I—ah—work for the city transit department.

HAIRDRESSER

I'm a—hair designer!

JUDGE

What does your job involve?

TOKEN CHANGER

A subway-token exchanger.

HAIRDRESSER

Washing, cutting, setting, teasing—hair!

JUDGE

Business address?

TOKEN CHANGER

IRT. Twenty-eighth Street. Uptown side.

HAIRDRESSER

Antoine's. Saks Fifth Avenue. Third floor—rear.

JUDGE

Perverts!

ALL

PERVERTS!!

HAIRDRESSER

So what if I do go out for a few social drinks with my customers? Their husbands know they can trust me!

TOKEN CHANGER

I have never, in my life, broken our rule against cashing anything over a five-dollar bill!

JUDGE

DID YOU KNOW THIS GIRL?

TOKEN CHANGER

(*Without thinking*)
Yes!

HAIRDRESSER

He did it, office-sore! I knew—he did it!

TOKEN CHANGER

Well, slightly, ever so slightly—but nevertheless, I knew her. To put it more honestly—and since we are in a court of law, honesty is the best information, though not always the most interesting . . .

ALL

STOP STALLING!!

TOKEN CHANGER

I SAW her—only saw her!

JUDGE

Then you did not know her?

TOKEN CHANGER

No! Saw her, spoke to her, but did not know her!

HAIRDRESSER

He said he knew her before—perjurer!!
(*He joins the other tenants, who move away and leave the* TOKEN CHANGER *and* JUDGE *in stage center.*)

TOKEN CHANGER

I saw her as she was trying to open her door. She must have just taken the apartment—she was having trouble with the door lock. All the locks at Grand Tenement are police locks, and they take a little getting used to.

SUPER

But don't get the wrong idea! Police locks are only a psychological protection; we don't really need them!

MODEL

God knows, we've been robbed so many times we haven't anything else to protect!

TOKEN CHANGER

I watched her for a moment, fumbling with the key. I didn't speak. I saw her legs were near perfect, her body was shaped like the inside curves of a wave, and I wanted to grab her ass and . . .

JUDGE

Please speak louder!

OTHERS

Please!

TOKEN CHANGER

I asked her if she needed any help—I didn't speak just then. I just stepped forward and took the key from her hand and opened the door. She was very thankful for my consideration. She smiled, and then I said, "Thank you." (*Murderer!*) I think it's very important to add to my testimony at this point that a transit changer working for the IRT, Twenty-eighth Street and Seventh Avenue, uptown, does not receive many smiles! (*Murderer!*) I've been working for the city there for sixteen years, and I could count on my right hand the number of "Thank-you's" I've gotten for tokens! (*Murderer!*) I sit there daily in that barred booth waiting to say, "You are welcome!" (*Murderer!*) I have been given that opportunity four times in sixteen years, and a smile—never! (*Murderer!*) So you can see— I am hardly going to kill someone who finally, after waiting sixteen years in an enclosed booth, smiles at me! Someone who can make me say not, "You are welcome!" but rather someone who gave me something to say "Thank you" for. She made it all worthwhile— even though she quickly ran into her apartment and slammed the door—WAIT!!

(*He tries to flee but is grabbed by the* JUDGE.)

OTHERS

(*Running to apartments*)
WAIT!!

FOLK SINGER

Wait!—Your Honor.

JUDGE

Yes?

FOLK SINGER

I think I may have some vital information for the case. A person was climbing out of apartment seven's window shortly after she took occupancy!

JUDGE

Is that person in this court?

FOLK SINGER

Yes, Your Honor. (*Others turn guiltily away.*) Myself! (*They turn back.*) I wanted to be the first to tell you. I'm a musician, and I rehearse from the hours of nine to one daily. My apartment, unfortunately, is situated next to a very noisy mattress belonging to . . .

MODEL

Objection! We agreed, no names in this hearing!

JUDGE

Objection granted!

ALL

Damn!!

FOLK SINGER

Any sound is disturbing when you're trying to create, and in particular the sound of a mattress spring bouncing up and down. Sex and art do not mix! So I used the empty apartment to rehearse in. The window bars were broken years ago and the management never bothered to fix it.

SUPER

An oversight, I'm sure. We've always had trouble with that apartment! People have never lived there long!

FOLK SINGER

She came running into the apartment and was just about to scream. You see, I always feel more creative if I rehearse naked! But then when she saw me . . . (*Murderer!*) . . . when I saw her . . . (*Murderer!*) . . . she thought . . . (*Murderer!*) I thought (*Murderer!*) . . . we both thought (*Murderer!*) . . . she was my (*Murderer!*) . . . I was her . . . (*Murderer!*) . . . sister (*Murderer!*) . . . . . . brother (*MURDERER!!*) . . . NO!! She had a brother who ran away to New York, and I have a sister whom I haven't seen for eight years—since I left home when I was fourteen, though I have kept close contact with home. I knew she wanted to come to New York because she wrote me how she wanted to get out of the house, Mother is a strict Catholic convert who used to be an Episcopalian lady wrestler! We even spoke. (*Murderer!*) I told her

about the call I was waiting for. (*Murderer!*) I still thought . . .
(*Murderer!*) . . . she still thought . . . (*Murderer!*) . . . she was my
. . . (*Murderer!*) . . . I was her . . . (*Murderer!*) . . . but then. . . .

OTHERS

But then?

FOLK SINGER

I realized it wasn't! My sister has blue eyes, and she doesn't read
newspapers—and my sister does not lie, Your Honor! She's like
myself. Well, realizing my mistake, and none too soon, I quickly
grabbed my clothes and left, the way I came in. I wanted to admit
that—as I am an honest person!
(*Stewardess begins to run for the exit.*)

OTHERS

GRAB HER!!
(*She is brought back by two of the men.*)

JUDGE

And where were you going, apartment five?

STEWARDESS

For a glass of water! Mystery makes me—thirsty!

JUDGE

Where were you at 1:32 P.M.?

OTHERS

Where were you at 1:32 P.M.?

STEWARDESS

Oh—I'd just gotten back from Hong Kong! I go there eight times
a year. No, no, I don't really like Hong Kong that much, but I'm an
airline stewardess. Would you like some coffee? (*NO!*) tea? (*NO!*)
milk? (*NO!*) I'd just gotten back an hour before this horrible, horrible thing happened. Yes, I was in my bathroom when she
screamed, washing out my smile—I mean, brushing my teeth.
That's one of our regulations—have to brush after every kiss. It was
a very rough flight back and I had to comfort all the passengers, and
what is more relaxing than a good Japanese kiss? That's like a

French kiss, only it also includes a massage, and you have to do it lying on the floor. Of course, a lot of the women passengers do go a little demented on me, but a regulation is a regulation!

JUDGE

Pervert!

STEWARDESS

Say what you may, but TWA is the friendliest airline in the skies! Well, there I was, brushing my teeth seventy-eight times—the plane was half empty—when I heard this scream! Would you like a pillow? (*NO!*) Blanket? (*NO!*) The latest magazines? (*NO!*) I knew someone was dying—I know that sound! I survived one accident. It wasn't in the air—we were taking off. Do you know that ninety-two percent of air accidents are on the land, either taking off or landing?

OTHERS

YES!

STEWARDESS

You did?

OTHERS

BLAH!

STEWARDESS

Ninety-three percent?

OTHERS

STOP STALLING!!
(*Others advance and surround the* STEWARDESS, *completely obscuring her at the end of her lines.*)

STEWARDESS

Oh! (*Murderer!*) Oh, yes! (*Murderer!*) I had heard that scream before! (*Murderer!*) Twelve girl students I didn't know, except for a formal hello, died in that accident! (*Murderer!*) There were twelve different screams, but it was one sound! (*Murderer!*) I am not interested in killing people! (*Murderer!*) I am instructed to comfort people in panic! (*MURDERER!*) That is one of the regulations!

INTERVIEWER

Keeping on the beautification idea, if they gave you control to better Harlem, what would you do?

MRS. PRESIDENT

Let's go back and speak of screwing, Bob!

JUDGE

Which of you two were fighting at the time of the murder?
(*Tenants back away, leaving the* WIDOW *and the* HAIRDRESSER *in center stage.*)

ALL

Which of us two were fighting at the time of the murder?

WIDOW

Me!

HAIRDRESSER

Me again!

WIDOW

He won't get off my party line!

HAIRDRESSER

See the terror I must face every day!

JUDGE

What do you do?

WIDOW

I am a widow. I scream out of windows at lovers, curse at cops, and throw an occasional bag of water at juvenile delinquents! A widow has to protect herself before she's attacked!

HAIRDRESSER

Don't worry, honey, you haven't a chance!

WIDOW

See the terror I must face every day—and I'm a widow!

HAIRDRESSER

And I'm innocent! I was talking to Clarence!

WIDOW

I'm innocent! I've lived here twenty-three years!

HAIRDRESSER

Claire is my only friend!

WIDOW

You get used to these things after twenty-three years!

HAIRDRESSER

Claire and I both moved here together from Chicago!

WIDOW

No, I did not say you can accept them, but you get used to them!

HAIRDRESSER

I don't think I have to answer that question! Claire and I are— friends!

WIDOW

I say, do unto others before they do unto you.

HAIRDRESSER

We're very close—that's all! Is friendship a crime?

WIDOW

So I bitch, and people are cautious and stay their distance!

HAIRDRESSER

You have to be close to someone in your life!

WIDOW

I like being a safe distance from others now!

HAIRDRESSER

You need someone! You can't go to the opera by yourself!

JUDGE

What do you do?

WIDOW

I said, I am a widow.

HAIRDRESSER

Yes, that is correct! I am unmarried!

WIDOW

I met my husband, an American lieutenant, in London during the war. He was discharged one year before the end, due to three battle wounds—for which he was awarded three Purple Hearts. Three Purple Hearts is the limit they will give; so, according to military rule, he was given an honorable discharge.

HAIRDRESSER

No, I have not served in the military forces.

WIDOW

He brought me to this country and we found this apartment in 1944.

HAIRDRESSER

I had asthma! I tell you—IT WAS ASTHMA!

WIDOW

I was younger, and did not mind the stairs—and it was only going to be temporary.

HAIRDRESSER

That's right, but I'm only working there temporarily until I get enough customers to open my own salon.

WIDOW

The rent was very reasonable, and war heroes make no more than cowards. As I said, it was only going to be temporary.

HAIRDRESSER

So I've worked there eight years, but it's only . . .

WIDOW

We were going to look for a larger place immediately, but he—my husband—started getting terrible leg cramps! His arms would become rigid! He could not move!

HAIRDRESSER

. . . temporary. I'm not stuck there forever! Next year I'm going to open my own salon, and Claire is going to be my business manager. He's my only friend.

WIDOW

I called the doctor, but it was a weekend and no doctor could be reached—only their answering services.

HAIRDRESSER

But sometimes, when Claire is—busy—he lets his answering service pick up.

WIDOW

I called two of my husband's friends—to help me carry him to the St. Vincent's emergency ward.

HAIRDRESSER

I know he's home, but he lets the service pick it up! Anybody who makes seventy-five dollars a week on temporary typing who has an answering service is a pretentious queen, Your Honor!

WIDOW

We got him to the emergency ward but had to wait in turn. There was a UN riot that night and four people were badly knifed! We had to wait our turn.

HAIRDRESSER

So I ask them to let it ring through—I wait until he picks it up. Sometimes he doesn't, but I know he's there! So I let it ring for hours. If he's going to drive me crazy, I'll drive him crazy!

WIDOW

I waited with him there for five hours. When the interns finally got to us, they took one look and nodded. His Purple-Heart wounds were infected! They said it was only a matter of time!

HAIRDRESSER

Time after time I've warned him to stop seeing her! I found out! I may not have an awful lot of friends, Your Honor, but I know a lot of people who talk! He's trying to prove something with that girl. Only when she's there, he lets the service pick up the phone!

WIDOW

Only a matter of time, before—before—— They suggested that he remain in the hospital. It would be easier that way, they said. After

all, he was in a coma. They said he would never regain consciousness!

HAIRDRESSER

I don't know who she is—never saw her! Someone he met in one of
the four hundred offices Claire's worked in!

WIDOW

So I went home—I could not face death then. Death was something that happened to other people—then.

HAIRDRESSER

He promised me he'd never see her again!

WIDOW

I kept vigil at home—called the hospital. They still said it was only
a matter of time!

HAIRDRESSER

Now don't get me wrong—jealous, I'm not! Other men I don't
mind. We've got a workable relationship. But a woman—that's
hitting awfully low, Your Honor!

WIDOW

It was three weeks. They had said it would only be a matter of
time. He recovered completely, asked for a divorce, and ran off
with a St. Vincent's nurse's aide! And I've never seen her!

HAIRDRESSER

He promised me he'd never see her again, but I know when I call
sometimes and the answering service picks up, she's there. And
I've never seen her.

WIDOW

So you can see, Your Honor,

HAIRDRESSER

We are innocent.

WIDOW

Our testimonies prove . . .

HAIRDRESSER

We did not know this girl!

BOTH

We've never seen her!

INTERVIEWER

But part of the beautification program is city planning, and the great problem of the cities today is that the center becomes all Negro and the whites are moving out into the suburbs. That is now creating some sort of social confrontation and mass physical demonstrations. Is there any way by which, through city planning, this problem can be solved? What are you doing about this?

MRS. PRESIDENT

Prayer, Bob! In these tense times, when everyone is dropping out on drugs, some of us have to stay alert and pray! This is my book of patron saints—here it is—patron saint of mass physical demonstrations, St. George! My, he must be a busy man! It's a hard question, Bob, but I believe we will solve it in time, and a lot of candles!

INTERVIEWER

Now, you were in Detroit last year before the riots . . .

MRS. PRESIDENT

Isn't it time for another commercial, or something?
(*The* WIDOW *and the* HAIRDRESSER *hurriedly leave center stage, but their place is immediately taken by the* SUPER, *busy scrubbing the floor.*)

INTERVIEWER

No!

MRS. PRESIDENT

All right.

INTERVIEWER

On your tour there, did you have any inkling that the city was bubbling with discontent, and would soon break out into such a violent rebellion of murder and savagery?

MRS. PRESIDENT

No! I did go to Detroit last year to talk to a garden club and to do a little shopping. Of course, I never went into the black areas.

INTERVIEWER

Why not? If you are an extension of your husband, why didn't you go into those areas?

MRS. PRESIDENT

I'm from the South, Bob, and I know my place. The Ku Klux Klan wasn't formed as a garden-party club!

JUDGE

Super!

SUPER

Don't mind me! Just go on with the others! I'm just the super! (*Being pulled to her feet*) Flunkies don't kill!

JUDGE

Am I wrong, or is there someone missing?

ALL

You are wrong, but there is someone missing!

SUPER

The teeny-bopper fucker——(*Yeah!*) I mean, apartment ten!

JUDGE

Get out here!

SUPER

Yeah! Get out here!

OTHERS

GET OUT HERE!!

PROFESSOR

I beg your pardon!

OTHERS

GET OUT HERE!!

PROFESSOR

That's what I thought you said.

SUPER

Those intellectual types will do it every time!

JUDGE

Where were you at 1:32 P.M.?

SUPER

Yeah! What were you doing?

OTHERS

WHAT WERE YOU DOING?

PROFESSOR

Lower your voice! It's a telltale sign of barbarism. Certified New York teachers are able to ignore barbarism. We have to or it might get us down. What I was doing is confidential. What I do is general knowledge. I teach.

SUPER

I wash.

PROFESSOR

A private girls' school on Park Avenue.

SUPER

The halls, the windows, but not the johns—that's the tenants' responsibility!

PROFESSOR

I am twenty-nine years of age.

SUPER

I'm old enough to stay out in a bar as long as I want!

PROFESSOR

Graduated from Fordham, Ph.D. in history, minor in sexology. Irish descent.

SUPER

P.S. 49, eighth grade, then graduated cum-lard-a from a mail-correspondence high school. Third-generation Puerto Rican and Armenian gypsy.

PROFESSOR

I am interested only in the minds of youth!

SUPER

I am interested only in a better detergent!

PROFESSOR

Knowledge cleanses the brain, soothes the soul! You learn this after college.

SUPER

Ajax is only a psychological cleaner; Spic and Span does the job. You learn this after a lot of floors!

JUDGE

You son of a bitch!

PROFESSOR

So what if I have taught at seven girls' schools in the short period of three years?

SUPER

So what if I don't wash the halls some weeks?

PROFESSOR

It was due to unfair accusations, and the stupidity of school boards on progressive education!

SUPER

Sometimes I get tired. It's due to my back. I have psychological arthritis!

PROFESSOR

Sticking to the old is the greatest disease we have today!

SUPER

Psychological arthritis is much worse! Real arthritis, you can rub in Ben-Gay; I could afford that. Psychological arthritis, you got to go to a psychiatrist! I can't afford that!

JUDGE

What about your——

BOTH

Don't bring her into this!

PROFESSOR

I don't want one of my pupils brought into this!

SUPER

I don't want my daughter brought into this!

PROFESSOR

Men of intellect do not waste their time killing!

SUPER

Flunkies don't have the time, either! On Monday, I wash the top floor, and by Sunday I've made it down to the first, then back up...

PROFESSOR

I am only interested in mental progress!

SUPER

... and back down. It's a vicious cycle, but it keeps me out of trouble.

JUDGE

What about your——

BOTH

DON'T BRING HER INTO THIS! PLEASE!

PROFESSOR

She was one of my pupils!

SUPER

She was my only daughter!

PROFESSOR

So she made me angry because she didn't join in extracurriculars!

SUPER

So she made me angry because she didn't come home a lot of nights!

PROFESSOR

Just because she failed in most of my classes—Modern Contraceptives I, Feminine Masturbation II, and V.D. Can Be Cured—for freshmen! As I said, I believe in progressive education!

SUPER

Just because she went out every night with a different man! She never brought them home; she took them down to the basement! I believe a girl should bring her friends home!

PROFESSOR

Mathematics and English cannot teach you how to guard yourself against life!

SUPER

There are rats down in Grand Tenement's basement!

PROFESSOR

But she was young—she still had time to learn how to apply herself!

SUPER

She still had time to learn how to control herself!

PROFESSOR

No, I did not have an affair with her!

SUPER

No, I never beat her!

JUDGE

Then why?

PROFESSOR

They are trying to dismiss me on the grounds of suspicion! I never touched her!

SUPER

She got those bruises when she fell down the basement stairs! I did not beat her!

PROFESSOR

I gave her special time only trying to help her reach the level of the others! Sexual knowledge can only save you!

SUPER

She knew too much. That was her trouble!

PROFESSOR

We can only learn from the past!

SUPER

I didn't know nothing at her age. I came out all right!

PROFESSOR

I warned her if she didn't protect herself with knowledge she'd be destroyed!

SUPER

I warned her if she didn't watch her step, she'd wind up just like me—and her first child would be illegitimate, just like herself!

JUDGE

THEN?

BOTH

She had the nerve——

PROFESSOR

. . . to tell me in front of the whole class, "You are wrong!"

SUPER

. . . In front of her friends, she told me, "Ma, all you do is pick up other people's garbage!"

PROFESSOR

I am not wrong! I believe in what I teach!

SUPER

I do not pick up garbage—that's the tenants' responsibility!

PROFESSOR

So, naturally, I had to defend my teachings. I invited her up to my apartment for a lesson and made her fall in love with me, so to speak. Stupidly she became pregnant, her parents sent her to a bad abortionist, and she died. You can only learn when it becomes a personal experience, unfortunately.

SUPER

So, naturally, I beat the shit out of her! I'll take anything but ungratefulness! I'm looked down on by enough people, without my own daughter—I had to make her watch her mouth! She could think I was a flunkie, but she wasn't going to say it! That's only for me to say. O.K., so I did beat her! I'm her mother! She ran away last month, got involved with narcotics, and the last I heard she fell out of a window during a party. (*Murderer!*)

PROFESSOR

You can see, Your Honor——

SUPER

We're innocent! (*Murderer!*)

PROFESSOR

We may have our problems——

SUPER

But killing is not one! (*Murderer!*)

PROFESSOR

Teaching is my problem!

SUPER

Washing is my problem! (*Murderer!*)

PROFESSOR

I'm too busy with my pupils!

SUPER

I'm too busy trying out different detergents! (*Murderer!*)

BOTH

. . . to get involved with a girl I don't even know!

(*Men advance to form a ring around them; the* SUPER *slips away and her place is taken by the* MODEL.)

INTERVIEWER

I'd like to go back for a moment to the President.

MRS. PRESIDENT

And just when we were getting to know each other!

INTERVIEWER

His first year after his election was enormously successful, and more bills were passed than ever before in American history. Since then, the situation has changed, and now he must feel quite frustrated.

MRS. PRESIDENT

It's harder to do it when you're over fifty, Bob. Of course, in other ways it's not hard at all. But, no, I don't think he's quite frustrated. He never thought that he would have an unbroken stream of Congressional success!

INTERVIEWER

I was talking about the war!

MRS. PRESIDENT

Now, Bob, you promised!

INTERVIEWER

What about Vietnam?

MRS. PRESIDENT

I'm not allowed to talk about that, Bob!

INTERVIEWER

WHAT ABOUT VIETNAM?

MRS. PRESIDENT

That was the condition on which I accepted this interview! NBC is a company of its word. I should know—I own part of it.

INTERVIEWER

WHAT ABOUT VIETNAM?
(*Men surround the* MODEL, *making clicking noises to simulate the clicking of cameras.*)

MODEL

Can I ask you a relatively simple question? Where were you when I called? I was robbed this morning. I've been robbed six times in my six months here—by the same thief! The only things I have come to depend upon in my life are, once a month I get a robbery and a menstrual attack! So—I called. They said they would send a man right up. I've been waiting for a long time. No man came right up for me. Yet! A girl screams! A girl dies! And in the flash of one second, a man comes right up! Do you only come right up when the dead call—when you really can't do any damn good?

A maniac, obviously a dope addict, broke into my apartment again this morning while I was sleeping, tied my hands, tried to rape me —but, thank God, I rationalized myself out of that! I mean, it was so early in the morning for that. And then he robbed me of everything I had left—a Westinghouse clock-radio, a Lady Schick, and four packs of super-long Benson & Hedges. I make ninety-five dollars before taxes on Seventh Avenue as a fashion mannequin. I cannot afford any more robberies this year! Not on that salary! So I called. They said they would send a man right up. I wait—I don't even know how long, because some goddamn maniac stole my sixth Westinghouse clock-radio and there's not a smoke in the place! I'm a very patient person, but there are some lines you must draw! You'd better draw this one, doll! (*Murderer!*)

No, I am not insensitive. (*Murderer!*) A girl is dead (*Murderer!*), murdered possibly (*Murderer!*), maybe suicide (*Murderer!*), maybe a Red Chinese running loose happened to pick her window to throw a knife through. (*Murderer!*) Somehow she is dying (*Murderer!*), somehow she is being murdered (*Murderer!*), and following the standard procedure of such an unlucky and uncomfortable circumstance (*MURDERER!*), she screams that one final scream, and you instinctively know that special sound! That's when you come right up! Well, what about my scream? Will you only come up when it's the last? I called. They said they would send a man right

up. They do, but not for me, and then the man they send holds me on suspicion, when I should be going to an audition to try and make some extra money so I can buy back the blood I've been robbed of six times! I am waiting for my answer. Where were you when I called?
(*Smiling, the girl falls dead.*)
Oh, thank you! You will come the next time!

HAIRDRESSER
Yeah! Where were you when she . . .
(*He is choked off by the* JUDGE *and the other men, who have been grouped in a circle about him.*)

INTERVIEWER
WHAT ABOUT VIETNAM?

MRS. PRESIDENT
See! It says here, "No questions will be asked about Vietnam."
(*The Grand Tenement tenants create the atmosphere of a noisy Italian wedding party, except for the* SEAMSTRESS, *who moves to stage center.*)

SEAMSTRESS
I don't like this! Tension makes people do crazy things. I've got someone else to consider besides myself now. (JUDGE *advances toward her.*) I don't go out at night any more 'cause I can't take any extra chances. There are thousands of degenerates waiting around dark corners who get their kicks beating up defenseless people like me. (JUDGE *strikes at her swollen stomach.*) Stop it! Stop it! Listen, if you don't be careful, you're going to bust my balloon! (*Padding falls from beneath her dress, revealing her to be un-pregnant.*) So? I wanted someone to marry me. I'm thirty-two and a half next Tuesday afternoon. You can wait just so long for security to find you, but when you're thirty-two and a half next Tuesday afternoon, you gotta start laying traps! So he would find out after the marriage? A trap like this is not subtle, but after the marriage they always find out a lot of things they never knew before—and is one more little thing going to hurt that much? I can't afford to be subtle any more; I'm going to be thirty-two and a half next——

OTHERS

We know already!

SEAMSTRESS

I may have a few tricks up my dress, but not murder!

JUDGE

Where were you at 1:32 P.M.?

SEAMSTRESS

I was on the phone with Louie. I'm always on the phone with—I love Louie, Your Honor! A person who loves is not capable of killing!

JUDGE

We'll decide that!

OTHERS

Liar!

SEAMSTRESS

All right, so I did know her! What does that prove? She was a friend of a friend of Louie's. I met her at a wedding!
(*Sounds of a noisy wedding.*)

JUDGE

Order in the court! Order in the court!

SEAMSTRESS

This friend of a friend of Louie's married this dizzy carhop from Trenton. She was there. She had to be there! Of ALL THE PLACES SHE COULD HAVE BEEN, SHE HAD TO BE . . .

JUDGE

Factual statements!

OTHERS

All we want are factual statements!

SEAMSTRESS

She and I talked a little. She was young, pretty, but she talked funny. I asked her a friendly, social question like "What are you doing in New York?" She answered, "Nothing!" (*Nothing.*) Then

Louie came back from the john—men's room—and asked me—us—
what we wanted to drink. She wanted "Nothing." (*Nothing.*) I
wanted a Scotch with a lot of water! Then I felt a lull in the conversation and I tried again, "Well, what do you want to do, to be?
Want some silly little dream tucked away somewhere?" "Nothing."
(*Nothing.*) And suddenly, I started screaming at her, "That's ridiculous! You must want something! You're trying to make a fool out
of me!" But she said nothing. (*Nothing.*) She wasn't a very good
conversationalist—not that I'm the best, but at least I try. Oh, she
was depressing me, Your Honor. I'm a fun person, usually, but if
the people I'm around aren't stimulating, I lose excitement. If they
don't want something, I start doubting what I want. I want Louie
to marry me, and I'm going to get him to! I'm not going to sew up
miniskirt hems at Union 109 for the rest of my life! I was never
faced with so much negativism in my life! And I couldn't afford to
get depressed in front of Louie! He likes me because I'm a fun
person, loving, expansive! Some people look gorgeous depressed,
but not me—and Louie seemed to be getting turned on by her.
Stupidity makes him very horny! (*Muted party sounds until the word
"headache"*) Yes, she was depressing me and enchanting Louie, so—
so—I got a headache! (*Ahhhhhhh!*) What else could I do? But Louie
didn't want to go. He reached into his pocket and said, "Here, take
two Anacins!"—and that's when I faced him and said, "Louie, I'm
pregnant!" (*MURDERER!*) It just slipped out. I'm not a calculating
person by nature—but it worked! He took me right home. The last
thing I said to her, while Louie was getting my coat, was, "Where
do you live?"—and I knew the answer to that and she said it—
"Nowhere!" I mean, anyone who wants nothing can't live anywhere,
right, Your Honor? So I yelled to her as Louie and I were walking
out the door together, "There might be an apartment for rent where
I live!" Of course, I didn't think she'd take me up on it and I never
mentioned where I lived. But I did try to be helpful! She was a
friend of a friend of Louie's—it was the least I could do! (*Loud
party noises resume, reaching a crescendo.*) Stop it! Stop it! I love
Louie, Your Honor. A person who loves is not capable of killing!
(*Tenants scramble back to their apartments and freeze.*)

MRS. PRESIDENT

It says here, "No questions . . ."

INTERVIEWER

I'm sorry. The war must weight you and your husband down terribly as it is.

JUDGE

Do you have anything to say before the jury arrives at your verdict?

INTERVIEWER

In a summary, Mrs. President, would you answer my final question?

TOKEN CHANGER

Yes!

MRS. PRESIDENT

Yes—if it's the one we rehearsed!

TOKEN CHANGER

I promised myself that in twenty years, when I'm very tired, I'll take a two-year vacation and go somewhere where there are only two colors, green and blue.

INTERVIEWER

What have you come to want from life?

TOKEN CHANGER

And I'll lie there between the two and remember only the happy moments I've known, and after those two years I'll die a happy death.

MRS. PRESIDENT

Well . . .

TOKEN CHANGER

But comes one ugly fear in your life which you know you can never erase, which annihilates all the beautiful moments you've saved.

MRS. PRESIDENT

What I've wanted from life has not changed over the years: to understand more, to try to cope with things better, to try to listen to others . . .

TOKEN CHANGER

And you try to kill this ugly fear, only to become a murderer, and the master plan you wanted for yourself is ruined!

FOLK SINGER

I don't take that kind of truth from anyone!

STEWARDESS

I've already killed twelve girls because of my own panic. There's no reason for me to stop now!

PROFESSOR

It was merely an educational experiment!

STEWARDESS

The punishment for one more cannot be any greater!

PROFESSOR

I was curious to see if man really has a conscience!

SUPER

She was patronizing me 'cause she thought I was a flunkie!

PROFESSOR

I feel nothing!

SUPER

She didn't listen to me, just smiled at everything I said!

TOKEN CHANGER

That smile made me very ugly!

SUPER

Nobody patronizes me just because I'm a flunkie!

TOKEN CHANGER

It destroyed all my hopes, and yet it wasn't something I could hold onto!

WIDOW

Someone had to pay for the twenty-three years I've been condemned to one window!

TOKEN CHANGER

She gave me something, only to rob me of everything I had!

HAIRDRESSER

Just because someone like her is there——

WIDOW

Took my husband!

HAIRDRESSER

. . . when I call!

TOKEN CHANGER

When a person has nothing——

SUPER

I wash!

PROFESSOR

I teach!

COLUMNIST

I write!

WIDOW

I scream!

SEAMSTRESS

I wait!

TOKEN CHANGER

. . . he becomes—she made me very ugly!

SEAMSTRESS

Because of her, I had to make up one little lie that has made my life one big deception!

MODEL

I'm so tired of other people getting in my way, getting what I deserve!

SEAMSTRESS

All the love I'd saved for Louie turned into hate!

MODEL

I thought maybe if one was eliminated, my turn would come sooner. I've always suffered from elimination!

HAIRDRESSER

I've waited for hours!

FOLK SINGER

I've waited for days!

WIDOW

I've waited for years!

SEAMSTRESS

And she was there!

MODEL

So I told myself it was time—now!

ALL

NOW!!

MODEL

I eliminate!

ALL

There was nothing personal about it!

MODEL

I was only trying to kill fear!

JUDGE

The jury has arrived at its verdict. You will be sentenced for the remainder of your lives to the positions you are now in!

INTERVIEWER

This has been an NBC live color presentation. Stay tuned . . .
(*From the time of the* MODEL's *lines,* MRS. PRESIDENT *has left the peacock area and wanders through the tenants as through Tussaud's waxworks. She now goes to apartment seven and discovers the letter opener stuck in the girl.*)

MRS. PRESIDENT

Here it is! My letter opener! I knew I brought it with me, because I never open letters without it. *He* gave it to me. Goodbye! It was very pleasant!

(*She exits into the audience, passing out of the hall after the following song and slamming the door.*)

FOLK SINGER

> Where is the warm?
> Where is the quiet?
> Why all the hawks out?
> Why all the riot?
> Spring
> sprung
> somewhere else
> this year.

A RAT'S MASS

by Adrienne Kennedy

A RAT'S MASS was first produced in March, 1965, by the Theatre Company of Boston under the direction of David Wheeler. La Mama Troupe performed the play on tour in Europe the following summer. The play was revived at La Mama in New York in September, 1969, under Seth Allen's direction. Another version was prepared by Ching Yeh for the newly re-formed La Mama Troupe's European tour in the spring and summer of 1970.

ADRIENNE KENNEDY was born in Pittsburgh in 1931 and grew up in Cleveland. She attended Ohio State University but found the social structure so opposed to Negroes that she did hardly any academic work. She started writing at twenty, but her writing received no real recognition until she joined Edward Albee's workshop in 1962. She won an Obie award for *Funnyhouse of a Negro*, done Off Broadway in 1964, and received a Guggenheim fellowship. *In His Own Write*, an adaptation of the writings of John Lennon, was presented at the National Theater in London in 1968, and *Cities in Bezique* was produced by Joseph Papp's Public Theater in New York in 1969. Her other plays are *A Lesson in Dead Language*, *The Owl Answers*, *The Beast Story*, and *Sun*. Most recently she has been working on a movie of *Funnyhouse of a Negro* with Pablo Ferro.

Sister Rat   Brother Rat   Rosemary

(BROTHER RAT *has a rat's hand, a human body, a tail.* SISTER RAT *has a rat's belly, a human head, a tail.*

Mass said in prayer voices that later turn to gnawing voices.

They were two pale Negro children.

SCENE *is THE RAT'S HOUSE. The house consists of two black chains, a red carpet runner and candles. The light is the light of the end of a summer's day.* BROTHER RAT *is kneeling facing the audience to the right of the chains. At the far left of the house, a procession of* JESUS, JOSEPH, MARY, *two wise* MEN *and a* SHEPHERD *stand.* SISTER RAT *stands at the end of the red aisle.*)

BROTHER RAT

Kay, within our room I see our dying baby, Nazis, screaming girls and cursing boys, empty swings, a dark sun. There are worms in the attic beams.
(*Stands*)
They scream and say we are damned. I see dying and gray cats walking. Rosemary is atop the slide. Exalted!
(*He looks at the space between the chains. Kneels again.*)
Kay, within our room I see a dying baby, Nazis, again they scream . . .
(*Stands again.*)
. . . and say we are damned. Within our once Capitol I see us dying. Rosemary is atop the slide exalted.
(*He looks again at the space. Chains swing silently.*)

SISTER RAT

We swore on Rosemary's Holy Communion Book.

BROTHER RAT

Did you tell? Does anyone know?
(*Chains, the* PROCESSION *watches*)

SISTER RAT

Blake, we swore on our father's Bible the next day in the attic.

BROTHER RAT

Did you tell, Sister Rat, does anyone know?
(*Kneels before the space.*)
It was Easter and my fear of holy days—it was because it was
Easter I made us swear.

SISTER RAT

Brother Rat, it was not Easter. It was night after Memorial Day.

BROTHER RAT

No, it was not after Memorial Day. It was the beginning of winter.
Bombs fell. It was the War.

SISTER RAT

It was the War.

BROTHER RAT

Our father said everyone was getting hung and shot in Europe.
America wouldn't be safe long.
(*Remains kneeling. Chains cease.* PROCESSION *marches across the
House to center.*)

SISTER RAT

Remember—we lived in a Holy Chapel with parents and Jesus,
Joseph, Mary, our wise men, and our shepherd. People said we were
the holiest children.
(*Chains go.* BROTHER RAT *turns face front.* SISTER RAT *comes down
the aisle.* PROCESSION *is still.* SISTER RAT *walks.*)
Blake, our parents send me to Georgia. It is a house with people
who say they are relatives and a garden of great sunflowers. Be
my brother's keeper, Blake. I hide under the house, my rat's belly
growing all day long I eat sunflower petals, I sit in the garden,
Blake, and hang three gray cats.
(*Stands before* BROTHER RAT)
Blake, I'm going to have a baby. I got our baby on the slide.
(*Falls*)
Gray cats walk this house all summer. I bury my face in the sand
so I cannot hear the rats that hide in our attic beams. Blake, why
did the War start? I want to hang myself.

BROTHER RAT

Kay, stop sending me the petals from Georgia. Stop saying our mother says you have to go to the state hospital because of your breakdown. Stop saying you have a rat's belly.
(*Chains cease.* PROCESSION *marches across sound of* RATS.)

BROTHER *and* SISTER RAT

The Nazis!
(*Marching,* BROTHER *and* SISTER RAT)
The Nazis have invaded our house.
(*Softer, chains again*)
Why did the War start? We want to hang ourselves.
The rats.
(*Sound*)
The rats have invaded our Cathedral.
(*They rapidly light more candles.* PROCESSION *returns, marches to the center.*)
Our old Rosemary songs. Weren't they beautiful! Our Rosemary Mass.
(PROCESSION *watches. Silence.*)
Yet we weren't safe long.
(*They look at* PROCESSION.)
Soon we will be getting shot and hung.
Within our house is a giant slide. Brother and Sister Rat we are.

SISTER RAT

Blake, remember when we lived in our house with Jesus and Joseph and Mary?

BROTHER RAT

Now there are rats in the church books behind every face in the congregation. They all have been on the slide. Every sister bleeds and every brother has made her bleed. The Communion wine.

BROTHER *and* SISTER RAT

The Communion wine. Our father gives out the Communion wine and it turns to blood, a red aisle of blood. Too, something is inside the altar listening.
(SISTER RAT *kneels.*)
When we were children we lived in our house, our mother blessed

us greatly, and God blessed us. Now they listen from the rat beams. (*Sound rats. They remain kneeling. Sound rats.*) It is our mother. Rosemary, Rosemary was the first girl we ever fell in love with. She lived next door behind a grape arbor her father had built. She often told us stories of Italy and read to us from her Holy Catechism Book. She was the prettiest girl in our school. It is one of those midwestern neighborhoods, Italians, Negroes and Jews. Rosemary always went to Catechism and wore Holy Communion dresses.

BROTHER RAT

Where are you going, Rosemary? we say. And she says, "I have to go to Catechism." Why do you always go to Catechism? "Because I am Catholic." Then, thinking, she says, "Colored people are not Catholics, are they?"

SISTER RAT

I don't think many.

BROTHER RAT

Well, I am. I am a descendant of the Pope and Julius Caesar and the Virgin Mary.
"Julius Caesar?"
Yes, Caesar was the Emperor of all Italia.
"And are you his descendant?"
Yes, she said.

BROTHER *and* SISTER RAT

We wish we were descendants of this Caesar, we said, how holy you are, how holy and beautiful. She smiled.

BROTHER RAT

Our school had a picnic in the country and she took my hand. We walked to a place of white birch trees. It is our Palestine she said. We are sailing to Italy I said. She was the prettiest girl—the only thing, she has worms in her hair.
(*Chains*)

SISTER RAT

Great Caesars my brother and I were. Behold us singing greatly, walking across our Palestine—my brother holding my hand and I am holding his and we are young before the War O Italia.

Rosemary was our best friend and taught us Latin and told us stories of Italy. O Rosemary songs.

BROTHER *and* SISTER RAT

My sister and I when we were young before the War, and Rosemary our best friend, O Rosemary songs. Now we live in Rat's Chapel. My sister and I.
(BROTHER RAT *stares down the aisle.*)

BROTHER RAT

It is Rosemary.
(*Stares*)
Did you tell? Does anyone know? Did you tell? Does anyone know? You started to cry. Kay and I struck you in the face with our father's rifle.
It was the beginning of summer, just getting dark. We were playing and Rosemary said, "Let's go to the playground." After you lay down on the slide so innocently, Rosemary said if I loved her I would do what she said. Oh, Kay.
After that our hiding in the attic, rats in the beam.
Now there is snow on the playground, ambulances are on every street, and within every ambulance is you, Kay, going to the hospital with a breakdown.

SISTER RAT

Blake, perhaps God will marry us in the State Hospital. Our fellow rats will attend us. Every day I look under our house to see who is listening.
(*Chains cease. Aisle bright.* PROCESSION *marches out.*)
I cry all the time now . . . not sobbing . . . Blake, did we really go on that slide together? What were those things she made us do while she watched?

BROTHER RAT

We hide in the attic like rats.

SISTER RAT

I cry all the time now.

BROTHER RAT

Within every ambulance is you, Kay.
Sister, all the time.
(*Sound*)

SISTER RAT

I am waiting for you, Blake, under the hospital so the Nazis won't
see me.
(PROCESSION *marches to center.*)

BROTHER RAT

The rat comes to the attic crying softly within her head down. She
thinks she's going to have a baby. If I were a Nazi I'd shoot her.
On the slide she said, Blake, I am bleeding.
Now there is blood on the aisle of our church. Before rat blood
came onto the slide we sailed. We did not swing in chains before
blood, we sang with Rosemary. Now I must go to battle.
(*Heil. Salutes* PROCESSION.)
Will you wait for me again at last spring?
(PROCESSION *does not answer.* BROTHER *and* SISTER RAT *fall down
and light candles. Silent chains.* BROTHER RAT *stands.*)

BROTHER RAT

(*Stares down aisle.*)
Will they wait for me at last spring, Rosemary?
(ROSEMARY *comes down red aisle in her Holy Communion dress.*)

ROSEMARY

Blake, the Nazis will get you on the battlefield.
(ROSEMARY *and* BROTHER RAT *stand before each other.* SISTER RAT
remains kneeling.)

BROTHER RAT

Rosemary, atone us, take us beyond the Nazis. We must sail to the
Capitol. Atone us. Deliver us unto your descendants.

ROSEMARY

The Nazis are going to get you.

BROTHER RAT

If you do not atone us, Kay and I will die. We shall have to die to forget how every day this winter gray cats swing with sunflowers in their mouths because my sister thinks I am the father of a baby. Rosemary, will you not atone us?

ROSEMARY

I will never atone you. Perhaps you can put a bullet in your head with your father's shotgun, then your holy battle will be done. (*The* PROCESSION *is at the edge of the house.*)

SISTER RAT

(*Kneeling*)
O HOLY Music Return.
(*The* PROCESSION)

ROSEMARY

Come with me, Blake.

BROTHER RAT

How can I ever reach last spring again if I come with you, Rosemary? I must forget how every day that winter gray cats swing with sunflowers in their mouths.

ROSEMARY

Perhaps you can put a bullet in your head.

SISTER RAT

I have a rat's belly.

BROTHER RAT

How I can ever again reach last spring if I come with you, Rosemary?

ROSEMARY

You must damn last spring in your heart. You will never see last spring again.

BROTHER *and* **SISTER RAT**

Then we must put a bullet in our heads.
(PROCESSION *marches out. Chains. Silence. They stare at Rosemary.* PROCESSION *returns.*)

PROCESSION

Goodbye, Kay and Blake. We are leaving you.

BROTHER *and* SISTER RAT

Jesus, Joseph, Mary, wise men, and shepherd, do not leave. Great Caesars, we will be again. You will behold us as we were before Rosemary with the worms in her hair. A spring can come after the War.

PROCESSION

What, Kay and Blake?

BROTHER *and* SISTER RAT

A spring can come after the War. When we grow up we will hang you so that we can run again, walk in the white birch trees. Jesus, Joseph, wise men, shepherd, do not leave us.

PROCESSION

We are leaving because it was Easter.

BROTHER RAT

No, no, it was not Easter, it was the beginning of June.

PROCESSION

In our minds it was Easter. Goodbye, Kay and Blake.
(*They walk out. A gnawing sound.* SISTER RAT *kneels.* BROTHER RAT *and* ROSEMARY *face each other. A gnawing sound.*)

ROSEMARY

In my mind was a vision of us, rats all.

BROTHER RAT

If only we could go back to our childhood.

SISTER RAT

Now there will always be rat blood on the rat walls of our rat house, just like the blood that came onto the slide.

BROTHER RAT

Beyond my rat head, there must remain a new Capitol where Great Kay and I will sing.
But no within my shot head I see the dying baby, Nazis and

Georgia relatives screaming, girls cursing, boys, a dark sun, and my grave. I am damned.

No . . . when I grow up I will swing again in white trees because beyond this dark rat sun and gnawed petals there will remain a Capitol.

SISTER RAT

A Cathedral.

BROTHER RAT

Now within my mind I forever see dying rats. And gray cats walking. Rosemary, worms in her hair, stop the slide. Our Holy songs in our parents' house, weren't they beautiful?

BROTHER *and* SISTER RAT

Now it is our rats' mass.
(*From now on their voices sound more like gnaws.*)

BROTHER RAT

She said, "If you love me, you will." It seemed so innocent.

She said it was like a wedding.

Now my sister Kay sends me gnawed petals from sunflowers at the State Hospital. She puts them in gray envelopes. Alone I go out to school and the movies. No more do I call by for Rosemary. She made me promise never to tell. "If you love me," she screamed, "you'll never tell." And I do love her.

I found my father's rifle in the attic.

Winter time . . . gray time. Dark boys come laughing, starting a game of horseshoes, gnawing in the beams. The winter is a place of great gnawed sunflowers. I see them in every street in every room of our house. I pick up gnawed great yellow petals and pray to be atoned.

I am praying to be atoned.

I am praying to be atoned dear God.

I am begging dear God to be atoned for the Holy Communion that existed between my sister and me and the love that I have for Rosemary.

I am praying to be atoned.

(*He kisses Rosemary. He comes down aisle, movements more rat-like, voice more like gnawing.*)

Bombs fall. I am alone in our old house with an attic full of dead rat babies. I must hide.

BROTHER *and* SISTER RAT

God, we ask you to stop throwing dead rat babies.

BROTHER RAT

(*Kneels*)
When I asked you yesterday, the day they brought my sister Kay home from the State Hospital, you said, God, Blake, perhaps you must put a bullet in your head. Then your battle will be done.
God, I think of Rosemary all the time. I love her.
I told myself afterward it was one of the boys playing horseshoes who had done those horrible things on the slide with my sister. Yet I told Kay I am her keeper, yet I told Rosemary I love her. It is the secret of my battlefield.

SISTER RAT

Here we are again in our attic where we once played games, but neither of us liked it because from time to time you could hear the rats. But it was our place to be alone, Blake. Now that I am home from the hospital, we must rid our minds of my rat's belly. Can you see it?
You did not visit me in the hospital, Brother Rat. Blake, I thought you were my brother's keeper.

BROTHER RAT

Everywhere I go I step in your blood.
Rosemary, I wanted you to love me.
(*He turns—chains—aisle bright—chains—gnawing sound—battle-field sounds.*)

BROTHER *and* SISTER RAT

God is hanging and shooting us.

SISTER RAT

Remember, Brother Rat, before I bled, before descending bombs and death on our Capitol we walked the Palatine . . . we went to the movies? Now the Germans and Caesar's army are after us, Blake.
(*He goes back to* ROSEMARY, *whose back is to him, and starts.*)

ROSEMARY

The Nazis are after you.
My greatest grief was your life together. My greatest grief.

BROTHER *and* SISTER RAT

(*Look up at chains.*)
Now every time we will go outside we will walk over the grave of
our dead baby. Red aisle runners will be on the street when we
come to the playground. Rosemary will forever be atop the slide,
exalted with worms in her hair.
(*They kneel, then rise, kneel, then rise.*)
We must very soon get rid of our rat heads so dying baby voices
on the beams will no more say we are your lost Caesars.

ROSEMARY

It is our wedding now, Blake.

BROTHER *and* SISTER RAT

Brother and Sister Rat we are, very soon we must.

SISTER RAT

We are rats in the beam now.

ROSEMARY

My greatest grief was your life together. The Nazis will come soon
now.

BROTHER *and* SISTER RAT

Every time we go out red blood runners will be on the street.
(*They kneel, then rise, kneel, then rise.*)
At least soon very soon we will get rid of our rat heads and rat
voices in beams will say no more we are your lost Caesars.

ROSEMARY

It is our wedding, Blake. The Nazis have come.
(*Marching*)
Brother and Sister Rat you are now. Soon you will become headless
and all will cease. The dark sun will be bright no more and no more
sounds of shooting in the distance.
(*Marching* PROCESSION *appears bearing shotguns.*)

BROTHER *and* SISTER RAT

We will become headless and all will cease. The dark sun will be bright no more and no more sound of shooting in the distance. It will be the end.

(*The* PROCESSION *shoots. They scamper. More shots. They fall.* ROSEMARY *remains.*)

END OF MASS

BLUEBEARD

A Melodrama in Three Acts

by Charles Ludlam

BLUEBEARD was first produced by the Ridiculous Theatrical Company at La Mama Experimental Theatre Club on March 24, 1970. It was directed by the author, with costumes by Mary Brecht, music by David Scott, sets by Christopher Scott, lighting by Leandro Katz, and the following cast:

SHEEMISH	John Brockmeyer
MRS. MAGGOT	Eleven
LAMIA THE LEOPARD WOMAN	Mario Montez
BARON KHANAZAR VON BLUEBEARD	Charles Ludlam
ANGELS	James Morfogen
	Frederick Teper
RODNEY PARKER	Bill Vehr
SYBIL BLUEBEARD	Blackeyed Susan
MISS FLORA CUBBIDGE	Lola Pashalinski
HECATE	Lohr Wilson

The Ridiculous Theatrical Company subsequently performed the play at Christopher's End and at the Gotham Art Theatre in New York City and on tour in Europe.

ACT I

THE EAVESDROPPER

SCENE: *The alchemical laboratory of* DR. BLUEBEARD *located on an island off the coast of Maine. The house is a lighthouse still in use. Revolving light, test tubes, and other laboratory equipment, including an operating table.* SHEEMISH, *the butler, and* MRS. MAGGOT, *the housekeeper, are dusting and sweeping.* MRS. MAGGOT *bumps the table, causing a test tube to fall and break.*

ACT I, SCENE 1: SHEEMISH, MRS. MAGGOT

SHEEMISH

Now, see what you've done! Clean it up at once, for if Khanazar the Bluebeard finds anything broken, he will surely send you to the House of Pain.

MRS. MAGGOT
(*Terribly frightened*)
No, no, not the House of Pain!

SHEEMISH
(*Sadistically*)
Yes, yes, the House of Pain. If I should mention the fact that you broke this little glass tube, I'm sure the master would send you to the House of Pain.

MRS. MAGGOT
(*More frightened*)
No, no, not the House of Pain! Please, Sheemish, don't tell, I beg of you.

SHEEMISH
(*Calculatingly*)
Very well. I will not tell . . . as long as you realize that I am doing you a favor . . . and that I will expect a favor in return.

MRS. MAGGOT
Anything, I'll do anything you ask, but please, please do not tell.

SHEEMISH

Replace the little glass tube. Substitute something for the sticky liquid inside. Do this quickly, for the good ship *Lady Vain* will dock here at three o'clock this afternoon, drop off a female passenger, and return to the mainland. We must prepare the guest room for tonight . . . and the bridal chamber for tomorrow.

MRS. MAGGOT

You mean he's found another . . . another . . .
(*She begins to weep.*)

SHEEMISH

Say it, Mrs. Maggot! Wife. Say it: Wife! Wife! Wife!

MRS. MAGGOT

I can't. I can't bear to say it. (*Falling to her knees*) Lord of my prayers! God of my sacrifice! Because you have done this thing, you shall lack both my fear and my praise. I shall not wince at your lightnings nor be awed when you go by.

SHEEMISH

Curse not our god, Khanazar the Bluebeard.

MRS. MAGGOT

Why should I not curse him who has stolen from me the gardens of my childhood?

SHEEMISH

Remember the House of Pain and hold your tongue. You have replaced the little glass. It looks exactly as it did before the little accident. Even the liquid is the same color and viscosity. You and I are the only ones who know. Come, the guest room. And Mrs. Maggot, forget the past.

MRS. MAGGOT

Since the operation I can't remember it, anyway.

SHEEMISH

And think as I do, of the future.

MRS. MAGGOT

The future is so very far.
The present is what must be feared.

For we are slaves of Khanazar,
And dread the wrath of the Bluebeard.

(*Exeunt*)

ACT I, SCENE 2: LAMIA THE LEOPARD WOMAN

(*Enter* LAMIA *the Leopard Woman, wearing more leopard than the costume designer thought advisable.*)

ACT I, SCENE 3: KHANAZAR THE BLUEBEARD

BLUEBEARD

(*Entering and seeing* LAMIA)
I thought I told you never to come to this side of the island again.
(*Draws gun and fires,* LAMIA *runs out.*)
Give up your passions, Bluebeard, and become the thing you claim to be. Is to end desire desire's chiefest end? Does sex afford no greater miracles? Have all my perversions and monstrosities, my fuckings and suckings led me to this? This little death at the climax followed by slumber? Yet chastity ravishes me. And yet the cunt gapes like the jaws of hell, an unfathomable abyss; or the boy-ass used to buggery spread wide to swallow me up its bung; or the mouth sucking out my life! Aaagh! If only there were some new and gentle genital that would combine with me and, mutually interpenetrated, steer me through this storm in paradise! (*The sound of a foghorn*) They said I was mad at medical school. They said no third genital was possible. Yang and yin, male and female, and that's that. (*Laughs maniacally.*) Science suits a mercenary drudge who aims at nothing but external trash. Give me a dark art that stretches as far as does the mind of man; a sound magician is a demigod. (*Foghorn again*)

ACT I, SCENE 4: GOOD ANGEL, BAD ANGEL, BLUEBEARD

GOOD ANGEL

On, Bluebeard, lay these thoughts aside,
and think not on them lest it tempt thy soul
and heap God's heavy wrath upon thee.
Take half—one sex, that's all—for that is Nature's way.
(*Foghorn*)

BAD ANGEL

> Go forward, Bluebeard, in that famous art
> wherein all nature's treasure is contained:
> Be thou on earth as God is in the sky,
> Master and possessor of both sexes.

(*Exit angels*)

ACT I, SCENE 5: BLUEBEARD

BLUEBEARD

> Love must be re-invented, that's obvious.
> Sex to me no longer is mysterious
> And so I swear that while my beard is blue,
> I'll twist some human flesh into a genital new.

ACT I, SCENE 6: BLUEBEARD, SHEEMISH, MRS. MAGGOT

SHEEMISH

Master, master.

BLUEBEARD

(*Enraged*)

Swine! How dare you enter my room without knocking? (*Lashes whip.*) Have you forgotten the House of Pain?

SHEEMISH

(*Clutching his genitals*)

No, no, not the House of Pain! Mercy, Master.

BLUEBEARD

How can I show you mercy when I am merciless with myself? I see in you nothing but my own failure, another experiment down the drain.

SHEEMISH

(*On his knees pathetically*)

Forgive me. (*Whimpers*)

BLUEBEARD

Aaagh, get up. Tell me what you want.

SHEEMISH

The good ship *Lady Vain* has docked here on the rock side of the island.

BLUEBEARD
(*Anticipating*)
Yes . . .

SHEEMISH
There are two women . . .

BLUEBEARD
(*In ecstasy*)
Ah, resolve me of all ambiguities. Perform what desperate enter-
prises I will!

MRS. MAGGOT
And a man.

BLUEBEARD
Huh? A man? There is no man! (*Lashes her with whip.*) You are
mistaken, there is no man.
(*Loud knocking at the door*)

MRS. MAGGOT
It's them.

SHEEMISH
(*Correcting her.*)
It is they.

BLUEBEARD
(*Looking through spy hole*)
Sybil said nothing about a man.
(*Loud knocking, howling wind, and the sound of rain*)

BLUEBEARD
Go away! Go away! Leave me in peace!

ACT I, SCENE 7: BLUEBEARD, SHEEMISH, MRS. MAGGOT, RODNEY PARKER,
SYBIL BLUEBEARD, MISS FLORA CUBBIDGE

RODNEY'S VOICE
Baron Bluebeard, please open the door!

BLUEBEARD
Leave me alone! Go away!

SYBIL'S VOICE

Dear uncle, please let us in, for the love of God. It's bitter without.

BLUEBEARD

(*Aside*)

And I am bitter within!

MISS CUBBIDGE'S VOICE

We'll catch our death of cold!

MRS. MAGGOT

(*In confusion*)

What should we do, Master?

SHEEMISH

(*Calling down from a lookout point*)

We must let them in, for their ship the *Lady Vain*, its sails big-bellied, makes way from our port. I think it will go down in the storm.

BLUEBEARD

Aaagh, very well, come in then. But you can't stay. (*Opens the door.*)

(*Enter* SYBIL, RODNEY, *and* MISS CUBBIDGE, *wet*)

SYBIL

(*Rushing to Bluebeard*)

Oh, Uncle Khanazar, my dear Uncle Khanazar, why wouldn't you let us in? How glad I am to see you. Who would have thought of you?

BLUEBEARD

Why, Sybil, I hope you always thought of me.

SYBIL

Dear uncle, so I do, but I meant to say of seeing you—I never dreamed I would while you were quartered here at . . . at . . . what is the name of this island, anyway?

BLUEBEARD

(*Lying*)

I don't believe it has a name. I've never thought to give it one.

RODNEY

The sailors called it "The Island of Lost Love."

SYBIL

It's true our ship was almost lost in the fog.

RODNEY

And we are in love.

BLUEBEARD

(*Aside*)
Grrr!

SYBIL

Oh, excuse me, Uncle, this is my fiancé, Rodney Parker.

BLUEBEARD

(*Icily*)
Howdyedo?

RODNEY

(*Running off at the mouth*)
Sybil has told me so much about you. She says you were the great misunderstood genius at medical school. But that you suddenly gave it all up, threw it all away to live here in almost total seclusion——

SYBIL

(*Interrupting*)
And this is Miss Cubbidge, my traveling companion and tutor.

MISS CUBBIDGE

(*Shaking his hand violently*)
I am incensed to meet you, Baron Bluebeard. Sybil told me that you were with her father at medical school when the terrible fire——

BLUEBEARD

(*Flaring up*) Don't squeeze my hand! I work with my hands. (*Then politely*) If you will excuse me. I expected only one guest. (*Turning to* MRS. MAGGOT *and* SHEEMISH, *who bow with sinister smiles*) Now there are extra preparations to be made. Mrs. Maggot and Sheemish will show you to your rooms. (*Kisses* SYBIL's *hand, shakes* MISS CUB-BIDGE's *hand, and ignores* RODNEY's *hand.*) We will sup when the moon rises over Mount Agdora. (*Exits.*)

RODNEY

Did you see that? I offered him my hand but he refused it.

SYBIL

I'm sure Uncle Khanazar meant nothing by it. He's so involved in his work and he's unused to human companionship.

ACT I, SCENE 8: SYBIL, RODNEY, CUBBIDGE, MAGGOT, SHEEMISH

RODNEY

(*Aside to* SYBIL)
What about these servants he keeps around here?

SYBIL

(*Aside to* RODNEY *and* CUBBIDGE)
Yes, of course. (*Then strangely*) But then they hardly seem human, do they?

MRS. MAGGOT

(*Dikey*)
This way to the washroom, ladies. Follow me to the washroom, ladies.

MISS CUBBIDGE

Shall we wash away that which we acquiesced during our long adjunct? I refer, of course, to the dust of travel.

SYBIL

Until dinner, Rodney dear.

RODNEY

Sybil, there is something that I must discuss with you.

SYBIL

Excuse me until then, dear Rodney. I must freshen up. (*Throws him a kiss and exits.*)

ACT I, SCENE 9: RODNEY, SHEEMISH

RODNEY

Ah, I'm convinced of it! Sybil is in love with him.

SHEEMISH

With whom?

RODNEY

Excuse me, I was thinking aloud. Thinking, thinking, thinking, that's all I ever do. My head thunders with thinking. I must stop thinking. I needs must shout it. (*Very loud*) Why did she come here? To look for him. Nothing I could do but she must come to look for him. I think this jealousy will drive me mad!

SHEEMISH

Shall I tell you between our two selves what I think of it? I'm afraid she'll get little return for her love; her journey to this foggy island will be useless.

RODNEY

(*Overjoyed*)
But what is the reason? Do tell me, Sheemish, what makes you take such a gloomy view of the situation?

SHEEMISH

His feelings are cold.

RODNEY

(*Enraged again*)
You think he will betray her innocent love?

SHEEMISH

He has no heart, that man.

RODNEY

But how could a gentleman do such a vile thing?

SHEEMISH

I have been his servant on this island nineteen years, and I will say this—just between us—that in my master, Baron Khanazar the Bluebeard, you see the vilest scoundrel that ever cumbered the earth—a madman, a cur, a devil, a turk, a heretic, who believes in neither heaven, hell, nor werewolf. He lives like an animal, like a swinish gourmet, a veritable vermin infesting his environs and shuttering his ears to every Christian remonstrance, and turning to ridicule everything we believe in.

RODNEY

But surely there's nothing between them. He wouldn't marry his own niece, Sybil. What a ridiculous idea! (*Laughs.*)

SHEEMISH

(*Ominously and with candor*)

Believe me, to satisfy his passion he would have gone further than that. He would have married you as well and her dog and cat into the bargain. Marriage means nothing to him. It is his usual method of ensnaring women! (*Sound of footsteps*) But here he comes taking a turn in the palace. Let us separate—what I have spoken I have spoken in confidence. I am his slave, but a master who has given himself over to wickedness is a thing to be dreaded. If you repeat a word of this to him, I will swear you made it up.

(*Exit Rodney.*)

ACT I, SCENE 10: SHEEMISH, BLUEBEARD

BLUEBEARD

I have been in my laboratory putting things in readiness, for I have found the ideal subject for my next experiment . . . or should I say, my next work of art?

SHEEMISH

(*With dread*)

Oh, Master.

BLUEBEARD

What is it?

SHEEMISH

I'm afraid. I'm afraid. I'm afraid. (*Leaps into* BLUEBEARD's *arms.*)

BLUEBEARD

(*Throwing him off*)

Down, down, you fool. Never mind the disagreeable things that may happen. Let us think of the pleasant ones. This girl is almost the most charming creature imaginable. Add to that a few of my innovations! I never saw two people so devoted, so completely in love. The manifest tenderness of their mutual affection inspired a like feeling in me. It affected me deeply. My love began as jealousy. I couldn't bear to see them so happy together. Vexation stimulated my desire and I realized what a pleasure it would give me to disturb their mutual understanding and break up an attachment so repugnant to my own susceptibilities.

SHEEMISH

Have you no desire for Miss Cubbidge?

BLUEBEARD

She is not without a certain cadaverous charm. (*Footsteps*) Shhh! Quickly, the spy hole, see who it is. (*Exit*)

SHEEMISH

The sun is in my eyes, but I know the sound of her footsteps—it is only Mrs. Maggot.

ACT I, SCENE 11: MRS. MAGGOT, SHEEMISH

(MRS. MAGGOT *and* SHEEMISH *bring on a table and chairs. Then they set the table for dinner.*)

MRS. MAGGOT

(*Carrying in a platter*)
Yum, yum, yum . . . I'm nibbling . . . yum . . . mutton good! Lovely . . . yum . . . yum . . . yum.

SHEEMISH

It is the first time meat has been seen in the palace in nineteen years.

MRS. MAGGOT

Twenty for me! Twenty years and never any meat. I've withered. You fed yourself on the fat in your hump, didn't you? Ach. Ouf. (*She is seized by a violent coughing fit.*) Swallowed the wrong way.

SHEEMISH

Heaven has punished you, glutton. Stop, before you eat the knives and the tablecloth.

MRS. MAGGOT

My illness, not my sin! Look, Sheemish, a chicken! Ah, the drumstick! (*With her mouth full*) Those who have a stomach eat; those who have a hump glue themselves to keyholes.

SHEEMISH

Watch what you say to me. My hump contains a second brain to think my evil thoughts for me. It hasn't forgotten the broken test tube and our little secret.

MRS. MAGGOT

You must teach me to spy through keyholes. Which eye does one use, the right or the left? They say in time one's eye becomes shaped like a keyhole. I prefer eavesdropping. There, see my ear, a delicate shell. (*She shows her trumpet.*)

SHEEMISH

When others are present, you are as deaf as a bat—but when we are alone you are cured and hear perfectly.

MRS. MAGGOT

It's a miracle! Look at that pork chop!

SHEEMISH

(*Grabs her and throws her onto the table. Climbing on top of her, he forces a huge piece of meat into her mouth.*) Here, glutton, eat this! Someday your mouth will be full of maggots and greenish pus.
(*Laughter of the dinner guests is heard off.*)
But here come the guests to dinner. Let us have a truce until the next time that we are alone.

MRS. MAGGOT

Peace!

ACT I, SCENE 12: MRS. MAGGOT, SHEEMISH, BLUEBEARD, RODNEY, SYBIL, MISS CUBBIDGE

(*The dinner guests and* BLUEBEARD *enter.* MRS. MAGGOT *and* SHEEMISH *just manage to get off the table in the nick of time.* MISS CUBBIDGE *enters on* BLUEBEARD'S *arm,* SYBIL *on* RODNEY'S *arm.*)

BLUEBEARD

Work, work, work. I have thought of nothing else these nineteen years. My work, my work, and nothing else.

SYBIL

Beware, Uncle, all work and no play makes Jack a dull boy.

MISS CUBBIDGE

True, Sybil, but all play and no work makes Jack a mere toy.

BLUEBEARD

No danger there. I never cease in my experimenting. My dream is to remake man, a new man with new possibilities for love.

SYBIL

Love for a man is a thing apart. Love for a woman is life itself.

BLUEBEARD

Won't you all be seated?
(BLUEBEARD *seats* MISS CUBBIDGE *at the table.* RODNEY *seats* SYBIL.)

MRS. MAGGOT

(*To Sybil*) Why, dearie, what an *unusual* locket.

SYBIL

Yes, it's lapis lazuli. My mother gave it to me the night she died when the terrible fire . . .

MISS CUBBIDGE

(*Interrupting*) No, Sybil.

SYBIL

I never knew my mother.

RODNEY

Strange, all the places are set to one side of the table.

BLUEBEARD

That is because of a little surprise I have for you. There will be an entertainment tonight, while we are taking our evening meal, a little play I wrote myself.

SYBIL

What, a play?

RODNEY

Jolly!

MISS CUBBIDGE

Wrote it yourself? You've a touch of erosion, I see, Baron. And yet you studied medicine?

BLUEBEARD

I write for amusement only.

MISS CUBBIDGE

Were you indoctrinated? I mean, did you receive the doctorate? On what theme did you write your dissipation? Which degree did you receive?

BLUEBEARD

I received the third degree.
(MRS. MAGGOT *places a platter of meat on the table.*)

RODNEY

This meat looks delicious.

BLUEBEARD

(*Having a seizure*)
Meat? Meat? (*Turning on* MRS. MAGGOT) You dare to serve them meat?

MRS. MAGGOT

Eh?

BLUEBEARD

(*In a blind rage*)
Take it away at once, blockhead! Do you want to ruin my experiment? (*He throws the meat at* MRS. MAGGOT *and then leaps up on the dinner table like a wild man roaring.*) What is the law?

MRS. MAGGOT *and* SHEEMISH

(*Bowing before him as though he were an idol on an altar, they link their arms together and chant, swaying back and forth rhythmically.*) We are not men. We are not women. We are not men. We are not women. His is the hand that makes. We are not men. We are not women. His is the House of Pain. We are not men. We are not women. That is the law!

BLUEBEARD

(*Rolling his eyes savagely*)
Now get out! (*Turning on the guests*) All of you!

MISS CUBBIDGE

(*Horrified*)
What about dinner?

BLUEBEARD

I've lost my appetite!

RODNEY

What about the play?

BLUEBEARD

I detest avant-garde theater.

ACT I, SCENE 13: BLUEBEARD, MISS CUBBIDGE, SYBIL,
RODNEY, SHEEMISH, MRS. MAGGOT, LAMIA

(*The face of* LAMIA *the Leopard Woman appears at the window.*)

RODNEY

Look, there's a face at the window!
(MISS CUBBIDGE *screams.* SYBIL *faints in* RODNEY'S *arms.* BLUEBEARD
fires his revolver at LAMIA. *Tableau vivant. The curtain falls.*)

ACT II

SCENE 1: SYBIL, RODNEY

SYBIL

Rodney, you have come to speak to me about my letter to you.

RODNEY

Yes, you could have told me face to face. People living in the same
house, even when they are the only people living on a deserted
island, as we are, can be farther apart than if they lived fifty miles
asunder in the country.

SYBIL

I have thought much of what I then wrote and I feel sure that we
had better——

RODNEY

Stop, Sybil . . . do not speak hurriedly, love. Shall I tell you what
I learned from your letter?

SYBIL

Yes, tell me if you think it is better that you should do so.

RODNEY

I learned that something had made you melancholy since we came
to this island. There are few of us who do not encounter, every
now and again, some of that irrational spirit of sadness which,

when over-indulged, leads men to madness and self-destruction. Since I have loved you, I have banished it utterly. Do not speak under the influence of that spirit until you have thought whether you, too, can banish it.

SYBIL

I have tried, but it will not be banished.

RODNEY

Try again, Sybil, if you love me. If you do not——.

SYBIL

If I do not love you, I love no one upon earth. (*Sits quietly looking into his face.*)

RODNEY

I believe it. I believe it as I believe in my own love for you. I trust your love implicitly, Sybil. So, come, return with me to the mainland and let us make an early marriage.

SYBIL

(*Strangely as if in a trance*)
No, I cannot do so.

RODNEY

(*Smiling*)
Is that melancholy fiend too much for you? Sybil, Sybil, Sybil.

SYBIL

(*Snapping out of it*)
You are noble, good, and great. I find myself unfit to be your wife.

RODNEY

Don't quibble, Sybil.

SYBIL

(*Falling to her knees*)
I beg your pardon on my knees.

RODNEY

I grant no such pardon. Do you think I will let you go from me in that way? No, love, if you are ill, I will wait till your illness is gone by; and if you will let me, I will be your nurse.

SYBIL

I am not ill. (*Her hands stray unconsciously to her breasts and yoni.*)

RODNEY

Not ill with any defined sickness. You do not shake with ague, nor does your head rack you with aching; but yet you must be ill to try to put an end to all that has passed between us for no reason at all.

SYBIL

(*Standing suddenly*)
Mr. Parker——

RODNEY

(*Deeply hurt*)
If you will call me so, I will think it only part of your malady.

SYBIL

Mr. Parker, I can only hope that you will take me at my word. I beg your forgiveness and that our engagement may be over.

RODNEY

No, no, no, Sybil, never with my consent. I would marry you to-morrow, tomorrow or next month, or the month after. But if it cannot be so, then I will wait . . . unless . . . there is some other man. Yes, that and that alone would convince me. Only your marriage to another man could convince me that I had lost you. (*He kisses her on the lips.*)

SYBIL

(*Turning away and surreptitiously wiping away the kiss. Smiling*)
I cannot convince you in that way.
(*Prissily wipes his lips on a lace hankie, carefully folds it and replaces it in his breast pocket.*)

RODNEY

(*Relieved*)
You will convince me in no other. Have you spoken to your uncle of this yet?

SYBIL

Not as yet.

RODNEY

(*Anxiously*)

Do not tell him. It is possible you may have to unsay what you have said.

SYBIL

No, it is not possible.

RODNEY

I think you must leave this island. The foggy air is no good for you. You need the sun, I think. You've grown so pale. You need a change.

SYBIL

Yes, you treat me as though I were partly silly and partly insane, but it is not so. The change you speak of should be in my nature and in yours.

(RODNEY *shakes his head and smiles. Aside*)

He is perfect! Oh, that he were less perfect!

RODNEY

I'll leave you alone for twenty-four hours to think this over. I advise you not to tell your uncle. But if you do tell him, let me know that you have done so.

SYBIL

Why that?

RODNEY

(*Pressing her hand*)

Good night, dearest, dearest Sybil.

(*Exit*)

ACT II, SCENE 2: SYBIL, BLUEBEARD

BLUEBEARD

What, Sybil, are you not in bed yet?

SYBIL

Not yet, Uncle Khanazar.

BLUEBEARD

So Rodney Parker has been here. I smell his cologne in the air.

SYBIL

Yes, he has been here.

BLUEBEARD

Is anything the matter, Sybil?

SYBIL

No, Uncle Khanazar, nothing is the matter.

BLUEBEARD

He has not made himself disagreeable, has he?

SYBIL

Not in the least. He never does anything wrong. He may defy man or woman to find fault with him.

BLUEBEARD

So that's it, is it? He is just a shade too good. I have noticed that myself. But it's a fault on the right side.

SYBIL

(*Deeply troubled*)
It's no fault, Uncle. If there be any fault, it is not with him.

BLUEBEARD

Being too good is not one of my faults . . . I am very bad.

SYBIL

(*Starry-eyed*)
Are you bad? Are you really bad?

BLUEBEARD

When I am good I am very, very good; but when I'm bad, I'm not bad. I'm good at being bad . . . I do it well.

SYBIL

(*Again as if in a trance*)

Tonight, at dinner, your words carried me away. (*Their lips almost meet but she yawns, breaking the spell, and he yawns sympathetically.*) But I am yawning and tired and I will go to bed. Good night, Uncle Khanazar.

BLUEBEARD

Good night, Sybil. (*Aside*) And rest, for a new life awaits you! (*Exit Sybil.*)

ACT II, SCENE 3: BLUEBEARD, MISS CUBBIDGE

MISS CUBBIDGE

Oh, excuse me, I didn't realize that the parlor was preoccupied. (*Starts out.*)

BLUEBEARD

Come in, Miss Cubbidge. I do not desire to be alone.

MISS CUBBIDGE

No, I think I'd better go and leave you to your own devices.

BLUEBEARD

Please stay. I think I know what you are thinking.

MISS CUBBIDGE

I'll do my own thinking, thank you, and my own existing.

BLUEBEARD

Miss Cubbidge, I don't think you like me.

MISS CUBBIDGE

I can sympathize with neither your virtues nor your vices.

BLUEBEARD

What would you say if I told you that I need a wife?

MISS CUBBIDGE

I do not believe in sudden marriages.

BLUEBEARD

People often say that marriage is an important thing and should be much thought of in advance, and marrying people are cautioned that there are many who marry in haste and repent at leisure. I am not sure, however, that marriage may not be pondered over too much; nor do I feel certain that the leisurely repentance does not as often follow the leisurely marriages as it does the rapid ones. Why, you yourself might marry suddenly and never regret it at all.

MISS CUBBIDGE

My health might fail me under the effects of so great a change made so late in life.

BLUEBEARD

Miss Cubbidge, how can you live without love?

MISS CUBBIDGE

It is my nature to love many persons a little if I've loved few or none passionately, Baron Bluebeard.

BLUEBEARD

Please, call me Khanazar, and may I call you——

MISS CUBBIDGE

(*Shyly*) Flora.

BLUEBEARD

Ah, Flora! It is only possible to be alone with you in nature. All other women destroy the landscape. You alone become part of it.

MISS CUBBIDGE

(*Aside*) Could any woman resist such desuetude? (*Giggling*) Why Baron Blue——

BLUEBEARD

(*Interrupting*) Khanazar.

MISS CUBBIDGE

(*Giggling*) Khanazar.

BLUEBEARD

Flora, you are part of the trees, the sky, you are the dominating goddess of nature. Come to me, Flora, you lovely little fauna, you.

MISS CUBBIDGE

(*Recovering herself*) Mr. Bluebeard, I shall certainly not come to you.

BLUEBEARD

(*Suddenly*) Look, do you see what it is I am holding in my hand?

MISS CUBBIDGE

(*Alarmed*) A revolver?

BLUEBEARD

Take it, press it to my temple and shoot, or say you will be mine.

MISS CUBBIDGE

(*Frightened with the revolver in her hand*) I can't shoot you but I cannot be yours either.

BLUEBEARD

It is one or the other. Blow my brains out. I will not live another day without you.

MISS CUBBIDGE

Recuperate your gun at once. It isn't loaded, is it?

BLUEBEARD

Pull the trigger! There are worse things awaiting man than death.

MISS CUBBIDGE

To what do you collude?

BLUEBEARD

All tortures do not matter . . . only not to be dead before one dies. I will not live without your love. (*He pretends to weep.*)

MISS CUBBIDGE

Don't weep, Baron Bluebeard . . . er . . . Khanazar. 'Tisn't manly. Try to be more malevolent.

BLUEBEARD

Marry me, marry me, Flora, and make me the happiest man on earth.

MISS CUBBIDGE

How can I marry you?

BLUEBEARD

(*Hypnotically*) Easily. Just repeat after me—I, Flora Cubbidge . . .

MISS CUBBIDGE

I Flora Cubbidge . . .

BLUEBEARD

Do solemnly swear . . .

MISS CUBBIDGE

Do solemnly swear . . .

BLUEBEARD

To take this man Baron Khanazar von Bluebeard as my lawful wedded husband . . .

MISS CUBBIDGE

To take this man Baron Khanazar von Bluebeard as my lawful wedded husband . . .

BLUEBEARD

To love, honor, and obey; for better or for worse, for richer or poorer; in sickness and in health; from this day forward . . .
(*He begins to undress her.*)

MISS CUBBIDGE

To love, honor, and obey; for better or for worse, for richer or for poorer; in sickness and in health; from this day forward . . .

BLUEBEARD

Until death us do part.

MISS CUBBIDGE

Till death us do part.

BLUEBEARD

(*Licentiously*) I may now kiss the bride.

MISS CUBBIDGE

What about your vows?

BLUEBEARD

Don't you trust me?

MISS CUBBIDGE

I do. I do. I do.
(*They begin to breathe heavily as they undress slowly. They move toward each other, wearing only their shoes, socks, stockings, and her merry widow. They clinch and roll about on the floor, making animal noises.*)

BLUEBEARD

Was ever woman in this manner wooed? Was ever woman in this manner won?

MISS CUBBIDGE

(*Aside*) There are things that happen in a day that would take a lifetime to explain.
(*There follows a scene of unprecedented eroticism in which* MISS CUBBIDGE *gives herself voluptuously to* BARON VON BLUEBEARD.)

BLUEBEARD

In my right pants pocket you will find a key. It is the key to my laboratory. Take it. And swear to me that you will never use it.

MISS CUBBIDGE

I swear! I must return to Sybil at once. She sometimes wakes up in a phalanx.

BLUEBEARD

Won't you sleep here tonight, with me?

MISS CUBBIDGE

No, I can't sleep in this bed. It has cold wet spots in it. Good night, Baron—husband.

BLUEBEARD

Good night, Miss Cubbidge.

MISS CUBBIDGE

Please don't mention our hymeneals to Sybil. I must find the right words to immure the news to her.

BLUEBEARD

Believe me, I'll confess to none of it.

MISS CUBBIDGE

Thank you. I believe that you have transformed me to a part of the dirigible essence. You have carried me aloft and I believe I am with Beatrice of whom Dante has sung in his immortal onus. Good night. (*Exit*)

ACT II, SCENE 4: BLUEBEARD

BLUEBEARD

It is a lucky thing for me that I did not take the vows or this marriage might be binding on me as it is on her. I cannot sleep tonight. There is work to be done in my laboratory. Good night, Miss Cubbidge, wherever you are. And good night to all the ladies who do be living in this world. Good night, ladies. Good night, sweet ladies.

ACT II, SCENE 5: RODNEY PARKER, LAMIA THE LEOPARD WOMAN

(*Entering surreptitiously*)

LAMIA

Shhh! Take care or the deaf one . . . she hears nothing of what you shout and overhears everything that you whisper.

RODNEY

What is it that you wish to tell me?

LAMIA

He is mad, I tell you, mad! And he will stop at nothing.

RODNEY

Who?

LAMIA

The Bluebeard—Khanazar. If you love that girl, convince her to leave this island at once.

RODNEY

But why?

LAMIA

Look at me. I was a woman once!

RODNEY

But you are a woman. So very much a woman. You are all woman.

LAMIA

No, no, never again will I bear the name of woman. I was changed in the House of Pain. I was a victim of his sex-switch tricks and his queer quackery.

RODNEY

Quackery—Sybil told me that he was a brilliant physiologist.

LAMIA

Even in Denmark they called him a quack. He wasn't satisfied with sex switches. He wants to create a third genital organ attached between the legs of a third sex. I am an experiment that failed.

RODNEY

(*Seductively*) You look like a woman to me.

LAMIA

I wish I could be a woman to you. (*Aside*) Perhaps when Bluebeard is defeated I will. (*Aloud*) He uses the same technique on all his victims. First he married me. Then he gave me the key to his laboratory, forbidding me to ever use it. Then he waited for curiosity to get the better of me. All women are curious.

RODNEY

Men marry because they are tired, women because they are curious.

LAMIA

Both are disappointed.

RODNEY

Does he ever use men for his experiments?

LAMIA

At first he did. Sheemish was the first. But when that experiment failed, he turned to women. We are all experiments that have failed. He has made us the slaves of this island.

RODNEY

(*Realizing*) The Island of Lost Love.

LAMIA

Save yourself and save the woman you love. Take the advice of the Leopard Woman and go.

RODNEY

How did a nice girl like you get mixed up in a mess like this?

LAMIA

I was entertaining in a small bistro night club called the Wild Cat's Pussy. I was billed as Lamia the Leopard Woman. It was only fourteen beans a day but I needed the scratch. I sang this song:

> Where is my Leopard Lover?
> When will I spot the cat for me?
> I'm wild when I'm under cover.
> Where is the cat who will tame me?
> Where is my wild cat lover?
> Leopard hunting is all the rage.
> Where is my wildcat lover?
> I'm free but I want to be caged.
> If you dig this feline
> Better make a beeline.
> I've got the spots, to give men the red-hots.
> Where is my wild leopard hunter?
> I'm game if you'll play my game.
> Where is that runt cunt hunter?
> I'm wild but I want to be tame.

After I sang my set he signaled and I sat at his table. He ordered a Tiger's Milk Flip. He was into health food. No woman can resist him, I tell you.

RODNEY

He seduced you?

LAMIA

Worst, worst, a thousand times worst. I didn't know if I was coming or going. He has a way with women.

RODNEY

Sybil, great Scott, no. Either you're jesting or I'm dreaming! Sybil with another man? I'll go mad.

LAMIA

His idealism . . . his intensity . . . the Clairol blue of his beard! His words carried me away. He had a strange look in his eyes. I felt strange inside. He and I were total strangers! If you love her, get her off this island before it is too late.

RODNEY

No, not Sybil. I am ashamed to listen to you. Yet she admires him so . . . I have gone mad!

LAMIA

He came closer . . . closer. Submit, he said, in the name of science and the dark arts. Submit. Submit.

RODNEY

(*In a panic*) Sybil is with him now. You are lying.

LAMIA

If you think that I am lying, look. (*She lifts her sarong.*) Look what he did to the Leopard Woman's pussy.

RODNEY

Eeeccht! Is that a mound of Venus or a penis?

LAMIA

(*Perplexed*) I wish I knew.

RODNEY

No, no, he can't do that to Sybil. I must kill him. What am I saying? This is madness. But what consolation is sanity to me? The most faithful of women is after all only a woman. I'll kill you. No, I am mad.

LAMIA

Go and stop him. Save her from the fate that has befallen me.

RODNEY

I will kill myself! No, I will kill her! Oh God, it is impossible. I have gone mad! (*He runs out.*)

ACT II, SCENE 6: LAMIA

LAMIA

(*Sings*)

I've lost my leopard lover—
A world of made is not a world of born.
Bluebeard will soon discover
Hell hath no fury like a woman scorned.

ACT II, SCENE 7: LAMIA, SHEEMISH

LAMIA

(*Calling after him*) Rodney! Rodney! Rodney! He is gone.

SHEEMISH

(*Appearing out of the shadows*) Are you afraid of being alone?

LAMIA

(*Fanning herself with a leopard fan*) How stifling it is! There must
be a storm coming.

SHEEMISH

I heard you telling the secrets of the island to Rodney Parker.
(*Spits.*)

LAMIA

(*Furiously*) Sneaking little eavesdropper! How dare you?

SHEEMISH

I love you.

LAMIA

(*Fanning herself*) What awful weather! This is the second day of it.

SHEEMISH

Every day I walk four miles to see you and four miles back and
meet with nothing but indifference from you.

LAMIA

Your love touches me but I can't return it, that's all.

SHEEMISH

(*Accusing*) But you came four miles here to tell the secrets of the island to Rodney Parker. (*Spits.*)

LAMIA

You are a bore.

SHEEMISH

(*Twisting her arm*) You are in love with him!

LAMIA

(*In pain*) Yes, it's true. If you must know. I do love him. I do! (*Aside*) For all the good it will do me. He loves Sybil.

SHEEMISH

(*Taking her in his arms roughly and humping her like a dog*) I want you.

LAMIA

(*Fighting him*) You stupid, vulgar, deformed nincompoop! Do you think I could ever fall for such a one as you? You are as ugly as sin itself. Besides, our genitals would never fit together.

SHEEMISH

(*Groping her*) We can work it out.

LAMIA

Evil cretin! God will punish you. (*She breaks away.*)

SHEEMISH

God will not punish the lunatic soul. He knows the powers of evil are too great for us with weak minds. Marry me!

LAMIA

I'd rather blow a bald baboon with B.O. and bunions than marry a monster! (*Exit* LAMIA *in a huff*)

SHEEMISH

(*Following her*) Lamia, be reasonable!

ACT II, SCENE 8: BLUEBEARD, SYBIL

(SYBIL *is seated at the spinette. She plays dramatic music.* BLUE-
BEARD *moves slowly, approaching her from behind. His eyes are
ablaze. She senses his approach. She plays with greater emphasis.
Her shoulders are bare. He begins kissing them. The music she is
playing rises to a crescendo. She stops playing suddenly.*)

SYBIL

This is ridiculous!

BLUEBEARD

(*Swinging a key on a chain back and forth before her eyes as
though hypnotizing her*) Here is the key to my laboratory. Take it
and swear to me that you will never use it.

SYBIL

(*In a trance*) Yes, master!

BLUEBEARD

Ah, my darling, my own one. You will be my wife.

SYBIL

Yes, Master!

BLUEBEARD

You will be the loveliest of all wives. (*Aside*) When I am through
with you.

SYBIL

Yes, Master.

BLUEBEARD

I am about to perform the magnum opus. The creation of a third
genital organ will perhaps lead to the creation of a third sex. You
will be my ultimate masterpiece of vivisection! (*He kisses her.*)

ACT II, SCENE 9: BLUEBEARD, SYBIL, MISS CUBBIDGE

MISS CUBBIDGE

(*Entering*) Sir, what are you doing with Sybil there? Are you making love to her, too?

BLUEBEARD

(*Aside to* MISS CUBBIDGE) No, no, on the contrary, she throws herself at me shamelessly, although I tell her that I am married to you.

SYBIL

What is it you want, Miss Cubbidge?

BLUEBEARD

(*Aside to* SYBIL) She is jealous of my speaking to you. She wants me to marry her, but I tell her it is you I must have.

MISS CUBBIDGE

(*Incredulous*) What, Sybil?

BLUEBEARD

(*Aside to* MISS CUBBIDGE) She won't listen to reason. The impressionable little creature is infatuated with me.

SYBIL

(*Incredulous*) What, Miss Cubbidge?

BLUEBEARD

(*Aside to* SYBIL) She won't listen to reason. The desperate old maid has got her claws out for me.

MISS CUBBIDGE

Do you . . .

BLUEBEARD

(*To* MISS CUBBIDGE) Your words would be in vain.

SYBIL

I'd . . .

BLUEBEARD

(*To* SYBIL) All you can say to her will be in vain.

MISS CUBBIDGE

Truly . . .

BLUEBEARD

(*Aside to* MISS CUBBIDGE) She's obstinate as the devil.

SYBIL

I think...

BLUEBEARD

(*Aside to* SYBIL) Say nothing to her, she's a madwoman.

SYBIL

No, no, I must speak to her.

MISS CUBBIDGE

I'll hear her reasons.

SYBIL

What...

BLUEBEARD

(*Aside to* SYBIL) I'll lay you a wager she tells you she's my wife.

MISS CUBBIDGE

I...

BLUEBEARD

(*Aside to* MISS CUBBIDGE) I'll bet you she says I'm going to marry her.

MISS CUBBIDGE

Sybil, as your chaperone I must intercept. It is past your bedtime.

SYBIL

Dear Miss Cubbidge, I have been to bed but I got up because I have insomnia.

MISS CUBBIDGE

So I see. Sybil, I must ask you to leave me alone with *my* husband. The baron and I married ourselves in an improvident ceremony earlier this evening.

BLUEBEARD

(*Aside to* SYBIL) What did I tell you? She's out of her mind.

SYBIL

Dear *Miss* Cubbidge, are you sure you are feeling all right? Are you ill?

MISS CUBBIDGE

(*Indignantly*) I've never felt more supine in my life. Sybil, it does not become a young *unmarried* woman to meddle in the affairs of others.

BLUEBEARD

(*Aside to* MISS CUBBIDGE) She thinks she is going to marry me.

SYBIL

It is not fit, *Miss* Cubbidge, to be jealous because the baron speaks to me. I am going to be his wife.

BLUEBEARD

(*Aside to* MISS CUBBIDGE) What did I tell you?

SYBIL

Baron, did you not promise to marry me?

BLUEBEARD

(*Aside to* SYBIL) Of course, my darling.

MISS CUBBIDGE

Baron, am I not your wife, the Baroness von Bluebeard?

BLUEBEARD

(*Aside to* MISS CUBBIDGE) How could you ask such a question?

SYBIL

(*Aside to the audience*) How sure the old goat is of herself!

MISS CUBBIDGE

(*Aside to the audience*) The baron is right, how pigheaded the little bitch is!

SYBIL

We must know at once the truth.

MISS CUBBIDGE

We must have the matter abnegated.

SYBIL *and* MISS CUBBIDGE

Which of us will it be, Baron?

BLUEBEARD

(*Addressing himself to both of them*) What would you have me say? Each of you knows in your heart of hearts whether or not I have made love to you. Let her that I truly love laugh at what the other says. Actions speak louder than words. (*Aside to* CUBBIDGE) Let her believe what she will. (*Aside to* SYBIL) Let her flatter herself in her senile imagination. (*Aside to* CUBBIDGE) I adore you. (*Aside to* SYBIL) I am yours alone. (*Aside to* CUBBIDGE) One night with you is worth a thousand with other women. (*Aside to* SYBIL) All faces are ugly in your presence. (*Aloud*) If you will excuse me, there is work to be done in my laboratory. I do not wish to be disturbed. Good night, ladies. (*Exits.*)

ACT II, SCENE 10: SYBIL, CUBBIDGE, SHEEMISH

SHEEMISH

(*Appearing out of the shadows*) Poor ladies! I can't bear to see you led to your destruction. Take my advice, return to the mainland.

SYBIL

I am she he loves, however.

MISS CUBBIDGE

It is to me he's married.

SHEEMISH

My master is an evil sadist. He will do you irreparable harm as he has done to others. He wants to marry the whole female sex so that he can take them to his laboratory and . . .

ACT II, SCENE 11: SYBIL, MISS CUBBIDGE, SHEEMISH, BLUEBEARD

BLUEBEARD

(*Popping back in*) One more word . . .

SHEEMISH

My master is no evil sadist. He means you no harm. If you ladies think he can marry the whole female sex, you've got another think coming. He is a man of his word . . . there he is, ask him yourself.

BLUEBEARD

What were you saying, Sheemish?

SHEEMISH

(*Aside to* BLUEBEARD) You know how catty women are. I was defending you . . . as best I could.

BLUEBEARD

(*To* SYBIL *and* MISS CUBBIDGE) She who holds the key to my heart holds the key to my laboratory. (*Exit*)

ACT II, SCENE 12: MISS CUBBIDGE, SYBIL, SHEEMISH

MISS CUBBIDGE

(*Aside*) Then he is my husband for he gave me the key.

SYBIL

(*Aside*) The key, I have the key! It is me he loves after all. (*Loud*) Good night, Madam. If you have the key, you are his wife.

MISS CUBBIDGE

Good night, Sybil. If it is to you he gave the key, you are his betrothed.
(*They both exit laughing.*)

ACT II, SCENE 13: SHEEMISH, MRS. MAGGOT

MRS. MAGGOT

(*Entering excitedly*) I overheard laughter. It is the first time laughter has been heard on this island in nineteen years. Who was laughing? Who is it that knows a single moment of happiness on the Island of Lost Love?

SHEEMISH

It was not with joy you heard them laughing, but with scorn. Bluebeard has got the young woman and her governess fighting like cats in the alley.

MRS. MAGGOT

I thought they always swore by each other.

SHEEMISH

It's at each other that they swear now. He's married both of them!

ACT II, SCENE 14: SHEEMISH, MRS. MAGGOT, SYBIL

MRS. MAGGOT

Look, here comes the young one carrying a candle, her long black hair unloosed, her lips slightly parted. A lovely flower that blooms for just one hour.

SHEEMISH

A sleepwalker, a somnambulist.

MRS. MAGGOT

Her eyes are open.

SHEEMISH

But their sense is shut. I believe he has mesmerized her. Let us conceal ourselves. I will keep my eyes peeled.

MRS. MAGGOT

And I my ears. I can't wait to find out what happens next!
(MRS. MAGGOT *and* SHEEMISH *hide.*)

SYBIL

I can control my curiosity no longer. I must see what lies behind the door to my lover's laboratory. I know he has forbade me ever to use this key. But how can I stand the suspense? Should not a woman take an interest in her husband's work?

MRS. MAGGOT

Shouldn't we try to save her?

SHEEMISH

Would you prefer to take her place in the House of Pain?

MRS. MAGGOT

No, no, not the House of Pain!
(SYBIL *unlocks the door and opens it.* BLUEBEARD *is discovered waiting for her.*)

ACT II, SCENE 15: SYBIL, BLUEBEARD, SHEEMISH, MRS. MAGGOT

BLUEBEARD

I trust you have kept your coming here a secret.

SYBIL

Baron!

BLUEBEARD

Curiosity killed the cat. (*Aside*) But it may have a salutary effect on the pussy. (*Aloud*) Look into my eyes, my little kitten, and repeat after me. I, Sybil, do solemnly swear to take this man Baron Khanazar von Bluebeard as my lawful wedded husband.

SYBIL

I, Sybil, do solemnly swear to take this man Baron Khanazar von Bluebeard as my lawful wedded husband.

MRS. MAGGOT

(*Moving her ear trumpet like an antenna*) I hear someone coming. Just in time! Rodney Parker will save her from the fate worse than death!

SHEEMISH

(*Aside*) My rival, Rodney Parker! Now I will have my revenge. (*To* MRS. MAGGOT) Detain him!

BLUEBEARD

To love honor and obey . . .

MRS. MAGGOT

Oh, cruel! Don't ask me that. I won't do it. Anything but that.

SYBIL

To love, honor, and obey.

SHEEMISH

Even the House of Pain? The test tube! Master, Master . . .

BLUEBEARD

For better or for worse; for richer or for poorer . . .

MRS. MAGGOT
I'll do it.

BLUEBEARD
In sickness and in health . . . from this day forward . . .

SYBIL
For better or for worse; for richer or for poorer . . . in sickness and in health, from this day forward . . .

ACT II, SCENE 16: SHEEMISH, MRS. MAGGOT, SYBIL, BLUEBEARD, RODNEY

(RODNEY *rushes onto the stage, mad.*)

RODNEY
Where is he? Where is he?
(SHEEMISH *roughly throws* MRS. MAGGOT *into* RODNEY.)

MRS. MAGGOT
Eh?

BLUEBEARD
Until death us do part.

SYBIL
Until death us do part.
(BLUEBEARD *blows out the candle and kisses* SYBIL.)

RODNEY
(*Shaking* MRS. MAGGOT *violently*) Where is Bluebeard?

MRS. MAGGOT
Eh?

RODNEY
Aagh! (*He throws* MRS. MAGGOT *aside.*)

BLUEBEARD
(*Pressing* SYBIL *to him, demented*) And now, ye demons, ere this night goes by I swear I'll conjure or I'll die!

RODNEY
(*Sees* BLUEBEARD.) Damn you, Bluebeard! Damn your soul!

SYBIL

Rodney! Ah! (*She faints.* BLUEBEARD *catches her and quickly carries her into the laboratory.* MRS. MAGGOT *trips* RODNEY, *then* SHEEMISH *and* MRS. MAGGOT *follow, slamming the door in* RODNEY's *face and locking it.* RODNEY *beats on the door and shouts.*)

ACT II, SCENE 17: RODNEY

RODNEY

Open the door, you pervert! You invert, you necrophiliac! Open up! Bluebeard! Bluebeard! BLUEBEARD!
(*Curtain*)

ACT III

SCENE 1: BLUEBEARD, SYBIL, SHEEMISH, MRS. MAGGOT

(*There is no lapse of time between* ACT II *and* ACT III. *The scene changes to the interior of* BLUEBEARD's *laboratory. Enter* BLUEBEARD *carrying* SYBIL *in his arms. He walks with a hesitant step, looking from side to side, his cheeks quivering, contracting, and expanding, his eyes intently focused.* SHEEMISH *and* MRS. MAGGOT *scurry about taking care of last-minute details. There is an air of great anticipation.*)

RODNEY'S VOICE

(*Offstage*) Bluebeard! Bluebeard! Bluebeard! Open this door or I'll break it down! (*Loud knocking*) Bluebeard!

BLUEBEARD

(*Laughing*) That door is lined with double-duty quilted zinc. No mortal arm can break it down. Even a man whose heart is pure and has the strength of ten could not break it down. But a delicate girl with just enough strength to lift a powder puff to her white bosom can open it . . . if she has the key.
(*More loud knocking*)

BLUEBEARD

Sheemish, take the girl to the operating room, bathe her, and prepare her for surgery.

SHEEMISH

No, Master, please, don't ask me to do that. Anything but that.

BLUEBEARD

And be gentle with her, I want no marks left on her lily-white body. If you so much as bruise her, you and I will make an appointment for a meeting here in the House of Pain, hum?

SHEEMISH

No, no, not the House of Pain! (*He carries* SYBIL *off.*)

ACT III, SCENE 2: BLUEBEARD, MRS. MAGGOT

BLUEBEARD

Mrs. Maggot, bring in the frog, the serpent, and the hearts, hands, eyes, feet but most of all the blood and genitals of the little children. Bring in the serpent first. I need it to trace a magic circle.

MRS. MAGGOT

Eh?

BLUEBEARD

Perhaps your hearing would be improved by a vacation. (*He covers her ears and whispers.*) In the House of Pain.

MRS. MAGGOT

No, no, not the House of Pain! (*She quickly hands him a bottle of blood and a paintbrush.*)

BLUEBEARD

(*Laughs.*) Thank you. Now leave me. Go and assist Sheemish. (MRS. MAGGOT *lingers.*) Is there something you want, Maggot?

MRS. MAGGOT

Yes, Master.

BLUEBEARD

Well, what is it?

MRS. MAGGOT

The lapis-lazuli locket the girl is wearing. May I have it?

BLUEBEARD

Yes, take it, scavenger!

MRS. MAGGOT

Do you think she will mind?

BLUEBEARD

No, she will not mind. She will remember nothing of her past life when the operation wears off. Now get out. (*Kicks her in the ass.*)

MRS. MAGGOT

Thank you, thank you, Master. (*Exit*)

ACT III, SCENE 3: BLUEBEARD

BLUEBEARD

(*Inscribing a circle in blood*)

> Now by the powers that only seem to be,
> With crystal sword and flame I conjure thee.
> I kiss the book; oh, come to me!
> Goddess of night: Hecate!

(*The sound of a gong is heard and a high-pitched cock crow that sometimes breaks from the most refined throat.* HECATE *appears in a flash of light and a puff of smoke.*)

ACT III, SCENE 4: BLUEBEARD, HECATE

HECATE

(*Wearing a blue beard*) Who summons the Slave of Sin?

BLUEBEARD

(*Laughing quietly aside*) Not for nothing have I worshiped the Dark One. (*To* HECATE) I called, Hecate, I, Khanazar von Bluebeard.

HECATE

How dare you? Don't you know that torture is the price you pay for summoning the Slave of Sin?

BLUEBEARD

All tortures do not matter: only not to be dead before one dies.

HECATE

What is it you want of me, my fool?

BLUEBEARD

Look, here are my books written in blood, there my apparatus. For nineteen long years I've waited and worked for this moment. In there, on the operating table, swathed in bandages, a new sex, waiting to live again in a genital I made with my own hands! (*Maniacally*) With my own hands!

HECATE

What about your own genitals?

BLUEBEARD

The male genital organ is but a faint relic and shadow, a sign that has become detached from its substance and lives on as an exquisite ornament.

HECATE

And what do you want of me, my fool?

BLUEBEARD

Good fortune.

HECATE

Do not seek for good fortune. You carry on your forehead the sign of the elect.

> Seek, Probe! Details unfold.
> Let nature's secret be retold.

If ever you mean to try, you should try now. (*She vanishes.*) (*There is a roll of thunder. Dramatic music from Bartok's* Castle of Bluebeard *begins to swell.* BLUEBEARD *dons surgeon's coat, gloves, and mask and enters the House of Pain.* MRS. MAGGOT *and* SHEEMISH *close the doors after him. There is the sound of loud knocking at the door.*)

ACT III, SCENE 5: MRS. MAGGOT, SHEEMISH

MRS. MAGGOT

Look, Sheemish, the lapis-lazuli locket. The master said I could have it. Pretty, ain't it?

SHEEMISH

What's with you and that locket?
(*A bloodcurdling scream issues from the laboratory. We may be sure that it is* SYBIL *writhing under the vivisector's knife. Both* SHEEMISH *and* MRS. MAGGOT *freeze for a moment in terror and clutch their own genitals in sympathy.*)

SHEEMISH

Listen, he has begun the operation.
(*There is another bloodcurdling scream. Again* MRS. MAGGOT *and* SHEEMISH *freeze and clutch their genitals.*)

RODNEY'S VOICE

(*Off*) What are you doing in there, you monster? (*He beats loudly on the door.* SYBIL *screams again off.*)

RODNEY'S VOICE

(*Off*) Open the door or I'll tear your heart out! (*Knocks loudly.*)

ACT III, SCENE 6: BLUEBEARD, MAGGOT, SHEEMISH

BLUEBEARD

(*Rushes on.*) The test tube! I need the test tube. Everything depends upon this sticky liquid now.
(*He snatches the test tube and hurries back to his work.* MRS. MAGGOT *and* SHEEMISH *exchange a guilty look. Another scream is heard. Suddenly* MISS CUBBIDGE *and* RODNEY *burst into the room.* MISS CUBBIDGE *brandishes the key.*)

ACT III, SCENE 7: MRS. MAGGOT, SHEEMISH, RODNEY, MISS CUBBIDGE

MISS CUBBIDGE

I could control my curiosity no longer.

RODNEY

I'll see to it that he goes to the guillotine. That will shorten him by a head.

MISS CUBBIDGE

He robbed me of my maidenhead. So it's not his head I'll see cut off him! I want him decalced.
(*Another scream is heard.*)

RODNEY

Let me at him. I'll maim the bloody bugger.

SHEEMISH

Don't be a fool. The girl is on the operating table. If you interfere now, she'll lose her life.

MISS CUBBIDGE

(*Aside*) With Sybil out of the way, the baron will be mine alone. (*Aloud*) We must save her, no matter what the danger.
(SYBIL *screams again.*)

RODNEY

I can't stand it. I'm going in there.

SHEEMISH

Are you crazy?

RODNEY

Yes, I'm crazy.

SHEEMISH

Can't you understand that we are powerless against a supernatural enemy?

ACT III, SCENE 8: BLUEBEARD, MISS CUBBIDGE, RODNEY, MRS. MAGGOT, SHEEMISH

BLUEBEARD

The time has come. The final stage of transmutation must be completed. Mars, god of war, and Venus, goddess of love, are conjunct in the twelfth house, the house of change and transformation.

Scorpio, which rules surgery and the genitalia, is at the zenith. This is the horoscope I have been waiting for. The signs are in perfect aspect. The third genital will be born under the most beneficent stars that twinkle in the heavens. Sheemish, bring in the girl, or should I say "subject"?

MISS CUBBIDGE

Khanazar, you have deceived me. I——

BLUEBEARD

Quiet! I have no time to talk to an idiot.

RODNEY

If anything goes wrong with this experiment, I swear I'll kill you.

BLUEBEARD

I have already sworn upon the Cross to enter into this experiment for life and for death.
(SHEEMISH *carries on* SYBIL, *who is wrapped in bandages like a mummy.*)

ACT III, SCENE 9: RODNEY, SYBIL, SHEEMISH, CUBBIDGE, MAGGOT, BLUEBEARD

BLUEBEARD

Gently, gently! Be careful, you fool.

MISS CUBBIDGE

(*Gasps*) Is she . . . is she . . . dead?

BLUEBEARD

(*Listens to* SYBIL's *heart and genital through stethoscope.*) No, she is not dead. She's just resting, waiting for new life to come.
(*There is the sound of thunder and flashes of lightning.* MRS. MAGGOT *and* SHEEMISH *light candles, incense. There are science-fiction lighting effects.*)

RODNEY

Is it a new life or a monster you are creating, Baron Prevert?

BLUEBEARD

The word is "pervert." I believe in this monster, as you call it.

RODNEY

So this is the House of Pain.

BLUEBEARD

How do you know when you unlock any door in life that you are not entering a House of Pain? I have thought nothing of pain. Years of studying nature have made me remorseless as nature itself. All we feel is pain. But we must take risks if we are to progress.

RODNEY

How could you? How could you?

BLUEBEARD

Do you know what it feels like to be God, Parker?

RODNEY

(*Spits in* BLUEBEARD's *face.*) I spit in your face.

BLUEBEARD

Do you think that the envenomed spittle of five hundred little gentlemen of your mark, piled one on top of the other, could succeed in so much as slobbering the tips of my august toes?
(*He turns his back on* RODNEY *and with the assistance of* SHEEMISH *begins unwinding the bandages that envelop* SYBIL. *When she is completely nude except for her fuck-me pumps, the genital begins to move.*)

BLUEBEARD

Look, it's moving. It's alive. It's moving. It's alive! It's alive!
(SYBIL *moves like the bride of Frankenstein with stiff, jerking movements of the head and neck. First she looks at* SHEEMISH *and screams with horror, then she looks at* BLUEBEARD *and screams with horror, then she looks at her new genital and growls with displeasure.*)

ACT III, SCENE 10: LAMIA, RODNEY, SYBIL, MAGGOT,
SHEEMISH, CUBBIDGE, BLUEBEARD

LAMIA

(*Enters and crawls toward* SYBIL *with catlike stealth and examines the third genital.*)

Now no man will ever want her! Rodney is mine.
(*She leaps toward* RODNEY. BLUEBEARD *fires on her and she falls.*)

BLUEBEARD

I told you never to come to this side of the island again.

SHEEMISH

(*Kneeling over* LAMIA's *body*) You killed the woman I love.

BLUEBEARD

(*Going to her also, feeling her pulse*) Woman? I wouldn't say she was a woman. She was a leopard, a wild cat. I couldn't make my leopard love me.

SHEEMISH

You killed the woman I love. Now you must die. (*He moves toward* BLUEBEARD *threateningly.*)

BLUEBEARD

(*Backing away*) No, Sheemish, no! Remember the House of Pain!

SHEEMISH

I no longer fear pain. My heart is broken. (*He seizes* BLUEBEARD *by the throat.*)

RODNEY

(*Looking at* SYBIL's *genital*) No man will ever want her?

MISS CUBBIDGE

(*To* MRS. MAGGOT) What are you doing with the lapis-lazuli locket? Sybil's mother gave it to her the night she died when the terrible fire . . . Sybil's real mother had a strawberry birth mark on her left kneecap.

RODNEY

I need never be jealous again!

MISS CUBBIDGE

Margaret, Margaret Maggot? Maggie!
(SHEEMISH *releases* BLUEBEARD *in amazement.*)

MRS. MAGGOT

The fire? Margaret Maggot? It's all coming back to me. I am Maggie Maggot. (*Turning on* BLUEBEARD) What have you suffered for that child that you dare to tear her from me without pity? Sybil is my daughter. I am her real mother. If you give me back my child, I shall live for her alone. I shall know how to tame my nature to be worthy of her always. My heart will not open itself to anyone but her. (*On her knees*) My whole life will be too brief to prove to her my tenderness, my love, my devotion.

BLUEBEARD

(*Kicking her over*) I detest cheap sentiment.

MISS CUBBIDGE

This exploits women!

MRS. MAGGOT

Women want an answer!
(*They seize* BLUEBEARD, *tie ropes to his wrists and stretch him across stage.* LAMIA *rises and begins strangling him slowly.*)

BLUEBEARD

Lamia! I thought you were dead.

LAMIA

My dear, didn't you know? A cat has nine lives.

SYBIL

(*The monster speaks haltingly.*) Stop . . . in . . . the . . . name . . . of love. The human heart . . . who knows to what perversions it may not turn, when its taste is guided by aesthetics?
(*The women drop the rope.* LAMIA *releases* BLUEBEARD. *The sound of the ship's foghorn is heard offstage.*)

SHEEMISH

(*Looking out the spy hole*) The *Lady Vain!* The *Lady Vain!* The *Lady Vain* has weathered the storm!

MISS CUBBIDGE

(*To* BLUEBEARD) I am leaving this moment. Tomorrow I shall be far away. I shall have forgotten everything that happened yesterday. It's enough to say that I will tell nobody, nobody. If, as I hope, you regret the words that escaped you, write to me and I shall despond at once. I leave without rancor and wish you the best, in spite of all. I am carrying your child. Would that your son will be your good angel. (*Hands him the key to the laboratory.*) Adieu! Come, Margaret, Sybil, Rodney. We must return to normalcy. (*They exit. There is the sound of a foghorn.*)

ACT III, SCENE 11: BLUEBEARD, LAMIA, SHEEMISH

BLUEBEARD

(*In a rage, shaking his fists at the heavens*)

I curse everything that you have given. I curse the day on which I was born. I curse the day on which I shall die. I curse the whole of my life. I fling everything back at your cruel face, senseless fate! (*Laughing*) With my curses I conquer you. What else can you do to me? With my last breath I will shout in your asinine ears: Be accursed, be accursed! I'm a failure, Sheemish, I'm a failure.

SHEEMISH

But, Master, you have heart, you have talent.

BLUEBEARD

Heart! Talent! These are nothing, my boy. Mediocrity is the true gift of the gods. (*Exit*)

ACT III, SCENE 12: SHEEMISH, LAMIA

SHEEMISH

Come, let us do the best we can to change the opinion of this unhappy man.
(*Exit with* LAMIA)
(*Curtain*)